D0342907

PENGUIN BOOKS

I CAN'T STAY LONG

Laurie Lee was born in Gloucestershire and educated at Slad village school and at Stroud Central School. At the age of nineteen he walked to London and then travelled on foot through Spain, where he was trapped by the outbreak of the Civil War – to which he later returned by crossing the Pyrenees (as described in his book *As I Walked Out One Midsummer Morning*).

During the Second World War he worked for the Ministry of Information and also made documentary films in Cyprus and India. In 1950–51 he was Caption-Writer-in-Chief and Curator of Eccentricities for the Festival of Britain.

Awarded the M.B.E. in 1952, he has published four books of poems: *The Sun My Monument* (1944), *The Bloom of Candles* (1947), *My Many-Coated Man* (1955) and *Pocket Poems* (1960). His other works include a verse play for radio, *The Voyage of Magellan* (1948); a record of his travels in Andalusia, *A Rose for Winter* (1955); his best-selling autobiography, *Cider with Rosie* (1959), and its sequel, *As I Walked Out One Midsummer Morning* (1969).

Fond of travelling and music, Laurie Lee finds he works best in his Chelsea garret, the muddy meadows of Slad, or certain mountain villages in Spain. He is married and has a daughter.

LAURIE LEE

I Can't Stay Long

*

PENGUIN BOOKS

Penguin Books Ltd, Harmondsworth, Middlesex, England
Penguin Books, 625 Madison Avenue, New York, New York 10022, U.S.A.
Penguin Books Australia Ltd, Ringwood, Victoria, Australia
Penguin Books Canada Ltd, 2801 John Street, Markham, Ontario, Canada
Penguin Books (N.Z.) Ltd, 182–190 Wairau Road, Auckland 10, New Zealand

—

First published by André Deutsch 1975
Published in Penguin Books 1977
Copyright © Laurie Lee, 1975
All rights reserved

—

Made and printed in Great Britain by
C. Nicholls & Company Ltd
Set in Monotype Baskerville

To Pen and Virginia
with love

Contents

Acknowledgements

Acknowledgements are due to the following publications in which essays included in this collection first appeared:

The Daily Telegraph Magazine, for 'Paradise', 'Arrack and Astarte' and 'Concorde 002.'

Encounter, for 'Ibiza High Fifties', 'A Wake in Warsaw' and 'A Festive Occasion'.

The Evening Standard, for 'The Firstborn'.

Leader Magazine, for 'A Drink with a Witch' and 'The Hills of Tuscany'.

Mademoiselle, for 'Love', 'Charm', 'Voices of Ireland', 'Spain, the Gold Syllable', 'Mexico', 'The Sugar Islands' and 'Gift from the Sea'.

The New York Times Book Review, for 'Writing Autobiography' and 'True Adventures of the Boy Reader'.

Redbook, for 'The Village that Lost its Children'.

Vogue, for 'First Love'.

The Geographical Magazine, London, for 'Whitsuntide Treat'.

The following essays have been broadcast by the BBC: 'Appetite', 'An Obstinate Exile' and 'Eight-Year-old World'.

Part One of 'The Firstborn' exists as a separate publication under the imprint of the Hogarth Press, which has kindly given permission for its inclusion in this collection. Part Two originally appeared elsewhere.

The author would like to thank Mr Nicholas Bentley and Mr John Raymond for their care and patience in helping him to make this selection and to prepare it for publication.

Preface

FOR some considerable time now I have had spread around my workroom floor odd piles and packages of manuscripts – the result of a generation of occasional prose writings – which have increasingly seemed to me, as I continued to trip over them, non-negotiable in more ways than one.

At last I thought that the best thing to do was to gather them into a book, or at least a selection of them – partly as a means of clearing the barnacled chaos of my room but also as a way of revisiting dimly remembered experiences and exercises.

I had not re-read a number of these pieces since first I wrote them – some as long as a couple of decades ago – and what strikes me most strongly about a lot of them now is their confident enthusiasm and unabashed celebration of the obvious.

There may be a simple explanation for this. When I first left my country village, at the age of nineteen, I found an outside world that was sparkling and new. The astonishment and pleasure at what I began to discover around me has continued almost undiminished to the present day. Hence the tone of voice of many of these pieces.

I suppose the selection, on the whole, is a kind of scrap-book of first loves and obsessions. It is roughly divided into three parts. Part One covers some early recollections of my country childhood and my departure from it. Part Two contains certain abstract considerations of love and the senses, and more immediate experiences of birth and death. Part Three is simply devoted to a series of voyages, arranged more or less in the order in which they happened. Many describe visits to places in which I found unclouded warmth and welcome, when to be a traveller was not yet to be just a labelled unit. They are therefore, for the most part, memorials to times and countries whose best is probably past and gone. Jet-tourism and war has finished off most of them. Prosperity has fortunately fattened but irradicably changed the rest. I think I was lucky to have known them when I did, before darkness began to fall from the air.

PART ONE

True Adventures of
the Boy Reader

ONE of my earliest memories is that of a small boy sitting in our village street surrounded by a group of grey-whiskered old men. Bored and fidgety, his mind clearly elsewhere, he is reading aloud in fluent sing-song the war news from a tattered newspaper.

This boy and I were of one generation and we shared the same trick of enlightenment: we were both the inheritors, after centuries of darkness, of our country's first literate peasantry. My mother and father, the children of a coachman and a sailor, read well and were largely self-taught. But their parents could do little more than spell out their names – which they were not often called on to do – and if given a book were likely to turn it over in their hands, cough loudly, and lay it aside.

Not that there were many books available at that time; our elders had little more to contend with, in the way of printed script, than their almanacs and their Sunday psalmbooks, which, of course, they knew mostly by heart. About the only other bound reading material available to greet the new gift of literacy were the widely-sold 'Penny Readers', which offered irreproachable love stories of an unearthly gentility, tales of martyrs and foreign missionaries, collected church sermons and strictures on drink, and certain moral epics devoted to the loyalty and devotion owed by the serving classes to the gentry.

Even so, the existence of these 'Penny Readers' created a revolution in home entertainment, and the gossip of grannies in chimney-corners began to be silenced by family readings-aloud. It was through this practice that I first knew the printed word, its power and its glory, its persuasive magic and ready gift of hallucination.

Many a winter's night we would settle round the lamp-lit kitchen, after supper had been cleared away, while our mother took down one of her 'Penny' volumes and read to us by the hour. Through mother's voice, and the awful tales she read, we saw the world through crystal casements, never doubting that this was the way it looked or that its peoples were less than the noblest. Alas, I can remember but two volumes now (perhaps they were all we had). One was *J. Cole*, the life-story of a footman who became a butler through thrift and prayer; and the other, called simply *Although He Was Black*, a posthumous tribute to a young Negro house-boy who, in spite of his colour, made good as a servant by sacrificing his life to his employer in a fire. These tales, in spite of their frequent readings, never failed to bathe us in tears.

Perhaps through over-indulgence in mother's fireside entertainments I was myself a tardy reader. When I was lent my first book, by a rich old neighbour, I thought she was off her head. It was called *Aikman's Scotland* and was bound in red leather and was just a three-dimensional object to me. Then one day the old lady stopped me in the street and asked me how I was enjoying the book, adding that she only lent it to me because she knew I loved reading and that I would treat it with special care. I was astonished; it had never occurred to me to read it; I had used it as a tunnel for my clockwork train.

At that time, in those Cotswold villages of the 'twenties, we may have been literate, but were by no means literary. We had no regular newspapers and of course no radio or television, and were as yet unracked by their tortuous linguistics. We were the inheritors still of an oral tradition of language, and the stream, though thin, was pure. Outside our own class, which was that of farms and cloth mills, hardly anyone spoke to us save from the pulpit. Our vocabulary was small, though naturally virile; our words ancient, round, warm from the tongue. If we were affected by any literary influence at all, it was from the King James Bible.

Such was my background, and in some ways it still rules

me. I am made uneasy by any form of writing which cannot readily be spoken aloud. From my earliest years, as soon as I could read, I was at home only with those particular classics which approached in style our country speech and the Bible. The three books that continue to stand out like megaliths in the empty reaches of my early reading are *Pilgrim's Progress*, *Robinson Crusoe* and *Gulliver's Travels*. As I read them then, so I read them now – with instant recognition. There are old folk still living in the village today who continue to address each other with the austere formalities of Christian addressing the demons. Robinson Crusoe's is the voice of a local bachelor-farmer boasting how he got through the year single-handed. The satirical fantasies and crudities of Gulliver are still much the mood of our village inn.

I was at the village school when I read these books (having bought the three of them at a rummage sale for a penny). At the school itself there were few books, except things about Cats and Mats, or terse little pamphlets stating that Jill was Ill and Jack had Broken his Back. Those were innocent, crisp, monosyllabic days, of which I was the last to complain.

Then at the age of twelve I was sent to the school in the town, and my reading changed abruptly. Here were dog-eared books for every pupil, mostly the works of Sir Walter Scott. After the fat-bacon language of my earlier reading I hated Scott's dry, latinized prose, finding its false medievalism and over-wrought fretwork merely a grating for dust and boredom.

I was made to read Scott for over two years – and have managed to avoid him since. But instead of being put off books forever I developed a passion for out-of-school reading. This marked the beginning of an indiscriminate gorging that was to continue throughout my teens. There was no one to tell me what to read; there was no one I knew who knew. As it is for most adolescents it was a matter of prodigious intake, mountains of chaff for a grain of wheat.

On my way home from school I developed a special technique: at several pages a day, while loitering at the bookstall in Woolworth's, I found I could read most of their stock in a year. Behind the manager's back, in the town's other bookshop, I slyly repeated the performance. Zane Grey, Jack London, Nat Gould, Edgar Wallace – such was the good, plain fare of that time, presenting a picture of both the Old World and the New which has never been equalled for innocent violence.

Then suddenly, by chance, I stumbled on Dickens, finding his Collected Works on a bonfire. Some old neighbour had thrown them out, and the rain had saved them from burning. Though scorched and mildewed I stole them home, cleaned them up, and read through the lot. After tea, with a volume propped up on an oil-lamp, the damp pages steaming gently, I was borne straightway into the stews of old London, until I could no longer remember my own name.

Reading at home, with a family of seven in the room, required a special brand of abstraction. But one had it then; it was no trouble at all, a concentration both intense and happy, which brothers or sisters, with all their fighting and singing, could never hope to break through. (True, in summertime I could go and read up a tree, or hide tiger-like out in the grass. But this was less through the fear of distracted attention than of being given odd jobs to do.)

Up till now my reading had been in a large sense Victorian, and quite a lot of it even more dated. Then with a bang something happened that really shook my foundations – I discovered the public library. I think it had been in the town some years, but no one had thought to tell me. But late or soon, it was an explosive discovery, coming at my most inflammable time.

As I gazed at its great shelves of books – none chained to the walls, all free – the world of *J. Cole* slowly folded up and died, wrapped in its sheets of old maid's lavender. But reading by stealth had become a habit and a free library took a moment to get used to. I started by working straight through the poetry shelf, beginning with the books nearest the door. Yeats, D. H. Lawrence, James Joyce, T. S. Eliot – I'd never heard of any of them before. My mother, of course, had introduced me to poetry, but she knew of no one later than Tennyson. Now vibrant new voices assailed and alarmed me, cracked in my ears like whips, so that for weeks I moved only to their urgent drivings and tossed at night to their echoes. This sharp, hard language, with its attractive bitterness, seemed to cut me to the very bone, purging my heart of its romantic dews and generally stiffening the blood.

Amazed, to begin with, at finding such books in the town, I also fancied I was the first to discover them. They led me to a door marked 'Heresy and Schism', which till then I had sworn to fly from. I began to feel personally responsible for these authors' views, as though I had originally thought of them myself, and when the poems of Joyce and Lawrence took me to their prose the fat was truly in the fire.

From that moment I never glanced at another Western or thriller; my happy apprenticeship as a reader was over. Before, my books had been the playthings of the village; now they were my private and loaded bombs. Through the once-open fields of my Christian valley I wandered secretively, proud and alone.

My decline was now rapid, and damnation near. It was finally completed at age fifteen. I had started work as an office boy in the town, and one day a travelling salesman came in and offered me my own library for a shilling a week. I ordered Lawrence, Shaw, Huxley's *Brave New World*, Gogol, Engels and Marx. I knocked up a bookcase from a rabbit's hutch and nailed the library to my bedroom wall.

Things were never quite the same again; the snug days had gone for good. Then the vicar discovered me reading *Brave New World* and took it away and burnt it. It was the end, in a way, of my country childhood and of its carefree acquiescence.

Whitsuntide Treat

In the kitchen there is a fierce bubbling of flames and water, and rainbows of reflected sunlight on the ceiling. My brothers and I, washed and anointed with brilliantine, turn and run out into the yard.

We are met by blades of heat and bursts of cuckoos, and the garden is a turmoil of bees and scratching hens.

Tense with the enjoyment of the hour, we walk along the road. There is a smell of tar and lilac in our nostrils, the road looks rich like a new carpet, we strike sparks with our boots as we walk and look luxuriously about us.

Girls are gathering flowers in the gardens, shoes are being blacked and ribbons tied, Joe Partridge practises his flute and a cart goes by with a pile of flags.

Now, in the steep field, with ropes and several ladders, we survey the trees. Bullock, the builder, trumpeting his cigarette, looks up and frowns at the lofty limbs. Each year it is the same problem, and each year we make the same bold decisions. A ladder sweeps into the air, a searching spear into the remote no-man's-land of the upper branches. The thick ropes, smelling of oakum and the sea, are trailed aloft and knotted into place. The seat is shaken to the ground and the whole thing hangs ready, a swaying, dangerous engine of delight.

'That'll do,' says Bullock. 'Like a go?'

I grip the rope and pull myself into the broad and slippery cockpit. Bullock stands behind me and I shoot like a rocket from his hands, soaring out over the valley and up among the strange knots and powdery shadows of the creaking oak. Each sweep is a sickening ordeal of fear and death, but I am having the First Swing, and the bully, Walt Kerry, that unscrupulous pirate of every pleasure, is outmanoeuvred and confounded.

At the Recreation Hut the flags are coming out. We go there and sit on the wall and watch. Here is a rich and splendid sight which never fails to ring the first gay bell of celebration. Across the green bank lie the flags in all their multitude; striped, squared and circled with traditional emblems; ensigns, Union Jacks, tricolours, crescent moons, and all the stars and suns of the orient.

And the girls are there, crouching and chattering, their mouths full of flowers and string, intent on the decorations. Upon the grass are piles of staring moon-daisies, and branches of lilac and intoxicating elder-blossom. The girls are arguing and crying out to one another and tying the blooms to the top of each flagpole, and the remainder will be bound with leaves into their hair. As they kneel on the ground among all the precious coloured rags we forget their tiresome tricks and schoolroom tempers; they flame in their dresses and are strange among the flowers.

And there against the wall, with its stained but glowing picture of 'The Good Shepherd', stands the Banner, the vanguard of our splendour. It is already topped with flowers, and its tall yellow poles, its ropes and gilded tassels, are woven thick with ivy leaves. To hold a pole, or at least a string of this banner, is the summit of our pride, and we scheme for it, secretly, weeks in advance.

But gazing at this emblem I am suddenly aware of Jenny King posturing beside it. She comes from a wild family of drunks and poachers, and she is my squaw, my secret. Elder-blossom hangs from her ears, and she holds a tall red flag in her hand and is smothering it with lilac. Thick swathes of scent curl up from the yard, and I forget the Banner and swear I will carry her flag or die.

We gather round the Cross in sweating groups, dancing our flags and scrambling for position. Six boys hold up the Banner, and Walt Kerry is prominent among them. Scowling, he clutches a coveted pole, militant, forbidding, and covered with warts like a riveted battleship.

The band arrives, spitting through pipes and flourishing

silver valves, and we form up behind them. I look everywhere for Jenny's scarlet flag and suddenly catch sight of it. It waves in the hands of a Painswick youth and her lilac is scattered on his coat. Cold with rage I trip him up, snatch the flag and hide it in my shirt. Then the band strikes up with a bumping burst of noise, the signal for a general armistice and the march to begin. The Banner lifts and leans into the sky, and pushing our flags forward we follow, exulting.

How the drums shake, how the trumpets prance, how bright is the sun and how gay the assembly! We sweep down the road and into the village and the people come to their doors and gaze at us in awe. We stamp our feet, our music thunders, and Jenny's flag is like a flame in the sky.

We are a mighty army, a host of Midian, we are ten thousand strong, valiant and splendid every one, oh, there is no end to us. We march in ecstasies of drums and cymbals, we are all twelve feet high and terrible as Turks.

When we reach the field the musicians sit round on forms and blow. The flags are hung in the trees, and with Joe's flute flying like a pigeon overhead the girls dance in a circle, their flowers dropping on the ground and their feet treading the petals into a paste of honey.

The boys watch, then break up into groups, nuzzling the grass, dividing the bushes, and throwing paper darts at the trumpets.

And all the grown-ups arrive, fluttering babies and bottles of cider, settling themselves down in family herds upon the grass. The village spinster arrives with her trays of home-made toffee, the Squire scatters oranges among the girls, and the band plays and drinks beer and shakes out its spittle and plays again.

And above the hoarse and drowsy dances, the stuttering cuckoos, the howling swings and the cries of tribal warfare, we strain our ears, waiting on tiptoe for the first stroke of the signal bell.

When it rings we all pause, and across the valley a tower of white smoke rises from the Recreation Hut.

Like a wave we charge down the steep banks, jumping molehills, scattering cowslips, and feeling the grass beat and tug against our shoes. Walt Kerry is flying on before, as usual, but we follow him closely, leaping like grasshoppers. Suddenly he disappears, and I pass him lying on his face in a patch of blue thistles, crying and beating the ground with rage.

In the Hut the tables are spread and waiting. There are rows of cups and rows of teapots and plates piled high with buns and cake. A steaming urn stands in a corner and the air is exciting with smells of bread and currants. We break madly around the tables, we bellow grace and rattle cups, and the hot sweet tea passes up and down and the buns pass into the bottomless pit.

But poor Walt Kerry doesn't come at all. They say he fell flat into a cow pancake and had to go home to wash.

Cakes are put aside for him, but it is not the same.

Back in the field fresh ceremonies draw out the evening. Then, as the shadows strip the sun and the golden cock turns red above the church, a trumpet is blown and we line up for the races. We feel as heavy as elephants.

Bill Bullock and the Vicar call through their hands, the families cheer their young, the girls their champions, and we dash up and down among the nettles, gasping in the agony of competition.

There is a three-legged race for fun, and I find Jenny, her hair loose and her face yellow with buttercups from rolling on the grass. We tie our legs together with a rag, we wind our arms about our waists and run together in a dream, bound as if we belonged to each other, a strange fleet animal which is both of us.

After the races, and the diplomacies of the judges, the prizes are given; scarlet cricket balls, yellow bats, pistols and fascinating boxes, the final trailing feathers of the day. We are full and weary now, the swings are deserted, the flags have disappeared. Everything has been won and tasted and enjoyed. Blue twilight rolls like smoke down the valley, the musicians disperse, rubbing their sore lips, and we all start for home laden with trophies, and boasting.

Only the lovers remain among the bushes, their time just beginning.

Eight-Year-Old World

My eight-year-old world has no language problems, no passports or barriers, no restraint and no money. It is as flat as a ribbon, about a million miles long, and scarcely wider than the garden path. It begins in the corner of the bedroom, among stuffed elephants and German helmets, and throws into space a gaudy coloured line – a line throbbing with circus freaks and horrors.

In the perspectives of this world there are no distances or vistas, only details of animals and men, close at hand and awfully regarded.

Conjured up by the tales of uncles, by black nights in bed, by facts half heard, half understood, its countries and continents, teeming with crazed inhabitants, lie as compact as railway stations along the path of my journey. And through this world I travel alone, armed with eyes for stretching, tongue for drying up, sticks for prodding, and legs for flying fast when things get out of hand.

The world begins, as I said, in the bedroom corner, which is the harbour of all departures and returns. And the world itself lies open to exploration by all kinds of conveyances – by feet, by memory, by hope and speculation.

First of course comes England, the home country, the limit of what is familiar. The entire realm lies immediately outside the house and stretches no further than the village edge. It consists of a few wild flowers, a mass of jungly grass, an ant-hill, an oak tree, a bees' nest, and a flake-stone quarry clustered with Roman snails.

This detailed landscape is all I know of England. It is home, the country we sing at school; and every event of

history can be sited somewhere among its fields. King Charles
once hid in that oak tree, King Rufus was murdered in that
dusty wood, all battles were fought on that brambled bank,
and every Queen was born here. I accept all these facts
without question, for England, beyond the boundaries of the
familiar parish, is unimaginable.

It is past these frontiers, past the stream and the quarry
and the end of the land, that the strange lands begin, the
world of foreigners and abroad.

It begins in a cloud of darkness, in a grove of evergreens a
mile away, deep down in a neighbouring valley. For that is
the home of the Druids, tall green-faced men in silver shirts
who spend their days motionless among the pine cones pluck-
ing at tinny harps and sneezing. I avoid that grove as I
would the dark of hell, for it is the first pit in the path of the
world traveller. Once fall into the hands of these lank-limbed
men and you are lost for ever. For they will choke you with
larch dust, poison your eyes with berries, kill you to a slow
music, and thread your head on a harp string like a bead. It is
a terrible place, as my grandmother has made quite clear.

Yet go beyond these evergreens and you are still not out of
the wood. For here lies a country of still more mortal danger,
where live the Welsh, the terrors of these valleys. They are
short-legged men, cunning as Blackfoot Indians, and they run
like foxes through the twilight grasses, their mouths stuffed
full of chicken feathers and their hands with strangled rabbits.
When they are not raiding the fields they run up and down
hills singing. I am not a Welshman, and when I hear this
singing I have been taught to fly. Otherwise I hide in bushes
and watch them closely as they pass, feeling my scalp tingle
at their strangeness and thanking my stars I am neither fowl
nor rabbit.

Outside the village walls these Welsh and Druids press
upon one closely and are the first denizens of the foreign
world. But beyond their territory and over the hill there lies
a grey stone town where an aunt lives among the savages.
The women of this town make strong wines by boiling such
things as oak leaves, harebells, dandelions and mice. The
men wear sacks and gaiters, talk with stones in their mouths,

and kick dogs from their path as they walk. They shout a lot, too, and smell of horses, and spend their time either fighting each other with cabbage stalks or sleeping drunkenly in sunny graveyards. To me these men, with their capacity for noise, sparks and violence, are a species of giant gods, remarkable and hair-raising. They are primeval monsters of the outside world, bursting with whiskered muscle, but made slightly less terrifying by the fact that my aunt lives here amongst them.

By the time one has skirted the Welsh and penetrated to the town of my aunt one has reached, as it were, the regions of Ultima Thule, the limits of the known lands. Beyond, the world is charted only by legends, an abyss of magic and mystery.

First there is a hundred miles of howling void, a desert of nothingness about which nothing is known. Then, out of this steamy untracked wilderness, the city of London raises its scarlet towers, floating in space like an enchanted island. This London, of course, with its hollow, drum-like name, is neither England nor abroad but something on its own, a walled fantasy of remembered tales. Within its limits stirs the greatest concentration of life ever to have been witnessed by human eyes. A roar is heard, as of a great pot boiling, chimneys pour sulphur into the heavy sky, banners and gory heads droop from the walls, and the streets are full of crusaders and crooks, poets and pick-pockets, and slit-eyed Chinamen smoking opium on the pavements. It is neither night nor day here, but a rouged perpetual twilight, during which several notable calamities are all happening at once. There are at least a dozen houses on fire, all burning merrily. A plague cart of corpses creaks its way to the river. A policeman drops into a sewer after a spy, while a heretic roasts slowly on a spit nearby. Buses, horse broughams and Roman chariots jostle each other on the crossings; pale queens in black ride weeping to the Tower, and large on a rooftop, livid against the sky, a headman fondles his shining axe. London, in fact, is neither place nor city, nor the abode of mortal men: it is a depository of fact and drama, a rag-book history lying in the flames, its black charred pages turning slowly

But leaving London and striking far afield, we are next confronted by the hot damp wastes of Africa. Africa, to my eight years' eyes, is no more than a tangled trail through a forbidden wood, but limitless in length, a sick green country of apparitions, a hunter's hell and paradise. One hacks one's way through tunnels of wild gooseberries, through barbed-wire tangles of bleeding briars, through fevered banks of nightshade. The pathway is stamped with fearsome tracks and throbs with drums and headache. Coils of black snakes unlace one's boots and the wet tongues of crocodiles lick one's blistered feet. All the animals of Noah beset this Afric path: their eyes in the undergrowth ripen like poisoned berries, their teeth shine like thorns, their voices scream and chuckle. Huge elephants flap their rhubarb leaves of ears, rhinos raise oak-tree snouts out of the swamp, the sky is black with leaping apes and leopards, and a jaguar, growling in his hole, sucks the warm juices from a hunter's head.

This Africa is a test for heroes, hostile, deadly, reeking of fangs and fevers. One never travels here except with a sense of mission, to effect a rescue, to explore new territory, to find a new mountain or an ancient treasure. Again there are no visible distances here, only the narrow trail and the taunting jungle. And night and day one travels it alone, feeling neither hunger nor exhaustion, conscious only of the threat in every leaf, the pitiless continent hungering for one's bones.

But worse than the bare-toothed beasts in the undergrowth, worse even than the Druids back home, are the multitudinous bushmen that infect one's path. They come at you from all sides and in all sizes – knee-high pygmies blowing darts, Congo-cannibals with poisoned spears, bouncing Bantus with butchers' knives, and giant Zulus dressed all in blood and feathers. They hunt you tirelessly, abandoning everything to the joy of the chase. They taunt you with drums and lead you into swamps hissing with adders. They hang from the trees and whisper in your ear, promising you untold torments. And finally they surround you, their eyes in every bush – and you know at last you are trapped.

But the beauty of this great Africa – so large it seems to cover half the world, so full of threats of unspeakable deaths –

is that as soon as things get too hot for you there is always a pathway down which you may turn to arrive back home in a couple of minutes.

Let us leave Africa now to its solitary hunters, to its lizards, rocks, and monkeys' tails encircling the moon. The cannibals lick their lips and steal away, the death drums fade, the lions yawn and sleep, made fat on our lost friends. But we are alive, and the world waits, and Africa will keep.

For next to Africa we have the Sea, that great surge of adventure, that deep blue space among the islands, through which we sail on an upright elm tree, peering high from its topmost boughs for pirate sails and serpents. The seas of the world are legends through which we ride immortal. Here we assume the mastery of our fates, climb rigging, give orders, sail nowhere, and clash continually with passing ships in brave and bloodless warfare. In these deep waters, storm-whipped and mountain high, ships sink but to rise again and no one ever drowns. Enemies may be bound, blindfolded, cast overboard and fed to the fish, but they always reach the shore alive, or return to fight again. And disasters here are like bank holidays, frequent but never fatal. Whales and sharks seize vessels in their teeth, crush them like biscuits and tear them like paper bags. Rocks writhe like living beasts to impale one's timbers. Volcanoes open in the waves to engulf one with steam and fire. Yet somehow one always escapes scot free. For this sea is a friendly monster, designed only to excite, and after each calamity the waves are dotted with the rafts of mariners happily drifting home.

Beyond and among the seas lie the countries discovered by my uncles. One is India, another the Arctic, and they both lie cheek by jowl. India approaches in the shape of a jewelled elephant, with a tiger on its back. On the back of the tiger rides my Uncle Charles, fighting the beast with his bare hands. I am glad to see him and in no way surprised at his occupation, for his great brown hands were made for fighting tigers. He is as good as a circus, is Uncle Charles, and his tough, leather-skinned body is tattooed all over with exotic fancies. Cobras are coiled around his arms, there are palm trees and temples upon his chest, birds and flowers climb up his back, and a half-clad dancing girl writhes on the mobile muscles of his belly. He is a king of India, tamer of elephants and rider of wild black horses. His friends are the dark magicians who live in the sandy caves. They produce bells out of the air, swallow smoke and flames, beat drums, sing, and run swords through their bloodless hearts. This India is more fun to be in than anywhere else. It smells of hot tea and pepper, and everything one sees is a conjuring trick. Snakes dance to music, cows wear beads and speak, hawks fly to your hand with rubies in their mouths, and the wildest tigers, at a word from my uncle, immediately become hearthrugs. It is a good place to be.

Nearby, in the Arctic, I meet another uncle, who is squat, hairy and old. It is a white place here and sparkling cold, for this is the storage house of all our winters and all the frosts and snows of the world fly here when the thaws set in. My arctic uncle has silver whiskers and is dressed like a bear. He cuts holes in the ice and pulls out shining fish. When he speaks smoke pours out of his nostrils, and standing in the snow he looks like an ancient photograph, smudged black with lines and creases.

I like it in the Arctic for it is white and curved like the top of a balloon. Through the ice one can see the broad brown faces of Eskimos, smiling and eating candles. Polar bears, like snowmen, swim around under water. There are dogs and wolves and houses of ice like bells; but the best of this place is the abundant cold and the fact that one is higher here than anywhere else on earth.

As for the rest of the world it is spread out thin, more distant, and rarely observed, lacking in uncles. There is Australia, of course, where men and rabbits walk like flies on the ceiling fields. There are the underground regions, full of molten fire and skeletons. There are islands of golden sand, covered with bananas and liquorice, mountains gashed by stars, deserts of storm and whirlwind, lakes full of billowing princesses and giants with hands like trees.

The furthest countries are the best and most fearsome. In far-off Spain for instance they will nail you to the wall, screw diamonds in your eyes and give you hot gold to drink. In

America they slice off the top of your head, or slash your veins and call you brother. In the jungles of Peru they make you King, fall down and worship you and feed you on roasted flies.

But beyond all these we come to the edge of the world, and the grass-grown cliffs drop sheer into the dark. Comets and stars roll musically by, and every thought has wings. I am armed now with a spaceman's eyes, with the nerve of a god and the hopefulness of angels. I have renounced all human associations. I am the Solitary, shining with light and power. The world is behind me. The garden path leads outward to the moon, and I have no idea when I'll be back.

A Drink with a Witch

IT was the brightest day of July, and at no time during the encounter did the light diminish or one cloud obscure the sun. Yet at four o'clock in the afternoon my tongue went dry and my thumbs pricked, and looking into her eyes I smelt wet crows, midnight and burning; and I knew I was with a witch.

It was not far from my home – or what remains of it – in a steep Cotswold valley; a fold in the limestone hills where the summer vegetation grows with all the matted fierceness of the Burmese jungle. Everything there seems more livid, greener, and more exotically lush than is decent to the general herbaceous smugness of the English countryside. In that valley wild parsley sprouts head-high, bearing great branches of sickly flowers that throw a dizzying fume into the nostrils. Garlic sprawls rank and oniony in the woods, orchids and fungi smoulder among sweating roots; elder-blossom piles up on the hedgerows like a hot-smelling snow; and the lakes, cloaked with green weed and pinned with dragonflies, break here and there with clusters of huge lilies that jag and sparkle like underwater explosions.

This valley is nameless and leads nowhere. There is one yellow road which dies early, and from there on only a grass-tufted cart-track winds among the rabbit warrens and flowering brambles. There are badger-runs in the brittle grass and in scattered quarries you will find the earths of foxes. Owls sit in the tops of the elm trees, snoring like pensioners in the sun, and water-otters, as smooth as seals, slip silently into the deep, shaded streams. You will find little other evidence of life up there, save for one broken, tile-spilling farm, inhabited by a bearded melancholy bachelor; and half a mile away – at the farthest fold of the valley – the tiny chapel, buried in its jungle.

This chapel had been deserted for as long as anyone could remember. When I was a boy, inspired by its rainbow-glass and vaulted roofs, we used it for several gaudy purposes: mock marriages, mock funerals, various initiations of which I can no longer speak, and once (oh, ghastly, unmentionable day) for the disposal of a dead cat we found lying there.

It was for the purpose of visiting again this unhallowed place that I was journeying that particular afternoon up the green, hot, seething valley. I had not been there for ten years, and as I pushed my way deeper into the tangle of brambles, I felt slightly affronted by the sight of the sprawling, insect-ridden wilderness. Each and every landmark we had made our own – Crusoe's cave, the path of the Blackfeet, the killing oak where we crucified our enemies and ate their heads with boiled potatoes – all were obliterated by a surging, indifferent tide of green.

As I skirted the ruined farm, however, I saw something which we, as children, had never been lucky enough to see. A white bullock, with black horns, lying dead under a wall.

At first I thought it was merely asleep in the sun, but as I approached I realised that this was not so. A buzz of flies circled its staring eyes and its pink tongue lay motionless between its teeth like a bitten rose. It was dead all right, and I left it with a faint, sinister feeling of privilege.

It was about ten minutes later, when I was clearly within the vicinity of the chapel – but lost – that I came upon the woman. I was stumbling about in the thicket of rank-smelling nettles, searching for once-known paths, when suddenly a creature rose up from the green-spiked depths like Venus rising up from the sea. I say Venus, because she was golden and unusually beautiful. She was about thirty years old, but much clearer in skin and more monumental in figure than the usual valley woman (whom the damp seems to smother and the steep hills to stunt). She had thick yellow hair, blue eyes, pale lips like alder leaves, and a long dress of yellow hessian tied round the waist with rope. Her cheeks and arms were yellow with dried earth and she clutched a few green weeds in her fingers.

We eyed each other in silence for a moment across the summer nettles; the valley rang with water and pigeons shuffled in the trees above. Then I said 'Good afternoon,' and she nodded.

'Where'm ye from, then?' she asked, not shifting her gaze. Her voice was deeper than hereabouts.

'From the village,' I answered.

'Did ye see ought a me beast, then – alive or dead?' she asked.

I thought of the bullock, but for some reason I felt compelled not to mention it.

'I saw no beast,' I answered.

She took a deep, convulsive breath, and looked at her hands.

'It's 'is wireless then,' she said. ' 'E thinks 'e's cotched me wi' it. But I'll beat 'im.' She tapped a locket of grilled silver that hung round her neck, and smiled to herself. It was a peculiar smile, slow and clear, like one who smiles asleep. I could not imagine what she was talking about so I began afresh.

'I came to see the chapel,' I said, 'but I don't seem to be able to find the path.'

'There ain't no path,' she said, then looked at me slyly. 'Save where me beast goes – an' 'e don't show, do 'e?'

I looked about the green, enclosing weeds, and said 'No.'

She tucked a handful of plants into her waistband and turned her back on me.

'If thee's want to see the place,' she said over her shoulder, 'come, I'll show 'ee. There ain't no law I know of.'

She pushed her way forward and I followed, and the nettles and parsley closed behind us like a broad, foam-crested sea. The chapel appeared suddenly on its bank, pointing up among a tangle of dog-roses. Outside the door stood a crooked crab-tree, thickly furred with lichen; and from one of its branches hung a harp.

The woman stood under the tree and looked up at it. The heavy shadows of the leaves fell over her face and body like a shower of black feathers. I could not think why I had never heard tell of her before. Strangeness and fascination began to creep over the surface of my skin.

'Do you play the harp?' I asked. She glanced at me sideways through a coil of hair.

'Aye,' she said harshly. 'By wind and wireless. When things be what they seem, 'e plays all right.' She swung round on me and raised her voice. 'You says you'm never seen ought a that beast. We'll find out, feller!'

There was not a breath of air in the valley, and the gold dust from the apple boughs stuck in my throat like pepper.

'You give me a drink and we'll talk about it,' I said.

The woman looked at me up and down, then turned to the chapel door and beckoned me inside.

There was the one bare room as I remembered it; the vaulted roof and the stained glass windows blazing. The sun threw the figures of saints like lantern-slides against the walls, and the woman, as she moved about before me, changed from blue to purple, from green to burning rose. Occasionally, like a mystic translation, the ghostly glowing face of some bearded prophet lay superimposed upon her own, and she looked at me with double eyes, through double features.

As I suspected, she lived here. The place had been cleared of its fallen stones. There was a brass bed, a table, jars of green water, a bucket of dried weeds, and a radio with a horn.

The woman told me to sit down, and poured me a cup of something from a jug. Then she placed a plateful of tiny strawberries before me and settled herself at the table. She grew suddenly arch, like a suburban hostess.

'Ye'll fancy a little wine on a hot day,' she said, patting her hair. 'It's ripe wine, kept long, and I makes a good brew, though I sez it.'

'What kind is it?' I asked.

'Bee-orchid,' she said. 'You'm never tasted that afore, I'll warrant.'

It glittered in the cup, transparent, cool, the colour of emeralds. I took a deep breath, and a gulp, and its taste was unearthly and undefinable. It was also very strong, and went immediately to the eyes. The room began to rock and smoulder and the woman to burn like a golden brand.

34

'Tell me of me beast!' she commanded suddenly, dropping her mincing manner. 'None sez they seen 'im, live or dead. But 'e ain't fer. I took'n to browse this marnin' an' 'e was 'arty. I looked for'n at noon, an' 'e was gone. You seen 'im, feller? Tell us, now.'

Among the hazy chapel fire that surrounded her, her eyes were blue and brilliant as ice. I was helpless, and I told her. 'It mayn't have been your beast,' I said. 'But he was dead, under a wall.'

She was rocking in her chair, her hands clasped tight.

'It's that whiskered chap up at the farm,' she said. ''E's been at'n – that I knows. 'E thinks I bled 'is pigs. But we'll beat 'im.'

'How could he have done such a thing?' I asked, not knowing rightly what he'd done.

' 'E works the wireless on me,' she said. 'But I know when 'e's at it. 'E can't begin a-twiddlin' but I knows.' She nodded across at the radio with its ancient horn. 'That tells when 'e's workin' on me. But I got one 'ere that's stronger every time.'

She put her fingers to her throat and raised the locket before her eyes, caressing it like a jewel. She suddenly looked very old.

'What is it?' I asked.

'I'll not show thee,' she said. 'But 'e's a strong 'un. 'E guards my beast agen 'em all.'

'But your beast is dead,' I said. 'It's a great pity. But no doubt you'll get compensation.'

'Aye, I'll get me compensation!' she cried. 'Beasts do live as are dead – an' them that lives can die. That whiskered un up there, wi' 'is sick visage – 'e'll know. 'E'll not work no more on me, not wi' all 'is wirelesses. Look 'ere, feller – d'ye want to know what this'n be? 'E be stronger than all. An' if things be what they seem, 'e'll show 'ee.'

She was rigid, intent, with the locket in her hands, and I had an immediate intimation that something was going to happen.

'Don't 'ee speak or move in the sun,' she said. 'Don't drink or breathe. 'Arken only. Things be what they seem.'

All her body seemed wrapped about the locket. The roots

35

of her limbs and fingers all led to it; her eyes burned upon it. There was a long pause. Then all of a sudden, distantly and dryly, the silver grill buzzed with a tiny noise. The woman's face went still and blind. With dreamy fingers she broke open the fragile cage and shook something out into the palm of her hand. It was a black horned beetle, quivering with rapid soundless wings. The woman put down her mouth to the throbbing insect; and whether it was the wine or a touch of the sun I cannot say, but as she crouched in that golden posture she seemed to me to be made of glass, a figure of fierce and formal beauty lit by some ghostly interior fire. Her hair webbed her shoulders like a dazzle of sun, and the beetle, in the nest of her hand, whirred softly against her lips. Then she raised her eyes and looked through me, listening intently.

'Don't move, feller,' she breathed. ''E's the sign an' the best of 'em all. Don't move, but 'arken!'

I listened, and there was not a sound to be heard. Not a bird in the trees, not a breath of wind in the stifling July woods. Even the bubbling pools and springs seemed to have died among their stones. Then – hardly noticeable at first – there rose a strange light moaning on the air, a trembling chord, far, faint and sweet – the throb of the harp in the tree. And almost immediately it was followed by stumbling footsteps in the wood, the solid tread of some heavy animal advancing towards us through the tangled nettles. I sat motionless, watching the woman. A shadow fell across her rapt, enchanted face. I spun round and saw a white bullock, with black horns, standing in the doorway.

My tongue went dry and my thumbs pricked, and as I turned to look into the woman's eyes I smelt wet crows, midnight and burning. And I knew I was with a witch.

First Love

It wasn't the discovery of sex, when I was a boy, that affected my life so much as the first occasion that I met it head on. . . .

I don't think I ever discovered sex, it seemed to be always there – a vague pink streak running back through the landscape as far as I can remember. This was probably due to my English country upbringing, where life was open as a cucumber-frame, and sex a constant force, like the national grid, occasionally boosted by thundery weather. There were the free, unpackaged animals and birds, constantly proving their tireless urges, all coolly encouraged and pandered to as one of the parish's more profitable drives. My childhood was cluttered with fumbling bees, loaded udders, and swelling fruit, with bellowing livestock, hypnotized hens, and bulls being led by the nose. Sex, in the country, was like grain in the wood, self-renewing as the daily paper, never obsessive, nor crowding the attention, but always going on if you cared to look for it.

On top of all this, I had three beautiful sisters who were my guardians from the cradle. They were about ten years my seniors, their graceful presence in the house a daily reminder of the delicate difference. Plump, pink, with fuzzy arms and cheeks, each one was flavour-packed, huge, rounded worlds to touch and play with, smoothly warm the whole year long.

My sisters by no means took the mystery out of sex but at least they cleared the mind, being free with my clothes as sisters are, having to bathe me on Saturday nights, and towelling me down with occasional exclamations of praise, always encouraging to a growing boy. . . .

So the twisted shock of a sudden sex-dawning was not a

problem I was asked to bear. My moment, after years of lazily inspecting the pitch, came when I was suddenly called on to play.

I couldn't have been more than fifteen at the time – I remember I had just left school. Our small Cotswold village was crammed with boys of my age, all coming to a head together – loose rangey lads, overgrown like weeds, top-heavy and multi-branched. We all seemed to steam or give off fumes like a furnace, heated more than we were wont to be heated, and, as there were few cars or motor-bikes to talk about, we were free to concentrate on sex.

Sex, and our questionable success at it, was the only status we sought, though virginity at that age, in spite of our boasted loss of it, was honoured more in the evasion than in the breach. So we squatted together in our rain-dark shed, painting the walls with our gaudy lies, playing competitive fantasies one against the other until we believed ourselves veterans.

Then one evening, walking home from such a gathering, I lost its cosy half-world forever. In a field near the vicarage, in a moment of terror and truth, I was confronted by a whole live girl. She stood in the grass, supposedly unaware, twitching her eyes like a grazing animal, indolently angling her flanks to the hunter, and closely watching me sideways.

I recognized her as a girl from a neighbouring village, a girl called Ellie, whom I'd known since a child. But she'd never directly looked at me before, and so I'd never really seen her. Seeing her now, brushing the grass with her hand, I was suddenly stung by brutish ambition. I thought of carrying this trophy back to the shed, laying it warm and real on the stones. I thought of the lads crowding round in a sudden miracle of silence. I also thought of Arnold.

Arnold was my closest friend at the time, and we used each other as whetstones. He was a year older than I; a thin, shifty lad who seemed specially constructed for scuttling down holes. We had competed together since we were infants and sucked the blood of each other's jealousies. Arnold must see this, I thought to myself. He wouldn't believe it otherwise.

'Seen any snakes?' asked Ellie. I made no reply, but strode

past her, mournfully whistling. I was wearing my brother's plus-fours and woollen stockings and the grass bounced off my legs like blow-darts.

The next day I steered Arnold up to the vicarage fields, and sure enough she was there again. But this time she was draped across the top of the stile so that there was no way of getting past her. She lay sprawled across it, her knees to her chin, a langorous and weighty road-block.

'Oo's 'er?' muttered Arnold, pulling up fast.

'I dunno,' I said, on needles.

'Some Bisley bird. Let's clip 'er earhole.'

'OK. Let's clip 'er earhole.'

Large, beautiful, with Spanish hair and eyes, skin tight with flesh as an apple, Ellie slipped from the stile and faced us boldly, smiling a slow, fat smile. I watched her closely as her eyes moved over us, heavy-lidded as a sleepy owl.

Her lazy gaze finally rested on Arnold. It was an excruciating moment of doubt. 'Push off, you,' she murmured. Arnold didn't argue; he gave a thin dry cough and went.

I was alone with the girl in a smell of warm rain, feeling handsome, jaunty, and chosen. Ellie stood thigh-deep in the glittering grass like a half-submerged tropic idol.

'Lift us up on that wall, come on,' she said. 'I'm dead scared of things in the grass.'

My hands sank deep into her armpits and she rose in the air like a bird. I wouldn't have believed it, or that I could do it, it was like lifting a healthy eagle.

The flat stone wall, backed by a twisted beech, seemed wider than any bed. We lay cradled together in its dusty silence looking down at the running grass.

'Ow's yer cousin?' said Ellie. 'We've 'ad some laughs. 'Er an' me. We thought we'd choke.' One side of my body was hot against her, the other was creeping cold. 'Ooh! – I'm falling.' She turned and held me – and I sank into a smell of doughnuts.

Holding this girl was advanced stuff indeed. She was sixteen and worked in the cake shop. She was more grown-up than any girl I'd yet touched – the others had only been children. Suddenly I was enveloped in her great bare arms;

39

the raciness went out of the encounter, her chatter quietened to almost maternal whispers, became little sounds of content and comfort.

I forgot the cowshed and the cowshed boys. Ellie was a revolution – a brimming generosity heaving with uncertainties and rounder than all my imaginings. So silent now, her wordless lips to my ear, her warm breadth turned towards me, she became not an adventure but a solemn need. Even Arnold went out of my mind. . . .

The June twilight came down and we disentangled our hair. The wall narrowed as we drew apart. Ellie's crumpled blue dress had moss in the folds like crevices filled with birds' nests.

'Look what I got,' she said, fishing behind the wall. She produced a bag full of crusty doughnuts. 'We won't need no supper. I get 'em from work. I live on 'em practically.' She gave me one and sank her teeth into another. 'You're a boy all right,' she said. 'You got a nerve.' She took another deep bite, and her teeth came out red with jam.

I couldn't forget Ellie after that, and there were vivid dreams at night, when her great brown body and crusty roundness became half girl and half groceries. My sleep knew the touch of gritty sugar on the lips and the crisp skin fresh from the bakery, enclosing who knew what stores of sweet dough, of what light dabs of jam hidden deep. . . .

I began to meet Ellie at frequent intervals, though I looked for her all the time. Perhaps a week would go by without seeing her, then she would suddenly pop up in the lane. 'Ah, there's my boy,' she'd say with a gurgle, and lead me away through the nettles. In the nests we made among the hedges, or in the quarries above the Severn, we lay innocently enough for hours together, eating each other or eating cakes.

I was oblivious now to the normal world and remote from its small affairs. Occasionally we were shadowed by some cowshed boys, but they might just as well have been sheep. Once or twice I saw Arnold watching us sharply through a hedge, but I felt neither pity nor anger. . . .

Then one evening Ellie leaned from her moving bus and called she had something to tell me. As soon as we met, on our frontier between villages, I could see that something was up. She'd done her hair a new way, in great piled-up coils, and her smile was bulging with secrets.

She said her mum and dad had gone away for a week and left her in charge of the house. To prove it, she opened the neck of her dress and produced a door key, large as a trowel. It was going to be lovely; she'd move down from the attic and sleep in the big brass bed. She'd be all by herself, just her and the cat. So I'd best not go near her, had I?

For the next couple of days I was quiet with decision, though I shook whenever I thought about it. What I had to do seemed so inevitable that I felt almost noble, like being called to war. But I took my time; I was older now, I thought I'd better not act like a savage. When the third night came, remote and still, I knew it must be the one. With the family in bed, I stole out of the house and lifted my bicycle over the gate.

I rode up the hill, through waves of warm moonlight, and crossed the common between our villages. I took long deep breaths, feeling heavy with destiny, going proud and melancholy to my task, wondering all the time, with salt on my tongue, whether I'd be changed when I returned this way, and thinking of the dark locked house at the end of my journey, with its enclosed and waiting girl.

Ellie's place stood alone at the edge of the village, a little way down a cart-track. It was silent, lampless, heavily loaded with moonlight and as pretty as one could wish. I buried my bicycle in a growth of nettles and crept, sweating, into the garden. I didn't pause for a moment to wonder what I was up to; every act seemed ordained by legend. I saw the open window above my head and started climbing the spout towards it. A roosting bird scurried out of a gutter, but I climbed boldly, alarming nature. What would happen when I leapt light-footed into the room and confronted the sleeping girl? Would she gasp with pleasure and open her arms, cry for mercy, or lose her reason?

I reached the window, and a wave of warm air, scented with Ellie, flowed out to greet me. I straddled the sill, wriggled my way through the casement, avoided a flowerpot, and I was in.

As my feet touched the floor I saw the moonlit bed and the white breathing weight of the girl. Her bare sleeping arms were like shining rivers, her nightdress like drifts of ice, and her long dark locks, coiled loose on the pillow, were deep canyons carving the Alps. She was more beautiful and mysterious than ever I'd seen her, achingly remote and magic, all cockiness left me – I wanted to kneel to her then, first to be dazzled, and then to love.

A floorboard creaked. Ellie sighed and stirred, then dreamily turned towards me.

'Oh, no!' she gurgled. 'Not *you* again, really! Arnold, you bad bad boy. . . .'

An Obstinate Exile

ONE bright June morning, when I was nineteen, I packed all I had on my back, left my native village, and walked up to London looking for gold and glory. That was some while ago, and I've been here on and off ever since. And I shall probably stay here for the rest of my life. Yet in spite of all that I still can't think of myself as a Londoner, nor ever will, nor ever want to.

For years I have lived in the flats, rooms and garrets of this city, the drawers in the human filing-cabinets that stand in blank rows down the streets of Kensington and Notting Hill. Yet when I talk of my home I still think of that damp green valley near Stroud where I was brought up. The boys I went to school with have long since grown and fattened, got married and gone bald, and they would probably have to give me a very long look before they recognized me if I turned up there again. But that is my home, and the image of it the day I left it is still more real to me than the long years in this crowded capital city.

Now why does one become an exile in the first place? And if one does, why be obstinate about it? Furthermore, if one is forced to be as disloyal about the place of one's adoption as I am going to be about London, why not simply go back away home?

Well, there are a lot of answers. I wasn't the first lad to run away to London. They've been doing it for generations, and their motives are usually ascribed to economic compulsions. But young men don't leave a lush creamy village life like mine solely for economic reasons. They do it to confound their elders, to show off, to prove their free will, and to win honours of the outside world – and they do it with the image always in their minds of returning one day, in the cool of the evening, to lay their trophies at the villagers' feet and watch the old boys gasp.

This ambition always goes awry, of course, because city honours are not village honours. Like certain wines, they do not travel; carry them back to the village and you find they are dust in your hands.

For village honours are still severely local. They include life-long success on the local dart-board, sharp wits in the cattle market, skill at growing whopping but useless vegetable marrows, weight-lifting, spitting, ringing bells, trapping foxes, cheating at draughts, winning at whist-drives or working one's way up to be postman or gravedigger.

Outside things don't count – and why should they? Take a train home, go to the pub, hand round cigarettes and re-mark that you've just been made Chief Inspector of Inkwells at the Ministry of Boil and Trouble, and what reaction do you get? They stick your cigarettes behind their ears, and then there's a silence, and then they say: 'Ah, but d'you 'ear about young Jim Hogg then? 'E's done well for isself, too. Caught three dozen rabbits last week in the vicarage grounds, an' sold back a dozen to the vicar. 'E's a lad. Har, har.'

No, when you leave your village as a young man you leave it for good. There's no going back at all. Unless, of course, you go and make a fortune in Australia, and then you might return as a sort of false Squire, and you'd have to spend the rest of your life standing everybody drinks and apologising.

I've said all this to explain why I'm an exile, why, having come to London, I have to stay here. I'm cut off from the country now in everything except heart. I've forgotten the tricks and trades of the village, and my hands have grown soft.

But I can't get used to London, or accept it, or make a home of it. My gorge rises at the weight and size and muddle of it, sterilising the ground from horizon to horizon. We seem to have forgotten that cities could once be beautiful; cities like Siena, like jewels in a landscape, like small glittering islands of carved stone lapped round by cornfields with wild flowers growing up their walls. In those days there was a balanced proportion between city and country; the shepherd on the hill was visible from the market square, the draper could stroll out into the fields on a summer evening and cool his feet in a brook. Just try and stroll out through the wilds of the Great West Road of an evening and see where you get to.

No, I've heard much about the spell and enchantment of London. I only wish it would work on me. Dr Johnson had a real affection for the place; so had Gay. But their London was a roaring, compact little city where everybody knew everybody else and there were country fields as close in as Kensington and Chelsea. But my London is gross, top-heavy, out of focus, and out of scale.

Of course, there *is* one great virtue in size; and of course, London *is* the greatest show on earth, for never have so many human characters been gathered together at one place. Here, in a day, you can see the world. Stand at the entrance to a main-line railway station, during rush-hour, and you see every possible human species scurrying past. One becomes amazed and transported by the multiplicity of the human face, by its infinite differences, by its almost prismatic graduations from ugliness to beauty, evil to good.

And you can't get this concentrated view anywhere but London. The sad, noisy clamour of life lived at close quarters; lovers in doorways, children in backstreets, singing on bus-tops on Saturday nights, whelk stalls, fish shops, cinemas, fairs, chimneys on fire, and the warmth in the winter streets generated by a million fires and a million bodies – it is this mass gregariousness, this feeling that one is at a non-stop party, that I like best of all.

Yet even this makes me long more for home. For this very gregariousness whets the appetite to know more of the human story, and in the country personal histories are everybody's property, but in London, Man is the most secret animal on earth.

Yes, everything I see in this city, even those things that give me greatest pleasure, I view always in terms of comparison with their country equivalents. When I look at the great Thames, I do not see the river god that rules the Port of London; I see a body of water, thick, brown, reechy, coated with tar and feathers, and I think only of the springs near my home where the young Thames rises, clear as bubbled glass from a bank of moss.

And this translation seems to me to be a symbol of the change which everything undergoes on its way from country to city. All things that grow, for instance, by the time they have reached the city seem to suffer such a loss of virtue that only by legal courtesy can they any longer be called by their original country names.

Why doesn't someone find a new name for city flowers and city vegetables? In my village, in the full tide of summer, we had to cut down the roses with a sickle to get to our front door. If you left them for a week they swept over the house like flames, cracking the windows and breaking through the roof. As they grew, in great blowsy perfumed masses all over the garden, you could jump on them, or hack them with knives, or even drive the cows through them, and still they flourished as persistent and lusty as weeds.

But look at those London roses – scentless, puny, plastic-coloured shades, mass-produced in market gardens, sold for a shilling and dead in a night. Fancy having to buy flowers anyway. I can never get used to it. We used to chuck them like rubbish at the neighbour. Primroses, tenpence a withered bunch; dry little violets sprayed with hair-oil. Step out of our back door and you'd tread on a pound's worth before you'd gone a yard. And cowslips – very rare in the London streets and costing a packet in season – we used to pick them by the bucketful and make wine out of them. I've even seen people selling cow-parsley and beechleaves up here. It's like selling the air.

And take new potatoes and mushrooms – both favourite victuals of mine. Something terrible seems to happen to London ones ; they come to the table like ghosts of reality, tasting of flour and water.

At home, when we wanted new potatoes for dinner, we went to the garden for a forkful, knocked the earth off, washed them under a pump, and threw them in the pot. When cooked they tasted of thyme and mint and summer, their texture as delicate as *marron glacé*. London potatoes are

46

just imitations, like plaster casts, dry and dusty, tasting of ash.

And if we wanted mushrooms we picked them before breakfast from tufts of wet grass in shining September fields. And when fried, they had the magic flavour of manna, neither vegetable nor flesh, a woody root-sweet tang, with an aura of orchids, sap and badgers' tongues. Theirs is a taste like no other in the world. But London mushrooms have no taste at all – blown up like rubber bubbles in derelict basements, or the dark of suburban Nissen huts, and empty of all virtue save the name.

But I talk too much of food. We all do. London has a spirit too, it has beauty, moods, shades, atmospheres; lingering sharp blue November afternoons, heavy rose-pink summer evenings, jaunty spring mornings, and star-bright winter nights. These moments of beauty are probably the worst of all. For a wet day of bedraggled ugliness leaves me in comfort, but the beauties of London of which I am most conscious are those days when the airs and hues of the country pile up and overflow and come sliding over the city roofs to remind me of what is going on in the fields and woods of home. Then I am most restless, and my days most demented.

Even the elements are somehow corrupted and made monstrous here. And to walk on a sun-baked pavement is torment; the heat seems rank and artificial, an affront rather than a blessing, and to see rain falling on a pavement is also torture. Grass in the rain smells of milk and honey; pavements in the rain smell of wet cigarettes and boots.

Another thing that makes me uneasy in London is the tameness of the pigeons. I like pigeons wild. I like to see them volley out of a high tree when they hear me coming and go swooping off discreetly to the neighbouring parish. It is a gesture to us both and balances our respect for each other. But in London there is none of that. Pigeons come padding after one like spivs, podgy, sly, looking for easy grub. They're fat and spoiled and scarcely even bother to fly any more. No, give me the remote, high-flying wood-pigeons every time, rather than these seedy Trafalgar Square touts with their crops stuffed full of pop-corn and bus-tickets. Letting themselves be photographed indeed! . . .

No, I shall never get used to London. But it has one sort of negative advantage. It is easy to work in such a muddled wilderness; it forces the mind and imagination to create the world it cannot offer. In a prison cell, as many writers have found, it is easy to work, for there is nothing else to do. And London is rather like that, a place which, in obscuring the moving forms of the seasons and blotting out the intimate features of the stars, keeps one in perpetual and vivid awareness of that perfect exiled world to which one can never return, and to which it is probably better one never should.

For here in London, I am like a radio receiver set up in a cellar, continually receiving messages from the other side of the lines. I can lie here in bed in the morning, with drawn blinds, and by the temperature of the air and the very quality of sound coming from the street, I know exactly what kind of day it is a hundred miles away: that there is frost on the fruit blossom, or that it is a perfect morning for harvest, or that on such a morning the sheep will be tumbled into the sheepwash and bleating under the shears. As I start my day, and acquaint myself with the congestion in the buses, I know already the scene in the distant village, white washing blowing in a brisk west wind, cows splashing among the bullrushes, foxgloves spearing the hedgerows, cornfields toasting in the sun under swooping storms of birds.

Yes, that place is still my home, which London can never be, in spite of all these years. And the reason is the obstinacy in the blood. I come from generations of Cotswold farmers. I have inherited instincts that are tuned to pastoral rhythms, to the moods of the earth, to seedtime and harvest, and the great cycle of the seasons. London cannot fulfil those instincts, and I for my part cannot lose them.

So London remains my cage, the door is open, but I cannot leave. Meanwhile, the cage is comfortable enough. And now, as I finish this somewhat ungrateful piece, if I am conscious of a faintly bitter taste in the mouth, it is, I must confess, my own fault. I have just been biting the hand that feeds me, and it tastes of soot.

Writing Autobiography

AUTOBIOGRAPHY can be the laying to rest of ghosts as well as an ordering of the mind. But for me it is also a celebration of living and an attempt to hoard its sensations.

In common with other writers I have written little that was not for the most part autobiographical. The spur for me is the fear of evaporation – erosion, amnesia, if you like – the fear that a whole decade may drift gently away and leave nothing but a salt-caked mud-flat.

A wasting memory is not only a destroyer; it can deny one's very existence. A day unremembered is like a soul unborn, worse than if it had never been. What indeed was that summer if it is not recalled? That journey? That act of love? To whom did it happen if it has left you with nothing? Certainly not to you. So any bits of warm life preserved by the pen are trophies snatched from the dark, are branches of leaves fished out of the flood, are tiny arrests of mortality.

The urge to write may also be the fear of death – particularly with autobiography – the need to leave messages for those who come after, saying, 'I was here; I saw it too'. Then there are the other uses of autobiography, some less poignant than these assurances – exposure, confession, apologia, revenge, or even staking one's claim to a godhead. In writing my first volume of autobiography, *Cider with Rosie* (1959), I was moved by several of these needs, but the chief one was celebration: to praise the life I'd had and so preserve it, and to live again both the good and the bad.

My book was a recollection of early years set against the village background of my Cotswold upbringing. The end of my childhood also coincided by chance with the end of a rural tradition – a semi-feudal way of life which had endured for nine centuries, until war and the motor-car put an end to it. Technically the book was not so simple. It took two years, and was written three times. In remembering my life, even those first few years of it, I found the territory a maze of paths.

I was less interested, anyway, in giving a portrait of myself, than in recording the details of that small local world – a world whose last days I had seen fresh as a child and which no child may ever see again. It seemed to me that my own story would keep, whereas the story of the village would not, for its words, even as I listened, were being sung for the last time and were passing into perpetual silence.

The village was small, set in a half mile of valley, but the details of its life seemed enormous. The problem of compression was like dressing one tree with leaves chosen from all over the forest. As I sat down to write, in a small room in London, opening my mind to that time-distant place, I saw at first a great landscape darkly fogged by the years and thickly matted by rumour and legend. It was only gradually that memory began to stir, setting off flash-points like summer lightning, which illuminated for a moment some field or landmark, some ancient totem or neighbour's face.

Seizing these flares and flashes became a way of writing, episodic and momentarily revealing, to be used as small beacons to mark the peaks of the story and to accentuate the darkness of what was left out. So I began my tale where this light sparked brightest, close-up, at the age of three, when I was no taller than grass, and was an intimate of insects and knew the details of stones and chair-legs.

This part of the book was of course easiest. I had lived so near to it, with the world no larger than my legs could carry me and no more complex than my understanding. I ruled as king these early chapters. Then the book moved away from me – taking in first my family, then our house and the village, and finally the whole of the valley. I became at this stage less a character than a presence, a listening shadow, a moving finger, recording the flavours of the days, the ghosts of neighbours, the bits of winter, gossip, death.

If a book is to stand, one must first choose its shape – the house that the tale will inhabit. One lays out the rooms for the necessary chapters, then starts wondering about the furniture. The moment before writing is perhaps the most harrowing of all, pacing the empty rooms, knowing that what goes in there can belong nowhere else, yet not at all sure where to find it. There are roofless books in all of us, books without walls and books full of lumber. I realized quite soon, when writing my own, that I had enough furniture to fill a town.

The pains of selection became a daily concern, and progress was marked by what was left out. The flowing chatter of my sisters, for twelve years unstaunched, had to be distilled to a few dozen phrases – phrases, perhaps, which they had never quite uttered, but bearing the accents of all that they had. A chapter about life in my village school also required this type of compression. Here five thousand hours had to be reduced to fifteen minutes – in terms of reading time – and those fifteen minutes, without wearying the reader, must seem like five thousand hours. In another chapter, about our life at home, I describe a day that never happened. Perhaps a thousand days of that life each yielded a moment for the book – a posture, a movement, a tone – all singly true and belonging to each other, though never having been joined before

Which brings me to the question of truth, of fact, often raised about autobiography. If dates are wrong, can the book still be true? If facts err, can feelings be false? One would prefer to have truth both in fact and feeling (if either could ever be proved). And yet. . . . I remember recording some opinions held by my mother which she had announced during a family wedding. 'You got your mother all wrong,' complained an aunt. 'That wasn't at Edie's wedding, it was Ethel's.'

Ours is a period of writing particularly devoted to facts, to a fondness for data rather than divination, as though to possess the exact measurements of the Taj Mahal is somehow to possess its spirit. I read in a magazine recently a profile of Chicago whose every line was a froth of statistics. It gave me a vivid picture, not so much of the city, but of the author cramped in the archives.

In writing autobiography, especially one that looks back at childhood, the only truth is what you remember. No one else who was there can agree with you because he has his own version of what he saw. He also holds to a personal truth of himself, based on an indefatigable self-regard. One neighbour's reaction, after reading my book, sums up this double vision: 'You hit off old Tom to the life,' he said. 'But why d'you tell all those lies about me?'

Seven brothers and sisters shared my early years, and we lived on top of each other. If they all had written of those days, each account would have been different, and each one true. We saw the same events at different heights, at different levels of mood and hunger – one suppressing an incident as too much to bear, another building it large around him, each reflecting one world according to the temper of his day, his age, the chance heat of his blood. Recalling it differently, as we were bound to do, what was it, in fact, we saw? Which one among us has the truth of it now? And which one shall be the judge? The truth is, of course, that there is no pure truth, only the moody accounts of witnesses.

But perhaps the widest pitfall in autobiography is the writer's censorship of self. Unconscious or deliberate, it often releases an image of one who could never have lived. Flat, shadowy, prim and bloodless, it is a leaf pressed dry on the page, the surrogate chosen for public office so that the author might survive in secret.

With a few exceptions, the first person singular is one of the recurrent shams of literature – the faceless 'I', opaque and neuter, fruit of some failure between honesty and nerve. To be fair, one should not confine this failing to literature. One finds it in painting, too, whose centuries of self-portraits, deprecating and tense, are often as alike as brothers. This cipher no doubt is the 'I' of all of us, the only self that our skills can see.

For the writer, after all, it may be a necessary one, the one that works best on the page. An ego that takes up too much of a book can often wither the rest of it. Charles Dickens's narrators were often dry as wafers, but they compèred

Gargantuan worlds. The autobiographer's self can be a transmitter of life that is larger than his own – though it is best that he should be shown taking part in that life and involved in its dirt and splendours. The dead stick 'I', like the staff of the maypole, can be the centre of the turning world, or it can be the electric needle that picks up and relays the thronging choirs of life around it.

PART TWO

Love

LOVE is; and makes all the rules itself, according to the multiple needs of the lover. We can all of us imagine what love should be, love being one of our earliest unshakeable certainties – having nourished it since childhood as a symbol of private magic, transfixed with our special demands and wishes. Our image of love is the spell we put on others – or fancy we do at least – in order to compel them to enter that particular part of ourselves which egoism has hollowed out to receive them. Indefatigable love-seekers all, spending the bulk of our energies to this end, why then are we so often defeated, finding durable love more difficult to win than almost any other ambition?

To be in love, of course, is to take on the pent-house of living, that topmost toppling tower, perpetually lit by the privileged radiance of well-being which sets one apart from the nether world. Born, we are mortal, dehydrated, ordinary; love is the oil that plumps one up, dilates the eyes, puts a glow on the skin, lifts us free from the weight of time, and helps us see in some other that particular kind of beauty which is the crown of our narcissism.

Love also brings into our lives that mysterious apparition called style, the special fluency of our acts and feelings, so that we are dressed, while it lasts, in the flashy garments of supermen, omnipotent, supercharged. Love is also disquiet, the brooding pleasures of doubt, midnights wasted by speculation, the frantic dance round the significance of the last thing she said, the need to see her to have life confirmed. At best, love is simply the slipping of a hand in another's, of knowing you are where you belong at last, and of exchanging through the eyes that all-consuming regard which ignores everybody else on earth.

Yet historically, they say, love is a modern invention, and largely an obsession of the temperate West. Whole nations and continents scarcely cater to it at all, and still live conspicuously well-knit lives. In much of Africa, the Mediterranean, South America and the East, love is a fiction, a light relief, its territory confined to the faintly fizzy narcotics of folk-tales and comic-strips. There, the mating of the sexes is considered too important a matter to be left to sentiment or the chance effects of moonlight, and so remains in the traditional hands of parents and brokers negotiating with such realities as cows or fig trees. If love or passion be present, this is a lucky bonus, the gilt-edge to the marriage bond; but it is real estate, rather than romantic whim, that is thought the best guarantee of a lasting match.

How then did we, of all people, fall into this dreamy snare, and put ourselves at the mercy of romantic love? For the Americans and the British are among the few in the world to order their fate at its fragile bidding, who stand ready and willing, at the first twinge of fancy, and with an almost total lack of further enquiry, to set up life together, expecting nothing more palpable in exchange than a pair of bed-sheets or an electric razor.

In this sense we are romantics, and are stuck with it I suppose, and everything seems conscripted to serve the illusion. It is propelled and fostered by almost all forms of our culture, popular pressures and social example – by art, entertainment, advertising, news, the influence of public heroes and private friends. Love's whim is the democracy by which we live, and in which we all stand nakedly equal, stripped of all possessions and all advantages save the chance favour we arouse in each other.

Love, that slick fever, strange convulsion of nerves at the physical presence of another; that incautious involvement sparked off by a trick of the light, chance propinquity, or a favourable arrangement of temperatures; that sudden release of tensions and sense of magical freewheeling through a world of new and unimaginable harmonies, set in motion by no more than a curve of a lip, posture, or tone of voice – such shaky beginnings are all that most of us need to say yes, to give ourselves up, to join another's life, without measure or doubt, and start founding careers and families.

But if we have chosen to live in the private grip of love – and it seems that most of us have – (and remembering at the same time that there are worse masters in the world) – perhaps we might ask what such love should be.

Not the seeking of ourselves in others, certainly, which can lead later to mutual rejection, but in acknowledging the uniqueness of the sexes, their tongue-and-groove opposites, which provides love with its natural adhesive. 'We are so much alike' is the fatal phrase, suggesting a cloudy affair with a mirror, when the real balance that binds us is the polar difference of sex and the magnetic forces that grapple between.

Perhaps the most useful service we can offer love is to respect that primitive gulf, which is a psychic need, like sleep and darkness, and the deepest store of emotional nourishment. This may not be so easy, in the general mix-up of today, with the enforced blurring of sexual identities; but man still should be man, and woman as female as she is able, so that both may know the best of their natures, and not be compelled to inhabit some neutral no-sex-land in which each is a displaced person.

Love should be an act of will, of passionate patience, flexible, cunning, constant; proof against roasting and freezing, drought and flood, and the shifting climates of mood and age. In order to make it succeed one must lose all preconceptions, including a reliance on milk and honey, and fashion something that can blanket the whole range of experience from ecstasy to decay.

Most of all it must be built on truth, not dream, the knowledge of what we are, rather than what we think it is the fashion to be. For no pair of lovers, no pair of leaves, was ever built to an identical programme. So beware of the norm, for no one is normal, and least of all sexually, and if this is assumed, through self-censorship or ignorance, it may only lead to intolerance, shock and outrage.

If love be true, love always consents (providing one is

honest and reasonably lucky) and never attempts to emasculate or straight jacket a passion simply because it fails to fit the conventional posture. In sexual love there is no one rule that demands what love should be, only – ideally – the dovetailing of oddities which love welcomes and combines.

Some of course are the possessors, and some the possessed; some placid, or deeply devious – seeking in the arms of the other their mother-daughter brides, or fathers, heroes, gods. Some need the spirit only, vessels for adoration, for comfort, peace and calm; while others must be taken physically with tooth and claw and can only be damaged by misplaced mercy.

All such is right, if love is right, and the anarchy is shared, and neither person is used simply as the other's victim but as one whose needs should also be cherished. Love approves, allows and liberates, and is not a course of moral correction, nor a penitential brainwash or a psychiatrist's couch, but a warm-blooded acceptance of what one is.

At the same time modern love offers another liberation which few societies can have known in the past: the union of two people exchanging equal rights, rather than the coerced mating of man and chattel. For the first time it is possible to imagine it even-handed, a true duality, freed from ancient divisions, when custom, superstition, poverty and fear set the sexes obscurely apart.

Here could lie the foundations of a new serenity, a new level of sexual pride; the girl knowing she was chosen for herself alone and so able to expand through all the versatilities of love, the man able to respond knowing that his choice was a woman and not a share in a flock of goats. The comforts of science, the release from animal drudgery, frees us if we wish it almost to make an art of love, giving us time to explore and balance our pleasures with a nice adjustment between passion and boredom.

The sum of love is that it should be a meeting place, an interlocking of nerves and senses, a series of constant surprises and renewals of each other's moods, a sharing of the gods of bliss and silence – best of all, a steady building, from the inside out, from the cosy centre of love's indulgencies, to extend its regions to admit a larger world where children can live and breathe.

This seems promising ground. Yet the hard fact remains that love today fails more often than it succeeds – a failure surely less due to original sin than to a tragic fault of the times. Or more likely to a combination of faults; the decay of instinct, a misunderstanding of love's basic nature, over-sophistication and loss of innocence, but chiefly the intolerable pressure of the age.

Love needs to seed in a certain space and quite – and even marriage requires some single-mindedness. The present machine-jigged world allows little for this, having lost the magic and mystery of distance, being shrunk, overcrowded, filled with the racket of voices, never still, never leaving man alone. Even worse, it provides us with all too much – inflation of experience and fragmentation of desire – stuffing our senses each day with so much more than we need that natural hunger is reduced to impotence.

Frantic mobility, mass-communications, the drug-fix of pop music (with its electronically erected virility) often keeps the lover at such a pitch of second-hand fever that normal flesh-and-blood contact palls. In the calm empty spaces of other times, a boy made good with the girl next door; now the crowded campus and swarming life of the city sees him half-paralysed by proliferation of choice. In Jane Austen's day the world was the parish and a pair of lovers could stand alone in the landscape; now, they share it with some thousand other eligible acquaintances in a dementia of equal temptation. Taking up, putting down, unable to decide or hold, constantly deluded by sight and surface – such conditioning, of course, is also the fracture of marriage, with the switching of partners like automobiles, a modern compulsion with little to show for the exchange save the junk-heaps on the edge of life.

We are all the victims of this; but perhaps the main cause of failure still lies in our attitude to love itself – that it is good only so long as it pleases, and that as soon as it drops one degree below the level of self-satisfaction it is somehow improper to attempt to preserve it.

This is but a natural expression of that contemporary

fallacy – the divine right to personal happiness, the rule of self-love, to be enjoyed without effort, at no matter what cost to others. Whoever gave us this right to be merely happy and what makes us think it such an enlightened idea? In claiming the sanction to withdraw from any relationship the moment our happiness appears less than perfect, we are acting out a delusion which results in the denial of everything but the most trivial kind of love. Worse still, it makes a paper house of marriage, flimsily built for instant collapse, haunted by rootless children whose sense of incipient desertion already dooms them to an emotional wasteland. Indeed, the interpretation of rights that allows the jettisoning of children in furtherance of their parents' right to happiness, not only cancels that happiness but makes more than reasonably certain that the next generation shall be denied it too.

Of all the pressures that threaten the wholeness of modern man, the fissures in love are the most foreboding. There is not less of love but less continuity in it, shallower grounds for its survival. Love must be deeper to adapt to the shifting sands of the world; able to withstand disaffections and occasional betrayals; be sufficiently constant, in the centre of orgy and bedlam, to create its own area of sacred quiet; and also be strong enough to take marriage, its toughest test, and to sink the best of its virtues in it, so that its children may be heirs of its proper kingdom rather than the frail castaways of its self-absorption.

Some readjustment of attitudes may be necessary of course. Such as the abdication of the need for power. And the giving up of the prize-fight relationship, which particularly in marriage consists of scoring points and knocking one another down. Also in no longer thinking of the woman as substitute mother or hostage, nor of the man as haltered stud-bull or mug, but in recognizing each as an extension of the other's honour where the impoverishment of one is a loss to both.

For love still has intimations of immortality to offer us, if we are willing to pay it tribute. If we can learn to forget the old clichés of jealousy and pride (which are just as hammy as the demand for happiness) and not be afraid to stand guard, protect, acquiesce, forgive, and even serve. Love is not merely the indulgence of one's personal taste-buds; it is also the delight in indulging another's. Also in remembering the lost beauties, perhaps briefly glimpsed in adolescence, of such simplicities as tenderness and care, in feeling able to charm without suffering loss of status, in taking some pleasure in the act of adoring, and in being content now and then to lie by one's sleeping love and to shield her eyes from the sun.

Appetite

ONE of the major pleasures in life is appetite, and one of our major duties should be to preserve it. Appetite is the keenness of living; it is one of the senses that tells you that you are still curious to exist, that you still have an edge on your longings and want to bite into the world and taste its multitudinous flavours and juices.

By appetite, of course, I don't mean just the lust for food, but any condition of unsatisfied desire, any burning in the blood that proves you want more than you've got, and that you haven't yet used up your life. Wilde said he felt sorry for those who never got their heart's desire, but sorrier still for those who did. I got mine once only, and it nearly killed me, and I've always preferred wanting to having since.

For appetite, to me, is this state of wanting, which keeps one's expectations alive. I remember learning this lesson long ago as a child, when treats and orgies were few, and when I discovered that the greatest pitch of happiness was not in actually eating a toffee but in gazing at it beforehand. True, the first bite was delicious, but once the toffee was gone one was left with nothing, neither toffee nor lust. Besides, the whole toffeeness of toffees was imperceptibly diminished by the gross act of having eaten it. No, the best was in wanting it, in sitting and looking at it, when one tasted an inexhaustible treasure-house of flavours.

So, for me, one of the keenest pleasures of appetite remains in the wanting, not the satisfaction. In wanting a peach, or a whisky, or a particular texture or sound, or to be with a particular friend. For in this condition, of course, I know that the object of desire is always at its most flawlessly perfect.

Which is why I would carry the preservation of appetite to the extent of deliberate fasting, simply because I think that appetite is too good to lose, too precious to be bludgeoned into insensibility by satiation and over-doing it.

For that matter, I don't really want three square meals a day – I want one huge, delicious, orgiastic, table-groaning blow-out, say every four days, and then not be too sure where the next one is coming from. A day of fasting is not for me just a puritanical device for denying oneself a pleasure, but rather a way of anticipating a rarer moment of supreme indulgence.

Fasting is an act of homage to the majesty of appetite. So I think we should arrange to give up our pleasures regularly – our food, our friends, our lovers – in order to preserve their intensity, and the moment of coming back to them. For this is the moment that renews and refreshes both oneself and the thing one loves. Sailors and travellers enjoyed this once, and so did hunters, I suppose. Part of the weariness of modern life may be that we live too much on top of each other, and are entertained and fed too regularly. Once we were separated by hunger both from our food and families, and then we learned to value both. The men went off hunting, and the dogs went with them; the women and children waved goodbye. The cave was empty of men for days on end; nobody ate, or knew what to do. The women crouched by the fire, the wet smoke in their eyes; the children wailed; everybody was hungry. Then one night there were shouts and the barking of dogs from the hills, and the men came back loaded with meat. This was the great reunion, and everybody gorged themselves silly, and appetite came into its own; the long-awaited meal became a feast to remember and an almost sacred celebration of life. Now we go off to the office and come home in the evenings to cheap chicken and frozen peas. Very nice, but too much of it, too easy and regular, served up without effort or wanting. We eat, we are lucky, our faces are shining with fat, but we don't know the pleasure of being hungry any more.

Too much of anything – too much music, entertainment happy snacks, or time spent with one's friends, creates a kind of impotence of living by which one can no longer hear, or taste, or see, or love, or remember. Life is short and precious, and appetite is one of its guardians, and loss of appetite is a sort of death. So if we are to enjoy this short life we should respect the divinity of appetite, and keep it eager and not too much blunted.

It is a long time now since I knew that acute moment of bliss that comes from putting parched lips to a cup of cold water. The springs are still there to be enjoyed – all one needs is the original thirst.

Charm

CHARM is the ultimate weapon, the supreme seduction, against which there are few defences. If you've got it, you need almost nothing else, neither money, looks, nor pedigree. It's a gift, only given to give away, and the more used the more there is. It is also a climate of behaviour set for perpetual summer and thermostatically controlled by taste and tact.

True charm is an aura, an invisible musk in the air; if you see it working, the spell is broken. At its worst, it is the charm of the charity duchess, like being struck in the face with a bunch of tulips; at its best, it is a smooth and painless injection which raises the blood to a genial fever. Most powerful of all, it is obsessive, direct, person-to-person, forsaking all others. Never attempt to ask for whom the charm-bells ring; if they toll for anyone, they must toll for you.

As to the ingredients of charm, there is no fixed formula; they vary intuitively between man and woman. A whole range of mysteries goes into the cauldron, but the magic remains the same. In some cases, perhaps, the hand of the charmer is lighter, more discreet, less overwhelming, but the experience it offers must be absolute – one cannot be 'almost' or 'partly' charmed.

Charm in a woman is probably more exacting than in a man, requiring a wider array of subtleties. It is a light in the face, a receptive stance, an air of exclusive welcome, an almost impossibly sustained note of satisfaction in one's company, and regret without fuss at parting. A woman with charm finds no man dull, doesn't have to pretend to ignore his dullness; indeed, in her presence he becomes not just a different person but the person he most wants to be. Such a woman gives life to his deep-held fantasies and suddenly makes them possible, not so much by flattering him as adding the necessary conviction to his long suspicion that he is king.

Of those women who have most successfully charmed me in the past, I remember chiefly their eyes and voices. That swimming way of looking, as though they were crushing wine, their tone of voice, and their silences. The magic of that look showed no distraction, nor any wish to be with anyone else. Their voices were furred with comfort, like plumped-up cushions, intimate and enveloping. Then the listening eyes, supreme charm in a woman, betraying no concern with any other world than this, warmly wrapping one round with total attention and turning one's lightest words to gold. Looking back, I don't pretend that I was in any way responsible; theirs was a charm to charm all men, and must have continued to exist, like the flower in the desert, when there was nobody there to see it.

A woman's charm needn't always cater to such extremes of indulgence – though no man will complain if it does. At the least, she spreads round her that particular glow of well-being for which any man will want to seek her out, and by making full use of her nature, celebrates the fact of his male-ness and so gives him an extra shot of life. Her charm lies also in that air of timeless maternalism, that calm and pacifying presence, which can dispel a man's moments of frustration and anger and salvage his failures of will.

Charm in a man, I suppose, is his ability to capture the complicity of a woman by a single-minded acknowledgment of her uniqueness. Here again it is a question of being totally absorbed, of forgetting that anyone else exists – but *really* forgetting, for nothing more fatally betrays than the sugges-tion of a wandering eye. Silent devotion is fine, but seldom enough; it is what a man says that counts, the bold declara-tions, the flights of fancy, the uncovering of secret virtues. Praise can be a jewel, but the gift must be personal, the only one of its kind in the world; while flattery itself will never be thought excessive so long as there's no suspicion that it's been said before.

A man's charm strikes deepest when a woman's imagination is engaged, with herself as the starting point; when she is made a part of some divine extravaganza, or mystic debauch, in which she feels herself both the inspirer and ravished victim. A man is charmed through his eyes, a woman by what she hears, so no man need be too anxious about his age. As wizened Voltaire once said: 'Give me a few minutes to talk away my face and I can seduce the Queen of France.'

No man, even so, will wish to talk a woman to death; there is also room for the confessional priest, a role of unstinted patience and dedication to the cause, together with a modest suspension of judgment. 'You may have sinned, but you couldn't help it, you were made for love. . . . You have been wronged, you have suffered too much. . . .' If a man has this quality, it is as much a solace to a woman as his power to dilate her with praise and passion.

But charm, after all, isn't exclusively sexual, it comes in a variety of cooler flavours. Most children have it – till they are told they have it – and so do old people with nothing to lose; animals, too, of course, and a few outdoor insects, and certain sea-creatures if they can claim to be mammals – seals, whales, and dolphins, but not egg-laying fish (you never saw a fish in a circus). With children and smaller animals it is often in the shape of the head and in the chaste unaccusing stare; with young girls and ponies, a certain stumbling awkwardness, a leggy inability to control their bodies. The sullen narcissism of adolescents, product of over-anxiety, can also offer a ponderous kind of charm. But all these are passive, and appeal to the emotions simply by capturing one's protective instincts.

Real charm is dynamic, an enveloping spell which mysteriously enslaves the senses. It is an inner light, fed on reservoirs of benevolence which well up like a thermal spring. It is unconscious, often nothing but the wish to please, and cannot be turned on and off at will. Which would seem to cancel the claims of some of the notorious charmers of the past – Casanova, Lawrence of Arabia, Rubirosa – whose talent, we suspect, wasn't charm at all so much as a compulsive need to seduce. Others, more recent, had larger successes through being less specific in their targets – Nehru, for instance, and Yehudi Menuhin, Churchill, and the early Beatles. As for the women – Cleopatra, Mata Hari, Madame du Barry – each one endowed with superb physical equipment; were they charmers, too? – in a sense they must have been, though they laid much calculated waste behind them.

You recognize charm by the feeling you get in its presence. You know who has it. But can you get it, too? Properly, you can't, because it's a quickness of spirit, an originality of touch you have to be born with. Or it's something that grows naturally out of another quality, like the simple desire to make people happy. Certainly, charm is not a question of learning palpable tricks, like wrinkling your nose, or having a laugh in your voice, or gaily tossing your hair out of your dancing eyes and twisting your mouth into succulent love-knots. Such signs, to the nervous, are ominous warnings which may well send him streaking for cover. On the other hand, there is an antenna, a built-in awareness of others, which most people have, and which care can nourish.

But in a study of charm, what else does one look for? Apart from the ability to listen – rarest of all human virtues and most difficult to sustain without vagueness – apart from warmth, sensitivity, and the power to please, what else is there visible? A generosity, I suppose, which makes no demands, a transaction which strikes no bargains, which doesn't hold itself back till you've filled up a test-card making it clear that you're worth the trouble. Charm can't withhold, but spends itself willingly on young and old alike, on the poor, the ugly, the dim, the boring, on the last fat man in the corner. It reveals itself also in a sense of ease, in casual but perfect manners, and often in a physical grace which springs less from an accident of youth than from a confident serenity of mind. Any person with this is more than just a popular fellow, he is also a social healer.

Charm, in the abstract, has something of the quality of music: radiance, balance, and harmony. One encounters it unexpectedly in odd corners of life with a shock of brief, inexplicable ravishment: in a massed flight of birds, a string of running horses, an arrangement of clouds on the sea; wooded islands, Tanagra figures, old balconies in Spain, the line of a sports car holding a corner, in the writings of Proust and Jane Austen, the paintings of Renoir and Fragonard, the poetry of Herrick, the sound of lute and guitar. . . . Thickets of leaves can have it, bare arms interlocking, suds of rain racing under a bridge, and such simplicities as waking after a sleep of nightmares to see sunlight bouncing off the ceiling. The effect of these, like many others, is to restore one's place in the world; to reassure, as it were, one's relationship with things, and to bring order to the wilderness.

But charm, in the end, is flesh and blood, a most potent act of behaviour, the laying down of a carpet by one person for another to give his existence a moment of honour. Much is deployed in the weaponry of human dealings: stealth, aggression, blackmail, lust, the urge to possess, devour, and destroy. Charm is the rarest, least used, and most invincible of powers, which can capture with a single glance. It is close to love in that it moves without force, bearing gifts like the growth of daylight. It snares completely, but is never punitive, it disarms by being itself disarmed, strikes without wounds, wins wars without casualties – though not, of course, without victims. He who would fall in the battle, let him fall to charm, and he will never be humbled, or know the taste of defeat.

In the armoury of man, charm is the enchanted dart, light and subtle as a hummingbird. But it is deceptive in one thing – like a sense of humour, if you think you've got it, you probably haven't.

Paradise

IT seems to me that the game of choosing one's Paradise is rarely a rewarding pastime; it either produces images of vast banality, or boredom on a cosmic scale: sometimes a kind of Killarney between showers, ringing with Irish tenors, or a perpetual Butlin's rigged for everlasting Bingo; for others an exclusive developed area in Stock Exchange marble surrounded by cottonwool and celestial grass. This last – perhaps the most popular and longest sold in the series – has always had its own unimaginable horror, where, in the glaring blue-white of the adman's heaven, the starched inmates have nothing whatever to do except sit down, stand up, walk around the draughty halls, or hide behind the classical pillars.

Indeed, through the ages, man's various conceptions of Paradise have seemed more often than not to teeter on the brink of hell. And with the common element of eternity thrown in, there wouldn't be all that much to choose between them – except that hell would seem to promise more entertainment.

Paradise, in the past, as a piece of Christian propaganda, never really got off the ground. Too chaste, too disinfected, too much on its best behaviour, it received little more than a dutiful nod from the faithful. Hell, on the other hand, was always a good crowd-raiser, having ninety per cent of the action – high colours, high temperatures, intricate devilries and always the most interesting company available. In the eyes of priest, prophet, poet and painter, Hades has always been a better bet than heaven. Milton's best-seller was *Paradise Lost* (while *Paradise Regained* was just a plate of cold potatoes). The sulphurous visions of Savonarola, Danté and

Hieronymus Bosch are something by which we have always been willingly and vigorously haunted. Of all the arts, only certain rare passages of music seem ever to have touched the fringes of a credible Paradise.

The difficulty of trying to suggest in any detail what one's personal Paradise should be is like suddenly coming into enormous wealth. There are no limits or disciplines to contain one's grandiose plans, and the results are generally unfortunate.

Having said that, and declared some of the flaws in the game, the time has come for me to outline my own banality. Paradise, for me, is a holding on to the familiar contained within some ideal scale of the past – an eighteenth-century thing, perhaps, in its grace and order (without its squalor and tribulations). I would have a landscape shelving gently between mountains to the sea, with pastures and woods between them. There would be a small city on the coast, a couple of villages in the hills, and a hermitage hanging from one of the distant crags – a place of sonorous mystery, never to be visited, but from which oracles would be issued once a week. The city would be walled, terraced and luminescent, intimate and without wheeled traffic. From its centre, the countryside would always be visible and could comfortably be reached on foot. Temperatures would be constant: 68° to 74° with no wind except a breeze from the sea. No rain either, except for unseen showers in the night, just enough to keep things green; or festive 'summer-rain days', known and predictable, when a light warm mist would drift through the streets and gardens, and lovers would fasten their shutters and spend long whispering afternoons accompanied by the sound of moistures dripping from rose to rose.

Weather, in Paradise, would be varied, yet tactful, never attempting to achieve any monotonous perfection. There would also be long Nordic twilights for walks in the country, beside river or reeded lake, whose rustling waters, standing with tall grave birds, would reflect the sky's slow shade towards night. The pastoral landscape itself would be lightened by tall flowering grasses, bee-orchids, button mushrooms and snails. Apart from songbirds, who would sing only at dawn and evening and the whisper of river and ocean – no noise: no explosion, public announcement, radio, hammering of buildings, motor-car, jetplane – only the deep, forgotten primeval silence which, like true darkness itself, is a natural balm of which man is now almost totally deprived.

Breaking this silence, or course, there would have to be music, for any place without music is a hearth without fire; not music of brass, I think, but music of reed and strings whose sounds are the most potent ravishers of the senses. This music would be based in the skull, to be switched on at will, and inaudible to others unless they wished to share it.

But what about people? Well mine would be a First Day Paradise, for a very solid reason. In it one would have no past, nor future, only the new-peeled light of the present, and so put the unthinkableness of eternity out of one's mind. The people of the city, fields and mountains – wits, sages, children, lovers – would shine for you with the original magic of first sight, as you yourself would shine for them. Recognition, but no remembrance, would ensure that they were members of a familiar society whom you could never accuse of repeating themselves; while their pleasure in the newness of you would spare you the purgatory of knowing that you might be boring them. It might be agreeable to imagine that everyone grew imperceptibly younger, like Cary Grant in his old TV films, but having no recollection, this wouldn't matter – each day would bring its fresh confrontation, each love would be first and only.

Paradise would also restore some of the powers we lost in that long descent from childhood to death.

Senses that failed would be returned to the keen, high level of their beginnings. The child's animal sharpness of taste and smell – which the adult knows only too well he's lost when he hears the adman trying to prove he still has them – the ability to take in the whiff of heat from summer grass in the morning, the oils in a leaf, the white dust on a daisy, the different spirits in wood, in clay, in iron, all of which allows the child to bind himself intimately to these objects, but from which the adult is inexorably exiled. Paradise would bring back these senses and the contacts they

offer – the special aura of a house as you open its door, a tang
which tells you its history and the character of all the people
in it; the awareness of an invisible animal close at hand in a
wood; the girlish texture of a young calf's mouth: and taste;
the brutality of nursery medicines, the delight in a common
caramel, the sharp bitter milk of the dandelion root, the
acrid horse-breath of straw in a barn.

Surely, with the handing back of these powers, one might
reasonably ask also for the restoration of appetite. Sacred
appetite, so readily blunted on earth – at least, three parts of
one's time to denying it, whether it be for food or love, not
for puritanical reasons but in order to sharpen it to the edge
when it could best celebrate the thing it longed for.

But one need'nt bother to ask what one would do in Paradise.
Timeless, without memory or sense of future, one would live
out each day new. An ideal landscape; mountains, fields and
woods, and the sea throwing up its light. A deep green silence
outside the walls of the city, or occasional sweet airs that
delight and harm not; within the city, companionship, the
sibilant pleasure of bare feet on marble; wine, oil, the smell of
herbs, brown skin; oceans mirrored in eyes that would be the
only eternity.

Above all, I think I'd wish for one exclusive indulgence –
the power to take off as one does in dreams, to rise and float
soundlessly over the bright tiles of the city, over the oak
groves and nibbling sheep, to jostle with falcons on mountain
crags and then sweep out over the purple sea.

On the rooftops, as I returned, silver storks, wings folded,
would stand catching the evening light. There would be
children in the patios playing with sleepy leopards, girls in
the windows preparing their lamps. Alighting on this terrace
of heaven I would join my unjealous friends and choose one
for the long cool twilight. Asking no more of the day than that
I should be reminded of my body by some brief and passing
pain; and perhaps be allowed one twinge of regret at the
thought of the other world I'd lived in, a sense of loss without
which no Paradise is perfect.

The Firstborn

I

SHE was born in the autumn and was a late fall in my life, and lay purple and dented like a little bruised plum, as though she'd been lightly trodden in the grass and forgotten.

Then the nurse lifted her up and she came suddenly alive, her bent legs kicking crabwise, and her first living gesture was a thin wringing of the hands accompanied by a far-out Hebridean lament.

This moment of meeting seemed to be a birthtime for both of us; her first and my second life. Nothing, I knew, would be the same again, and I think I was reasonably shaken. I peered intently at her, looking for familiar signs, but she was convulsed as an Aztec idol. Was this really my daughter, this purple concentration of anguish, this blind and protesting dwarf?

Then they handed her to me, stiff and howling, and I held her for the first time and kissed her, and she went still and quiet as though by instinctive guile, and I was instantly enslaved by her flattery of my powers.

Only a few brief weeks have passed since that day, but already I've felt all the obvious astonishments. New-born, of course, she looked already a centenarian, tottering on the brink of an old crone's grave, exhausted, shrunken, bald as Voltaire, mopping, mowing and twisting wrinkled claws in speechless spasms of querulous doom.

But with each day of survival she has grown younger and fatter, her face filling, drawing on life, every breath of real air healing the birth-death stain she had worn so witheringly at the beginning.

Now this girl, my child, this parcel of will and warmth,

fills the cottage with her obsessive purpose. The rhythmic tides of her sleeping and feeding spaciously measure the days and nights. Her frail self-absorption is a commanding presence, her helplessness strong as a rock, so that I find myself listening even to her silences as though some great engine was purring upstairs.

When awake, and not feeding, she snorts and gobbles, dryly, like a ruminative jackdaw, or strains and groans and waves her hands about as though casting invisible nets.

When I watch her at this I see her hauling in life, groping fiercely with every limb and muscle, working blind at a task no one can properly share, in a darkness where she is still alone.

She is of course just an ordinary miracle, but is also the particular late wonder of my life. So each night I take her to bed like a book and lie close and study her. Her dark blue eyes stare straight into mine, but off-centre, not seeing me.

Such moments could be the best we shall ever know – those midnights of mutual blindness. Already, I suppose, I should be afraid for her future, but I am more concerned with mine.

I am fearing perhaps her first acute recognition, her first questions, the first man she makes of me. But for the moment I'm safe: she stares idly through me, at the pillow, at the light on the wall, and each is a shadow of purely nominal value and she prefers neither one to the other.

Meanwhile as I study her I find her early strangeness insidiously claiming a family face.

Here she is then, my daughter, here, alive, the one I must possess and guard. A year ago this space was empty, not even a hope of her was in it. Now she's here, brand new, with our name upon her; and no one will call in the night to reclaim her.

She is here for good, her life stretching before us, twenty odd years wrapped up in that bundle; she will grow, learn to totter, to run in the garden, run back, and call this place home. Or will she?

Looking at those weaving hands and complicated ears, the fit of the skin round that delicate body, I can't indulge in the neurosis of imagining all this to be merely a receptacle for Strontium 90. The forces within her seem much too powerful to submit to a blanket death of that kind.

But she could, even so, be a victim of chance; all those quick lively tendrils seem so vulnerable to their own recklessness – surely she'll fall on the fire, or roll down some crevice, or kick herself out of the window?

I realise I'm succumbing to the occupational disease, the father-jitters or new-parenthood-shakes, expressed in: 'Hark the child's screaming, she must be dying.' Or, 'She's so quiet, she must be dead.'

As it is, my daughter is so new to me still that I can't yet leave her alone. I have to keep on digging her out of her sleep to make sure that she's really alive.

She is a time-killing lump, her face a sheaf of masks which she shuffles through aimlessly. One by one she reveals them, while I watch eerie rehearsals of those emotions she will one day need, random, out-of-sequence but already exact, automatic but strangely knowing – a quick pucker of fury, a puff of ho-hum boredom, a beaming after-dinner smile, perplexity, slyness, a sudden wrinkling of grief, pop-eyed interest, and fat-lipped love.

It is little more than a month since I was handed this living heap of expectations, and I can feel nothing but simple awe.

What have I got exactly? And what am I going to do with her? And what for that matter will she do with me?

I have got a daughter, whose life is already separate from mine, whose will already follows its own directions, and who has quickly corrected my woolly preconceptions of her by being something remorselessly different. She is the child of herself and will be what she is. I am merely the keeper of her temporary helplessness.

Even so, with luck, she can alter me; indeed, is doing so now. At this stage in my life she will give me more than she gets, and may even later become *my* keeper.

But if I could teach her anything at all – by unloading upon her some of the ill-tied parcels of my years — I'd like it to be acceptance and a holy relish for life. To accept with gladness the fact of being a woman – when she'll find all nature to be on her side.

If pretty, to thank God and enjoy her luck and not start beefing about being loved for her mind. To be willing to give pleasure without feeling loss of face, to prefer charm to the vanity of aggression, and not to deliver her powers and mysteries into the opposite camp by wishing to compete with men.

In this way, I believe – though some of her sisters may disapprove – she might know some happiness and also spread some around.

And as a brief tenant of this precious and irreplaceable world, I'd ask her to preserve life both in herself and others. To prefer always Societies for Propagation and Promotion rather than those for the Abolition or Prevention of.

Never to persecute others for the sins hidden in herself, nor to seek justice in terms of vengeance; to avoid like a plague all acts of mob-righteousness; to take cover whenever flags start flying; and to accept her frustrations and faults as her own personal burden, and not to blame them too often, if she can possibly help it, on young or old, whites or coloureds, East, West, Jews, Gentiles, Television, Bingo, Trades Unions, the City, school-milk or the British Railways.

For the rest, may she be my own salvation, for any man's child is his second chance. In this rôle I see her leading me back to my beginnings, reopening rooms I'd locked and forgotten, stirring the dust in my mind by re-asking the big questions – as any child can do.

But in my case, perhaps, just not too late; she persuades me there may yet be time, that with her, my tardy but bright-eyed pathfinder, I may return to that wood which long ago I fled from, but which together we may now enter and know.

II

She is now only a few months old and at the beginning of it all, rolling her eyes for the first time at the world. A dangerous temptation for any father, new to the charms and vanities of parenthood, to use her as a glass in which to adore his own image, to act miracles and be a god again.

Inert, receptive, captive and goggle-eyed, she offers everything for self-indulgence; her readiness, for instance, to restore one's powers to astonish, and to be shown the whole world new. She laughs easily already, demanding no effort of wit, gulping chuckles at my corniest gestures – a built-in appreciation so quick and uncritical it seems to promise a life-long romance.

But I am late to parenthood and I know I must beware; my daughter and I stand in mutual danger; so easy for either of us to turn the other's head, or for me to ruin her with too much cherishing. A late only child is particularly vulnerable, of course – a target for attentions she might be happier without, or liable to be cast into rôles that have little to do with her nature in order to act out some parental fantasy.

Nevertheless, here she is, just a few months old, clear clay to work wonders with. No doubt, if I could, I'd mould her into something wispy and adoring, but fortunately she'll have none of that. Like any other child, she is a unique reality, already something I cannot touch, with a programme of her own packed away inside her to which she will grow without help from me.

Even so, there is much I want to show and give her; and also much I would protect her from. I would spare her the burden of too many ambitions, and too many expectations, such as the assumption that simply because she is mine she must therefore be both beautiful and clever. I'll try not to improve her too much, or use her in games of one-uppance, or send her climbing too many competitive beanstalks; and I'd like to protect her from the need to go one better than her parents in order to improve their status by proxy. One can't help sympathising with the dad who says: 'I never had a chance myself, but my kid's going to have the best.' But the result very often is a stranger in the house, a teen-age aristocrat served by parent serfs, forced to talk and dress a cut above the old folks and to feel little save guilt and embarrassment.

At the same time I'd best protect her from the opposite kind of freakishness – that of using her as a sociological guinea-pig. For next to circus-trained animals, few creatures look so fundamentally awkward as children who have been forced into experimental postures of behaviour in order to indulge some theoretical fidget of their parents. One feels that children should be left to enjoy their conservative birthright, and not be conscripted as second-hand revolutionaries. A child can, and should, when the time is ripe, initiate its own revolutions.

What I want for my child is an important beginning, a background where she can most naturally grow. My own childhood was rough, but it was a good time too, and I want her to have one like it. I was lucky to be raised in a country district, rich with unpackaged and unpriced rewards; and although we were materially poor (and I don't wish that she should be poor) I believe there are worse things than that kind of poverty. There is, for instance, the burden of abundance, often as stultifying as want, when too many non-stop treats and ready-made diversions can mount almost to infanticide, can glut a child's appetites, ravish it of wonder, and leave it no space or silence for dreams. So I would like to give my child chances to be surprised, periods of waiting to sharpen her longings, then some treat or treasure that was worth looking forward to, and an interval to enjoy and remember it.

I was brought up in a village when childhood and the countryside were simply their own rewards, when electricity had not obliterated the old ghosts in the corners, and songs were not changed once a week. That time and condition can't come again, but I'd like my daughter to know what is left of it. For it still contains people undazed by street lamps, who know darkness and the movements of stars, and who can talk about mysteries the townsman has forgotten, and who are not entirely cut off from the soil's live skin by insulations of cement and asphalt.

I want to take my daughter to this surviving world – not as a visitor, but to be a native in it. So that she may accept it simply as part of creation, and take its light into her eyes and bones. To know the natural intimacy of living close to the seasons, where they are still the gods in possession; to feel the quick earth stir when she treads upon it, to take the smokeless wind in her mouth, to watch the green year turn, lambs drop and stagger, birds hatch, grass grow and seed. To have for her horizons the banks of woods rather than the rented air of office blocks, and to be accompanied on her walks by the coloured squares of fields rather than raddled posters for fags and petrol. Not later, but as soon as she can use her eyes, I'd like her to have this world to live in, so that she can know it and regard it as a place to belong to, and not just a piece of prettiness to be gawped at from a motor car.

I suppose the country can only properly be given to a child – as from birth it was given to me. And as it was given to me, so I'd like to show it to her, and see it again through her eyes – the veils of blue rain wandering up from Wales, streaking the sky before they hit the ground; copper clouds of thunder towering over the Severn, mist wiping great holes in the hillside, the beech-tops breaking into a storm of rooks, the light on the cows in the evening. . . . And there will be the naming of plants (if I can remember them), explaining the differences between daws and ravens, collecting woodlice, earwigs, frogs and grasshoppers; and the attempts to tame a fox. I must also refind the valley's traditional playground – the caves and holes in the quarries, Roman snails on the walls and fossilled fish in the stones, the bridge of willows across the stream, pools and springs and water voles, hooked burrs and thistle-seeds, the sharp free food of crab and damson, and the first mushrooms of a September morning. Best of all, at full moon, to be able to take her from her bed, and carry her down through the warm bright wood, to the lake where the heron stands like a spear of silver and the blue pike nibble the reeds. . . .

Children can often be grubs, even in a pastoral paradise, and I believe that I was one by nature. Relaxed and drowsy, content to sit in corners, I had to be taught to use my eyes. My mother, sisters and brothers taught me, though I wasn't aware of it at the time. But what they showed me then, I never forgot, and I hope my daughter will find it the same. Yet for all the milk-fed charms of country life, I want her to see it whole, to acknowledge the occasional savageries as well as the soft green days, the dark as well as the light. Unlike the secretive city, the country is naked, and displays most of the truths about us; but even the worst of these truths, being part of a primitive harmony, are seldom exploited and never morbid. So it is against this background, which neither conceals nor excuses, that I think my child can best balance her life, can look on birth and death in their proper relation – not taking them soiled or second-hand from the Press – and can accept the valley as real, not only in fat-cheeked summer, but also under the dead necessary face of winter.

Given this world to be in, where she can grow reasonably wild, she will also expect the comfort of some authority. To load any child with absolute freedom is to force it to inhabit a wasteland, where it must push its will to find the limits allowed it and grow frantic unless it does. Let her have the assurance, then, of a proper authority, and of a not too inflexible routine, within whose restraints she may take occasional refuge – otherwise I hope she'll be free. I want her to be free from fear to enquire and get answers, free to imagine and tell tall tales, free to be curious and to show enthusiasm, and free at times to invade my silences.

I hope she'll sing when she wants to, and be flattered when she needs it, and not get attention according to timetable. May our house not be so tidy that it inhibits her gusto, nor so squalid that she resigns her pride. She shall love God if she wishes, and have a place for saints and angels, or even dress shrines for the more unfashionable spirits. She shall not be condemned to grey flannel, nor kept for ever in jeans, nor treated as sexless or a pretended boy, but be given nice clothes early, and occasions to wear them, and be encouraged to value her mysteries. She will not be suppressed too much, nor yet spoiled I hope, but taught politeness, good manners and charm – not as affected graces but as ordinary gifts designed to make other people happy. She will not be the first in the family, nor yet the last, but a respected member of it; and when good things occur I'd like her to stay up and share them – and sleep late through the next dull day.

As for the arts, I hope she'll want some of these, but not too self-consciously. May she paint herself blue, and the walls and ceilings, but not as part of some art-school posture. And may she dance and spin for the pleasure her young limbs give her, but not with Dame Margot always in mind. She shall have music, too, not wherever she goes, but as an important embellishment of her life. A house without music is like a house without lights, but no light should burn night and day. Today's non-stop music, piped from shuddering plastic boxes, debauches the senses of one of its sacred pleasures. Music should be a voluptuous treat, like a deep hot bath, not a continuous shriek in the plumbing. I'd like my child to have music for consolation, excitement, and occasional exaltation, to think of it as an event and an extravagance of the senses and not just a background for chatter and peanuts. If it's good, I don't mind whether it's jazz or the classics, though I hope she'll feel free to like both. Best of all, may she succeed in playing some instrument herself, which is one of the most intense of musical pleasures. We are all listeners today, passive or otherwise, and for some it can be a genuine enrichment; but to play any instrument, no matter how badly, is worth a thousand hours of listening.

There remains the question of education, usually a subject for snobs or fanatics (I've still time to develop into either). But I would like to give her the sort that matches her curiosity and needs, and not one to make her life a misery. I'll not send her away if I can help it; she's bound to leave soon enough. I hope she'll stay at home, inky fingers and all, and be around where I can watch her grow. It is the privilege of the poor – and the very rich – to keep their children at home; I'm neither, but I'm too jealous of my daughter's childhood to wish to give it away to the pattern-makers. I've no mind to pack her off to some boarding-school, to lose sight of her for months at a time, only to get her back, stiff as a hockey post, and sicklied o'er with the pale thought of caste. . . . No, I hope she'll be content to get her conformity at a day school and to unravel it back home each night.

She may have other ideas; to be a blue-stocking, for instance, in which case I must give her the chance. But I'd rather she was less clever, and wholly a woman, than a brilliant scholar later frustrated by marriage. Meanwhile, I'll give her a house full of books, with none of them closed to her, but not expect her to prefer Proust to *Pam's Schooldays*. If she's a success I'll be pleased, but I'll not care if she isn't nor measure my approval in terms of her O Levels. May spontaneity and warmth be her main achievements, not gradings in academic abstractions. May she feel confident, wanted, take pleasure and give it, be artful (but not want to act), laugh easily, covet no one, forget herself sometimes, never be bored or feel the need to kill time, avoid painting-by-numbers, processed food, processed language, have an antenna for the responses of others, and learn that though animals are often much easier to love than men (and both worth it) loving man needs more talent. . . .

These are hopes, of course, rather than exact intentions. For who knows what my girl will be? She's only a few months old, and a surprise already – and I imagine I've got a lot more surprises coming. But in the end, I suppose, I just want to give her love and the assurance of a home on earth. This child was not born merely to extend my ego, nor even to give me unbroken pleasure, nor to provide me with a plaything to be fussed over, neglected, shown off and then put away. She was born that I might give her a first foot in this world and might help her to want to live in it. She is here through me, and I am responsible for her – and I'm not looking for any escape-clauses there. Having a child alters the rights of every man, and I don't expect to live as I did without her. I am hers to be with, and hope to be what she needs, and know of no reason why I should ever desert her.

The Village that
Lost its Children

'OCTOBER the twenty-first, man, nineteen hundred and sixty-six. At ten past nine in the morning, the last day of school, just as they were saying their prayers. . . .'

Returning to Aberfan, almost a year after the disaster, this was the first voice I heard, coming from an old Welsh miner who stood alone with his dog on the embankment looking over the ruins.

'Nobody was to blame,' he went on, ' – or all of us. . . .' The rain dripped black from his cap. 'Why, when I worked underground I filled many a truck for the tip. But not to knock down the school I didn't. . . . There have been worse than this, man. Those in Italy with the water, and that other place with the great big wind. Ay, there was worse – but this one was different. . . .'

His lilting chapel voice seemed to be addressed to the air or to anyone who cared to stop and listen, and I soon learned to recognize it as part of a village chorus rising all day from the streets and pubs, a kind of compulsive recitation of tragedy, perpetually telling and re-telling the story.

A winter and summer have gone, and it is still the main topic in the village – re-living the moment it happened. When no stranger is around it is told interminably to one another, but the presence of a stranger makes it easier. Then the face of the speaker grows trancelike, often oblivious to the listener, as the details are gone over again and again, as though the teller were alone, repeating the words of some riddle, some perverse mystery as yet unsolved.

'I was in the kitchen when I heard it. I didn't take much notice. I thought somebody was delivering coal. Then the neighbour came shouting, "Quick, the tip's on the school!" I just stared at her. I thought she was mad. . . .'

'We heard this swishing noise. "That's a jet," said me husband. "It's never going to take the mountain." Then he looked out of the window. "The school's down!" he said, "and your uncle and auntie's house has gone. . . ."'

'The muck slid over the road, carrying the school tiles on top of it, all neat, just as if a man had done it. . . . It was the water that saved us – it pushed the muck the other way. Otherwise we'd have gone like the others. . . .'

'After it'd happened, everything went quiet, like turning off the wireless. All those children inside, and you couldn't hear a whimper, not a sound, not even a bird. . . .'

'People were just standing. They couldn't take it in. We broke some windows and got out the first of the children. . . .'

'The women were cold as stone. It was the men who panicked. They was tearing at the muck with their hands – it was like wet rubber – a shovel wouldn't go into it. . . .'

'As they was bringing out the bodies, one of the women said, "There won't be a child left in our road. . . ."'

'Some of the little ones who got out – all covered in muck – they didn't cry, they just walked away. . . .'

'I was standing on something that moved. I pulled some of the stuff away and saw the face of me cousin. . . .'

'I still think of the farm up the field where the old woman and child were killed – they never found stick nor stone. . . . And the poor boy Michael carried dead on a mattress all down the mountain to the back door of the school. . . .'

'The next day I said to me husband, "Let's go from here." But he wanted to stay where the child was laid. . . .'

'I take charge of me granddaughter now. She's too much for me really, but her mother's in bed with nerves. Been in and out of hospital ever since the day it happened. Can't stop crying. I do what I can. . . .'

And so on and on – from women leaning out of windows, standing at their doors, or at their garden gates. After a year they seem to have found little rest or comfort, and few facile consolations. Most of them are still living in a state of shock, in a village which remains an open wound.

Few people had ever heard of Aberfan until disaster struck it. It was just another of the small mining ghettoes lying tucked away in the sump of the South Wales valleys – a huddle of anonymous terraced houses of uniform ugliness unrelieved except for chapel and pub.

Its heart was the coal-pit, and its environment like the others – the debris of a slowly exhausting industry: a disused canal, some decaying rail-tracks, a river black as the Styx, a general coating of grime over roofs and gardens, and the hills above blistered with a century of slag-heaps.

Such villages learned to accept a twilight world where most of the menfolk worked down the pits. Many died early, with their lungs full of coal-dust, and the life was traditionally grim and perilous. Disaster, in fact, was about the only news that ever came out of the valleys – the sudden explosion underground, miners entombed alive, or the silent death in the dark from gas. Wales and the world were long hardened to such news. But not to what happened in Aberfan. . . .

A colliery sends to the surface more waste than coal, and a mining village has to learn to live with it. It must be put somewhere or the mine would close, and it's too expensive to carry it far. So the tips grow everywhere, straddling the hillsides, nudging the houses like black-furred beasts. Almost everyone, from time to time, has seen danger in them, but mostly they are endured as a fact of life.

On the mountain above Aberfan there were seven such tips. The evening sun sank early behind them. To some of the younger generation they had always been there, as though dumped by the hand of God. They could be seen from the school windows, immediately below them, rising like black pyramids in the western sky. But they were not as solid as they looked; it was known that several had moved in the past, inching ominously down the mountain.

What was not known however was that the newest tip, number 7, was a killer with a rotten heart. It had been begun in Easter 1958, and was built on a mountain spring, most treacherous of all foundations. Gradually, over the years, the fatal seeping of water was turning Tip 7 into a mountain of moving muck.

Then one morning, out of the mist, the unthinkable happened, and the tip came down on the village. The children of Pantglas Junior School had just arrived in their classrooms and were right in the path of it. They were the first to be hit by the wave of stupifying filth which instantly smothered more than a hundred of them.

The catastrophe was not only the worst in Wales but an event of such wanton and indifferent cruelty it seemed to put to shame both man and God. . . .

The tragedy of Aberfan was one of inertia – of a danger which grew slowly for all to see, but which almost no one took steps to prevent. Now that the worst has happened, the process of healing also seems infected by the inertia of public authority and private grief – a dullness of shock and apathy which freezes the power of action.

Even today, a year later, the visitor needn't search hard for reminders; the stain of what happened is still nakedly visible. One sees the ineffectual little bulldozers, high on the mountain, patting and smoothing the remains of the tip. The black trail down the hillside left behind by the avalanche – a series of gigantic descending waves – is now covered by the fresh false innocence of grass which doesn't conceal its revolting power.

Where the waves broke on the village remains a terrible void, and little has been done to soften its horror. Sheered-off houses, broken walls and polluted back-gardens, a heap of smashed and rusty cars; these form a rim of wreckage around a central wilderness – the site where the school once stood.

Immediately after the disaster, in a kind of frenzy of outrage, all that was left of the school-buildings was savagely bulldozed. It seems to have been the last attempt to obliterate the pain. The scene of the tragedy today, where a hundred and sixteen children died, is just a sloping area of squalid rubbish, a trodden waste – lying derelict in the rain.

Someone, over the months, has aimlessly tried to enclose it with a few old railings and bits of broken wire. The barrier is ineffective and almost obscene and only stresses the desolation. Walk across the site and the ground itself seems stifled, choked and littered with trash – old shoes, stockings, lengths of iron piping, lemonade cartons, rags. Fragments of the school itself still lie embedded in the rubbish – chunks of green-painted classroom wall – all gummed together by the congealed slime of the tip and reeking sourly of sulphurous ash.

Even more poignant relics lie in a corner of the buried playground, piled haphazardly against a wall – some miniature desks and chairs, evocative as a dead child's clothes, infant-sized, still showing the shape of their bodies. Among the rubble there also lie crumpled little song-books, sodden and smeared with slime, the words of some bed-time song still visible on the pages surrounded by drawings of sleeping elves.

Across the road from the school, and facing up the mountain, stands a row of abandoned houses. This must once have been a trim little working-class terrace, staidly Victorian but specially Welsh, with lace-curtained windows, potted plants in the hall, and a piano in every parlour – until the wave of slag broke against it, smashed in the doors and windows, and squeezed through the rooms like toothpaste.

Something has been done to clear them, but not very much. They stand like broken and blackened teeth. Doors sag, windows gape, revealing the devastation within – a crushed piano, some half-smothered furniture. You can step in from the street and walk round the forsaken rooms which still emit an aura of suffocation and panic – floors scattered with letters, coat-hangers on the stairs, a jar of pickles on the kitchen table. The sense of catastrophe and desertion, resembling the choked ruins of Pompeii, hangs in the air like volcanic dust.

But the raw, naked, inexplicable scar on the village remains the site of the school itself – that festering waste of sombre silence from which no one can take their eyes. Why, one wonders, after all this time, has it not been cleared or decently covered? It seems that the people of Aberfan are made powerless by it, spellbound, unable to move. The ground is so seared with memory it has become a kind of no-man's-land, a negative limbo paralysing the will, something poisoned, sterile and permanently damned, on which nothing can be planted, nothing built.

The aftertaste of the macabre which still affects the village is strengthened further by its attraction for sightseers. The streets of Aberfan are narrow, and not built for traffic, so the bulldozed site of the Junior School itself has become the most convenient carpark for tourists. Almost any fine afternoon you will see them arrive, parents and children with cameras and balloons, clambering over the ruins and up and down the railway embankment eating ice-creams and photographing each other.

I remember young lovers arm-in-arm wandering around the devastated waste; a green-suited blonde posing against a slag-heap; another in shorts hitching a ride on a bulldozer; an elegant old lady poking at pieces of rubble.

They had come, they had seen it – the shock of Aberfan for an outing, to take home with their snaps and seaweed. Visitors from America, Canada and Australia, too, tip-toeing carefully with large round eyes. With a certain eagerness also exclaiming, 'My, wasn't it just terrible?' Approaching a miner with a hushed enquiry. 'Excuse me, please,' – pointing down – 'but are they still under there? . . .' 'What was it like – were you here that day?'

Most of the villagers seem in no way distressed by this, visitors are a comfort rather than an intrusion. The stories begin again for each newcomer, recited in a kind of dream. . . . Yet the trippers, scrambling over the slag in their bright holiday clothes, are on the whole not a lovely sight. As one old miner exclaimed, 'Why don't they bring their buckets and spades? There's plenty of dirt for them to dig.'

But some of the Welsh visitors, one notices – those from the neighbouring coal-valleys – are subtly different from any of the others. They come in silent families, without questions or cameras, but bringing their children too – walking them quickly over the ruins and holding on to their arms, feeling their living flesh. . . .

Aberfan cemetery lies up on the mountain, in the shadow of

the distant tips. Above the traditional huddle of colliers' tombstones, studded with slate-grey urns and angels, stretches the clean grassy bank, visible from all over the valley, where most of the children are buried. They lie side by side in two long lines of graves, each child marked with a painted cross. The pretty names shine clearly, black on white, delicate against the wood; Lynn, Carol, Gareth, Islwyn . . . most of them aged between seven and ten. Beneath the long rows of crosses, the mounds of red Welsh earth are deeply quilted in flowers, heavy-headed chrysanthemums, roses, daisies that are constantly changed and renewed.

Here and there among the blooms one sees the little groping symbols of identity – a plastic jet-plane, a china rabbit. . . . At the foot of one of the graves a miniature oil-lamp burns steadily. Another has a football fashioned from lilies. Others are decorated with little verses, resigned or otherwise, enamelled on pages of marble: 'God came one day to gather flowers. He came our way and gathered ours.' 'A day of memory sad to recall; Without farewell she left us all.' (Or, even more blankly: 'Safe in the arms of Jesus.') Here, more than anywhere, one feels the loss kept alive, the sense of brutal confrontation, the statistics laid out in these long flowered rows continuously freshened, swept and attended.

It is a hard climb from the village, but many of the mothers make it each day. There is little else of importance for them to do. Here they are nearest to their ghosts, and to each other – the only ones they don't have to explain to. They bring their bunches of fresh flowers, and water in lemonade bottles, and busy themselves almost domestically among the graves, chattering to each other and admiring one another's arrangements, fussing and giving advice.

In the evening the fathers arrive, carrying shears and sacking, kneel down and begin clipping the grass – each to his own small plot, his wife sitting nearby, the narrow grave with its cross between them. It is a mute routine, a dry-eyed companionship of grief, for the time being their only anchor.

There was a grave marked 'Sandra' with a young woman standing beside it, listless, as though waiting for someone.

She had a thin worn face and dark feverish eyes. Her dress was damp from kneeling on the grass.

'We were lucky,' she said. 'Some were just arms and legs. Our Sandra hadn't a blemish on her. Just a little pink spot up on her forehead, here. There were others much worse than us.'

Her husband joined us, scrambling up through the tombstones – a muscular young man freshly scrubbed from the pit. She gave him her empty lemonade bottle and he stuck it in his pocket and together they looked at the grave a moment. He was proud of the cross, which had been carved by a cousin and was more ornate than any of the others. 'It stands out,' he said. 'I dare say you noticed. I dotted in the words meself.'

A grey wall of rain began to roll up the valley, slowly covering the pits below. 'Run, man!' cried the husband, slapping his wife lightly on the behind. 'Get off home or you'll catch yer death.'

The wife slipped away quietly, and the rain presently stopped. The flowers on the graves began to steam with scent. The miner raked up some grass; then we walked back to the village along the bank of the old canal.

'We were lucky,' he said. 'We've still got the boy. He's thirteen. But it's worse for the missus. I took her away for a bit but she can't get over it. She's still bad. She lived for our Sandra.'

We went for a drink, passing the site of the school. 'That's our Sandie's place,' he muttered. Then over beer in the pub he talked for two hours, his half-closed eyes on the ceiling, his voice a steady staccato, searching, remembering, going doggedly back to the beginning.

'They called me from the pit about ten. I saw the missus in the street. Somebody was giving her a cup of tea. "Where's the boy?" I said. "The boy's all right," she said. "Where's the girl?" "The girl's in there." "Don't you worry," I said, "we'll get her out." But I didn't like the look of it – digging was hopeless. . . . I gave it till eleven o'clock. After all, we're miners, we can judge about slurry. At eleven o'clock I knew. They said there's no more you can do. I went off home.

Somebody said, "Would you like a cup of tea?" "I'm not fussy," I said. Somebody put a fag in my mouth. It was all over – I just stopped thinking. . . . Then somebody came in and said, "We've got her. Would you like to come down and identify her?" So I said "O.K." and got up. . . . I went to the chapel mortuary. She hadn't a mark on her. She was just as her mother had sent her to school. . . .

'Of course, we could have lost the boy too. He was on his way up Moy Road when he saw the houses falling towards him. He ran off home; and I couldn't get a word out of him for months. He had to go to the psychiatrist. . . . Just wouldn't talk about it, and wouldn't mention his sister either. And the two of 'em worshipped each other. They was always together; slept in the same room, holding hands. . . . He used to hide when we went to the grave. . . .

'Then one night – about four months later it was – we was round at our brother's place. The boy went outside to the lavatory, and I heard him call "Dad!" "Ay, what is it boy?" I said. "Come out here," he said. "Sure," I said, "what's the matter?" It was a beautiful frosty night. He said, "Look at that star up there – that's our Sandie, Dad." "Sure," I said, "that's our little Sandie. . . ."

'The boy's all right now, and I'm going to see he's all right. He's interested in machines and science. He comes to me and says, "Dad, there's a super Hawker down in the shop." I says, "How much?" He says, "Only £1." I says, "Here you are then, son." His granny says, "Why don't you let him wait till Saturday?" I says, "If I had £100 in my pocket I'd give it to him. He can have anything he wants. . . ." And I'll make damn sure he never goes down the pit. He's not going to grow up daft like me. . . .

'Ay, ay, but our Sandie. . . . Sometimes I'm lying with the missus and she turns to me and says, "Why?" "Why *our* girl?" she says. . . . I think that meself – but what in God's name can I say?'

The hotel where I stayed was the only one in the village. The ashtray by the bedside was a child's china boot. I shared my meals with a local bachelor, temporarily unhoused, who enjoyed the detachment of the completely deaf.

'Summer's nearly gone,' he'd say, over his evening chops. 'Another week – we shan't sweat after that. . . . They say there's a splendid lot of hazel-nuts up the mountain this year – of course, there's not the children, you know.'

Downstairs in the bar the miners came and went, treating their dogs to little bowls of beer. Or remained arguing in corners with their backs to the television which flickered madly with its sound turned off. On the day of the disaster the hotel had been a rescue centre, and was something of a headquarters of memory still. The landslide had come to a halt just outside the door, and the bar-room windows still looked on chaos.

Dai, the proprietor, was a jumpy young man, rhetorical, wracked with nerves. On the night I arrived he'd just thrown out a party of tourists, and his dark eyes were damp with fury.

'Asking if I'd sell 'em souvenirs – what do they think we are? I don't trade on the price of the dead. "Beat it!" I told 'em. "There's plenty of souvenirs out there. Help yourself. Genuine Aberfan muck!"'

Late that night, after a few drinks, it all seemed to hit him again, and he'd lean over the counter with his thick voice trembling.

'You don't get used to it, you know. Look round this bar and I'll tell you. . . . A cross section, the lot of 'em. That one by the dartboard – lost his seven-year-old daughter. The one under the window – he was at work at the time – lost his wife and his widowed mother. All of 'em quiet enough now, but I remember us crying in this bar, crying and clinging together. And some of my best friends up the road: young Glyn – *kaput* – his wife and his sister Doris. . . . What do they expect us to be then – idealists or what? Sometimes I still go down on my knees and weep. . . .'

His voice rose hot and loud, but no one in the bar took any notice. No doubt they were used to the young man's emotion. So he put a record on the gramophone and turned up the amplifier, flooding the room with Handel's *Messiah*. There were complaints, but he ignored them. 'I always play that when I'm angry. I haven't time to read bloody books.'

After a few days in Aberfan one begins to notice the less obvious gaps – the school outfitters with the price of its clothes marked down, or the lines of washing in back-gardens hanging with every kind of garment except for those aged between seven and ten. Here and there, though rarely, like the precious leaves of new growth, one sees a line of freshly laundered napkins; or the prams of the newborn appearing with an air of Cadillac luxury, glittering with chromium and canopies of lace. But the silence in so many of the houses is the silence of life taken from it, the coldness of a fire withdrawn. Fathers at work down the pits can somehow account for themselves, but the bereaved mothers seem to have no purpose.

Meanwhile in the midst of all this, like orchids among the slag-heaps, one comes across occasional groups of the children who lived. Prettily dressed and beribboned, riding expensive pedal-cars and bicycles, they are an élite, the aristocrats of survival – pampered, cherished, their lives nervously guarded, and also coveted by those who mourn. By luck, chance, and by no choice of their own, they are part of the unhealed scar-tissue of Aberfan. They have the run of the fish-and-chip shops, are loaded with toys and treats, and are invited away for free holidays. Perhaps more than anywhere else in guilt-ridden, sweet-bribing Britain, noted for its neglect of children, they have become the ice-cream-and-chocolate-coated symbols of our conscience, something we wish to placate at last.

It is understandable and right that they should be given the best – they had little enough before. Unhappily the bereaved can't help feeling their loss twice bitter when faced by these rewards of survival. 'Isn't it enough that they lived?' they often ask. 'What more do their parents want? . . .' The presence of the children who were spared adds to the tragic problem of Aberfan, as does the weight of world-wide good-will they carry. What kind of future will they have if they remain in the village? Will they be nothing but the ghosts of those who died? And will they ever feel the need to forgive their good fortune – or even to forgive themselves?

The Welsh are not like any other people in Britain, and they know how separate they are. They are the Celts, the tough little wine-dark race who were the original possessors of the island, who never mixed with the invaders coming later from the east, but were slowly driven into the western mountains.

For well over a thousand years they inhabited this remote other-world, protected by poverty and their mysteries of language, showing a talent for survival in the face of Anglo-Saxon encroachment, and remaining insular, tribal and necessarily devious – border-raiders at times, passive resisters at others – but content on the whole to be left alone.

And they might have remained so, being chiefly interested in sheep, but for the discovery of the rich coal seams in the south, which took most of the farmers and shepherds off their mountainsides and put them to work underground.

Here was raised a breed of men accustomed to toiling in darkness, who grew old robbed of half their daylight, condemned to an ugly, dangerous and second-class life, bringing up their families in the waste of the pits – semi-slaves, in fact, seeking consolation, like Negroes, in music, poetry and religion, in occasional outbreaks of protest of a rhetorical nature, but mostly in the hope of something better in the life to come.

Puritan, unpredictable, in some ways still pagan, they have had to exchange their pastures for the mining slum, where the little slate-grey chapels replace their sylvan temples, their passionate hymn-singing the light they lost. But their particular strength in privation has always been the old tribal tradition, reflected in a close-knit feeling for family. Misfortune to one carries a shock-wave to all more instinctively than anywhere else in Britain. Death and disaster have always been familiar to the Welsh, and in the past have only bound them closer. The special tragedy of Aberfan is that it possessed unprecedented cruelties that threatened for the first time to erode a community.

Aberfan, it is said, suffered from two disasters – first the landslide, then an avalanche of money. The number and innocence of the victims, and the bestial nature of their death, sent a trauma around the world, a sense of unease so great that people were compelled to do something about it. So they sent money, it seemed the least they could do. Money – and toys (incredibly enough) – poured into Aberfan even before the bodies were cleared, piling a second shadow above the stricken village almost as treacherous as the first.

It proved in many ways a cruel misjudgment based on a spontaneous wave of sympathy. Of all places in need of money and toys at that time, Aberfan was perhaps uniquely the last on earth. Cash could bring little comfort to sorrow of this kind, certainly no peace of mind; and the mountain of toys – no matter how kindly meant – was, to say the least, a macabre irrelevance.

The Disaster Fund grew quickly to a million and a quarter pounds and became the source of unhappiness and division. For almost a year it remained, practically untouched, a vast and dismaying fortune, sprawling over the village like some great golden monster which no one could tame or put to use.

The problem became a lingering sickness, disturbing a part of everyone's mind, subject of endless argument, rivalry and impotence. How was the money to be spent, and who exactly was it for – for the bereaved, or for the good of all? Many of the bereaved themselves were in no doubt about this. Why should those who escaped the tragedy benefit? The monstrous injustice of their loss could hardly allow them to feel generous, and they held unhappy meetings of protest.

The inertia of unspent wealth not only set troubled neighbour against neighbour, but also put a brake on Aberfan's power of recovery. Now, after months of unease, some solution has been arrived at, with some lifting of the intolerable burden. Each bereaved family, it has been agreed, shall get an immediate sum of £5000, with a fund of £100,000 set aside for the injured children. 'Now that the money issue has been settled,' said one of the parents, 'it may bring us a bit of peace.'

It may; but a deeper, more intangible sickness remains – the question of the cause of the disaster itself. Of all catastrophes to a community used to death in the mines this one was in every sense most vicious. Colliers' wives have always been accustomed to sending their men off to the pit, wondering if they'd ever see them again. Men's lives were traditionally part of the price of coal. But not those of the children, up on the surface.

Left to themselves over the months, time had drugged many of the villagers and they have been able to bury the worst of their questions. Then with the publication, last August, of the Government's report on the tragedy, every wound was re-opened, and the darkest doubts confirmed.

For the disaster, as all feared, need never have happened. It was the result of sloth, apathy and blindness. 'A terrifying tale,' said the report, 'of bungling ineptitude by many men charged with tasks for which they were totally unfitted, of failure to heed clear warnings . . . of men led astray by foolishness or by ignorance or by a combination of both.' Indeed, a tale of tips badly sited, recklessly maintained, and their perils blandly ignored.

Earthquake, flood, slaughter by the elements – any of these might have been accepted. But the tip that killed was not an act of God, it was put there by ordinary men, and everyone in the valleys feels somehow involved, and nobody can wholly accuse, or forgive.

Meanwhile, the lost mothers of Aberfan continue to live out their half-lives, wandering aimless round their empty houses, haunting their doorsteps, sitting dull-eyed in cafés, waiting for the afternoon climb to the graves. It is as though part of the chambers of their minds had collapsed inside them. One wonders if they will ever be entirely whole again.

I spoke to Mrs T. the local midwife, and she shook her head.

'Some have had new babies – but it doesn't replace. They always seem to be looking for the other one. "You're still young," I tell 'em, but they don't want to think about it. A lot of 'em are worse than they were, not better. And there's much bitterness, you know – they'll turn away from the other children, like they just can't bear to see them. . . . Some of these mothers seem hollow, not with it somehow; talk to 'em, and they look right through you. The "bereaved" – I'm beginning to hate the word. It's going to take a long time. . . .'

PART THREE

Hills of Tuscany

IN Florence the spring was over and the heat had come. The carved palaces quivered like radiators in the sun. Hot blasts of air, as from kitchen stoves, moved through the streets laden with odours of meat and frying oil. In the cheaper cafés brick-faced British tourists sat sweating and counting their crumpled money. But from the tower of the Palazzo Vecchio one could look out across the roasting roofs of the city and see the rising hills around – vistas of vine and olive, cool blue and frosted silver; a series of diminishing horizons, jagged and sparkling, floating south like icebergs in the fresh clear air.

I'd had my fill of Florence, lovely but indigestible city. My eyes were choked with pictures and frescoes, all stamped one on top of the other, blurred, their colours running. I began to long for those cool uplands, that country air, for the dateless wild olive and the uncatalogued cuckoo. I decided to walk to Siena, some fifty miles to the south, along the old road through the Chianti hills.

So I packed a rucksack, rolled up a sleeping-bag, bought a map, and left the city in a pair of stout shoes. It was noon, but it might have been midnight. The sun was blinding and the streets deserted. I took the Via Chiantigiana and walked in a daze for two hours. At two o'clock I flopped in the town square of Grassina and ate my lunch – bread, wine, fruit, and a memorable ice-cream.

In the café shade sat a row of old men with short silver hair, squeaking at one another like crickets. Nearby stood a row of mules, covered with wet sheets, and dozing. In a dry and rubbishy gutter the town idiot sat fishing with rod and line. Curly-haired children, with the gilded faces of angels, taunted him happily and baited his hook with orange peel. For some time I watched a procession of girls, in flaming red dresses, filling their kettles at the public tap. Then heavy with wine I staggered out of the town and slept for two hours on a bank of sage.

Through the late afternoon I walked six miles, climbing slowly into the hills. The road was white and deep with dust. The dust lifted like smoke on the evening wind and coated my hair and hands with tiny fragments of marble – marble of the Tuscan cities and their white cathedrals. The hedges were rimmed with dust and starred with jasmine and dog-roses, huge blossoms, heavy, dilating, fat as clotted cream, and bigger than any others I have ever seen. And at six o'clock rose the dog-rose moon and hung pure white in the daylight sky.

My bag grew heavy, and heavier as I climbed. But at last I reached the crest of the Campo dell'Ugolino and took a farewell look at the Florentine hills – classical backcloths slashed with cypresses, powdered with grape-bloom by the evening sun, and glittering with alabaster villas.

At last I felt I was on my way, I had reached the first of those magical horizons, and my feet were sound. Larks started up, and cuckoos called, and bright green lizards shot from stone to stone. Under the long evening shadows I entered Strada-in-Chianti, and marked it on my map.

Strada, strung out along its street, was cool and busy, engrossed in flashing needles. Groups of young girls sat on the pavements embroidering and making lace. Old men with sharp knives split withies as though they were flaying devils. Old women, toothlessly chewing, were plaiting straw hats with black and frenzied fingers. Only the young men were idle, squatting on their haunches outside the wine shop talking of football.

I had a meal here – spaghetti cooked with oil and butter, black wine of the village, and two fried eggs. The plump girl who served me leaned through the window and sang with voluptuous melancholy into the street. The street was full of swallows, diving low. The room was full of flies.

When I had finished, the girl helped me on with my rucksack, feeling the weight of it and puffing huge sighs of consolation through her wine-coloured lips. 'Why do you walk?' she asked. 'Are you German?' 'No,' said I. 'Then *why*?' she repeated, mystified. I hadn't the word, nor the heart, to answer her.

Now through the red of sunset I went out of the village to find a place to sleep. A wood or a ruin would do, and I walked three miles looking for it. An uneasy time, full of illusions of homelessness, as the daylight dies, and the rose-warm clouds go dull, like wet ashes, and I enter the dark country and am suddenly startled by the sight of my moon-thrown shadow walking beside me.

I found a wood at last and unpacked among the bushes. The ground was hard and covered with little stones and flowers. The air was thick with the scent of thyme and honeysuckle. I rolled myself up in my bag and tried to sleep.

I shall not forget that night – it was worse than lying in the heart of a modern city. The moon came up over the trees and shone into my face like a street-lamp. Then, as though at the turn of a switch, the whole countryside suddenly began to whirr and roar, to squeak and whistle. The expected silence of the night became a cacophony of bellowing frogs, blundering beetles, crickets and cuckoos, mosquitoes, mice, donkeys, dogs and nightingales. There was no sleep or peace till the sun rose, and then it was too late and I was too stiff.

At seven I drank my bottle of water, cooled by the night, and took to the road. I was some two hours from Greve, the heart of Chianti, and there I planned to drink a lot of coffee.

I was in high deserted country, with vast views sparkling all round me. Wild wheat grew everywhere, hanging its frail bleached spears. The sun was remorseless in the sky. I went down into a deep valley of oakwoods, past sad shut farms with shell-pocked walls, over broken bridges shored up with tree trunks. This is a country of broken bridges, and almost every house has its wound. Up all these valleys the long war ground its lacerating way, leisurely dynamiting, negligently tearing off roofs, harrowing the face of the land like the passage of an ice-age. That is also the tragedy one senses in these shot-up farms, in the tommy-gun scars on the cemetery walls. Murder done quietly, passionately, with rescue bogged down on the other side of a mountain, arriving so seldom in the nick of time. No neat dreams of Hollywood but the casual truth of war.

At the bottom of the valley I found a green river and bathed in it. Soap-suds floated down among the pebbles from a washerwoman upstream; and white-smocked children, as neat as cherubim, walked along the banks on their way to school.

On this road I met a vast flock of sheep, driven by a cloaked shepherd and a mad-eyed dog. The sheep tinkled with bells. Their hooves thudded in the dust like thunder-drops. An occasional ram slunk by, his head low under the coiled weight of his horns. And one single remarkable sheep caught my eye – was it mascot or mystic symbol? – its shorn hide tattooed with an elaborate crucifix and scarlet fleur-de-lys.

Here also among the wheatfields stood a crude memorial to a young man murdered there in 1899. A wayside cross decorated with flowers and skulls, and a legend lamenting the deed. And nearby, cutting the hedge, a merry roadman in a brilliant waistcoat embroidered with stars and roses.

At nine-thirty that morning I entered Greve, a town smelling of pure wine. Its outside walls were shattered with dynamite, but within was an ancient piazza quiet and arcaded like a cloister. Here I rested and took a late breakfast, while a woman set up a stall of cherries and a dog sniffed a snake-skin in the road. There was no one else to be seen.

Later, with a bottle of Chianti, some bread and fruit, I climbed four miles through the blazing morning and entered Panzano, a village roosting like a red hen on the top of a sharp hill.

I found Panzano full of fête and excitement. It was the day of the annual bicycle race. Young men, with brown legs and very short shorts, were limbering up or pinching their bicycle tyres. In the square there were stalls selling ice-creams, medicine, balloons, copper jars, looking-glasses, and American chewing-gum. There were flags and summer-looking girls everywhere. It was to be a great day.

But I left it and came down a steep hill that coiled into the heart of another valley. And my feet began to ache and thirst to plague me. The road forked, and there was no signpost. I asked an old woman for Castellina, and evilly she bade me take the left one.

In this valley I paused at midday by a stream that came tumbling cold from the hills. In this water I cooled my wine, put my cherries to wash in a little whirlpool, and hung my burning feet in the chill current among the tickling fishes. It was an ecstasy of mirage and delirium – to be experienced only after four hours of footing a white-hot mountain road. I drank the cool wine and ate my bread and cherries, then stretched myself out among the wheat which grew to the water's edge. The depth of the wheat was a tangle of wild flowers: moon-daisies, gentians, scarlet poppies; with columbines twining up the wheatstalks and hanging their blossoms among the ripening ears. It was a good place to be. Nearby, a charm of nightingales flooded the daylit branches of a wood. Slightly drunk, crooning and groaning, I sang myself to sleep.

When I took to the road again, and had walked some miles, the sun was not where it should have been. I had a feeling I was walking in the wrong direction. And I was.

Two country policemen appeared, unshaven, brandishing rifles, who bid me halt, examined my papers, sucked their teeth at me, inquired why in God's name I was walking, *on foot*, and then told me Radda was just round the corner. I didn't want Radda; it meant I had come nearly ten miles out of my way. But there was another road back to Castellina, along the top of the hills. 'Pleasant?' I asked. 'No, brutish,' they said.

They were right. First I climbed the cliff into Radda, sucking sharp lemons and grunting under my burden. Then for two and a half hours I walked the hog's back, through dust and rocks and thorns, but on top of the world, with the great blue distances south of Siena appearing for the first time.

It was hard going, but I wanted to sleep south of Castellina that night. I met no one on that road but snakes and lizards. I walked with sweat in my eyes and the devil of thirst in my mouth. But I passed through one of the most wild and beautiful stretches of country in the whole of middle Italy, the roof of those green and secret valleys where the grape-bubbles of Chianti swell and sweeten in the sun. That night I camped on a high plain two miles south of Castellina, on a platform of ground commanding great views. When the blue night came, the distances below me, with their many villages, sprang into clusters of light, like diamonds scattered on velvet. I lay down with my head against a bush, and in the bush there was a nesting bird. For some time she fluttered nervously with her wings, but in the end we slept at peace together; and I slept well.

When I woke late on that last morning the first thing I saw was a fantastic town of golden towers, surrounded by oak woods, lying some fifteen miles to the west. It was San Gimignano, that medieval parody of Manhattan, soaring, glittering, and unbelievable.

Then, as I moved my head, suddenly I discovered Siena, hiding behind the bush. I had been waiting for my first sight of it, and I had somehow missed it in the twilight of yesterday. It stood far off, but clear, a proper city, rose-red and ringed by a great wall, with cathedral and palaces topping its trinity of hills and all the green country rising and breaking round it. It was a city compact as a carved Jerusalem held in the hand of a saint. And behind it hung a folded mountain, blue, like a curtain nailed against the sky.

So I took the road once more – the last leg of my journey, and of my strength. The sun was inexorable, the landscape already quivering like water in the heat. I walked in a dream of thirst and aching muscles. Lizards and dragonflies sprang from beneath my toes. White oxen, with horns like swords, ploughed drunkenly in the fields, slicing the chocolate earth.

Then I spied a farm on the skyline, with two women herding pigs. I decided to beg for water. I came up the hill, blond, burnt, in my khaki slacks, bowed by my fool's burden. But the women saw me coming. '*Tedesco*! German!' they screamed. Pigs, goats, poultry were driven into the farm, doors slammed, windows shuttered. Guiltily I passed the shell-shot buildings, and silently they watched me.

A long morning of exhaustion and enchantment, sucking

dry lemon-skins, with the exquisite landscapes growing like dreams one out of the other. Vines and mulberries and moon-coloured olives; wayside Madonnas laced with dusty flowers; and steep little fields tilted towards the sun, full of red wheat and flickering salamanders.

By noon I had walked twelve miles and Siena stood above me. My three-day journey was almost over. Slowly I crawled towards its rusty walls. By now Siena had become for me a city of ice, of courtyards dripping with wet roses, of sparkling fountains and flashing fish.

It was not quite that; but it gave me a cool room, and chaste white wine, and a long sleep in a bed. It also gave me streets too narrow for Cadillacs, streets in which to walk and draw one's fingers along the walls of palaces, in which to hear the sounds of choirs, mandolines, and flutes, and cataracts of conversation. It was a city gilded with the patina of ancient devotions, the brooding celestial visions of its fourteenth-century painters, the gaunt glory of its supreme personality, St Caterina. It was a city that seemed all molten gold by day, and by night a ghostly silver, beaten out by a huge and antique moon. It was a city of pilgrimage, and one to which one must always return.

But next time I think I'll take a train, or perhaps a string of mules.

Spain:
The Gold Syllable

SPAIN is not Europe. It is not even Africa-in-Europe. It is an island cut off by pride and geography, by its indifference to its neighbours and by the presence of its three seas – Biscay, the Atlantic and the Mediterranean. On that island, as on other true islands, everywhere, ancient traditions of custom and character have developed to a point of excess.

Before the days of the aeroplane most people went to Spain by sea; most went as conquerors, and few escaped. Phoenicians, Romans, Visigoths, Moors – the country trapped them among the grills of its mountains, fried them in its oils, turned them a gentle brown, then served them up in a kind of racial *paella* that is still the symbol of the stockpot of Spain. Not even its present invader, the traveller's-cheque tourist, can pass through the country unmarked. Because Spain, self-closed in its arid square, remains one of the few countries in the world that do not adore change, that do not look towards the fatter nations with envy, that do not prefer the sterilized caution of the ice-box society to the rawer flavours of life-as-it-comes.

Spain is poor, crude, ignorant of much of the world; over half the country is mountain and wilderness; it knows a savage climate, vast aching skies, interminable landscapes of distance and silence. But within the bright walls of its towns and villages it has developed a gregarious and extrovert ritual of life in which there are few outsiders and little loneliness. The Spaniard believes himself superior, both in culture and morality, to any other people in the world, and believes this so steadfastly he neither boasts nor hates but welcomes strangers with a chivalrous warmth based on compassion for their benighted shortcomings.

Much more lies behind that gold syllable, 'Spain', than the bullfight and dance of the posters. It's neither as simple as that nor as trivial. It is an island, yes; it is also an archipelago; it is one name but many countries. They lie side by side, from Biscay to the Mediterranean, each separate in face and behaviour. Great mountains divide them, they are split by east-west rivers; their frontiers are the Sierra de Guadarrama, Sierra Morena, Despeñaperros, Nevada, the rivers Ebro, Douro, Tagus and Guadalquivir. Contained by these barriers, they have developed wide distinctions of habit; but they breathe one air, which is Spain.

In the north, for instance, are the Welsh-like Basques, who dig mines and write incomprehensible poetry; there are the north-west Galicians, who have Celto-Irish blood, inhabit green hills among the Atlantic mists, drink raw red wine, own the bones of St James and blow on bagpipes for strange formal dances. Eastward, in Catalonia, are the only Europeans in Spain – a brilliant, restless, politically agitated people whose city, Barcelona, is the most 'advanced' and is perhaps half in love with Paris. These three, the Basques, Galicians and Catalans, have independent dreams and separate languages.

In the middle of the country is something else again: the bare, almost mile-high plain of Castile, a place of ringing emptiness and rare blue air, whose solitary distances have bred cruelty and saints as well as the half-crazed idealism of Quixote. Much of it is desert, where hungers grow huge and put on flesh to torment the wanderer. But in the centre, like an anchored liner at sea, rides the fantastic city of Madrid.

Madrid is probably the first and best place for the hurried traveller to visit, for it contains all Spain, like an anthology. Until 1607 a neglected provincial town, it was commanded to exist, with one of those supremely royal gestures, by Philip III. Now it is the wonder of its two million inhabitants.

'When I die,' they say, 'let me go to heaven, but let me have a little window to look down on Madrid.' It is difficult to interpret the Madrileno's passion for his city but it doesn't take long to share it. It is in many ways an ugly place; its main streets are vulgar and pretentious, its public buildings swollen platitudes in stone, its slums worse than those of

Naples. But it is one of the few cities in the world still used as a frame for living rather than as a labyrinth in which to work and hide. There is at all times in the streets a palpable *alegria*, which all who come may share, arising from the warm, relaxed manners of a people who would rather make friends than money.

Spread on its plateau, under huge stars at night and by day within a sharp sight of the mountains, Madrid has a vigour that only high towns know. At no time during the day or night does the city seem to run down. The inhabitants move in clockwork tides to the pull of their traditional pleasures. As the night-lovers depart the dawn-markets wake up. The washed-down streets catch the edge of the sun. There are smells of fresh coffee and burning charcoal, and the market stalls are all noise and glitter, piled with great presses of vegetables and fish and streaming with rainbows of morning water.

After breakfast you walk – as does everyone else – and re-acquaint yourself with vertical man. To the parks, per-haps, with their frock-coated photographers, their starched children pretty as pies. Or to the Prado, stacked with its glowing Goyas – which like wine seem much headier here at their source than anywhere else on earth. Or to pick over the Rastro, the city's flea market, where one can buy anything unimaginable – a medieval soup pot, a tame flamingo, a sack of horseshoes or a suit of lights.

About noon (or at any moment you choose before it) you may stop at some cool-scrubbed tavern. The tide of apéritif drinkers – which includes most of Madrid – begins then to approach its flood. Glasses of sherry, manzanilla and ver-mouth line the bars like golden tulips. With each drink you will be served, from great blocks of ice, some of the best sea food in the world – oysters, lobsters, crayfish, prawns, sea snails, cockles and crabs. It is now the holy hour in Madrid, the peak of the middle day. There are rapturous reunions between dandy young men who have not seen each other for at least twenty minutes. Passenger trains all over the country have been halted or shunted into sidings in order that the crustaceans from Biscay, Vigo and Málaga may be rushed still alive to the city. And here, in the heart of the baking land, hundreds of miles from any ocean, the inheritors of Cristóbal Colón drink, pause, break the crust from a prawn and smell again the salt seas of past glories.

As well as the sea food with which any bar will provide you, there will also be a range of delicious hot morsels – fried tongue, baked sparrows, larks on a spit, stewed cow's belly and kidneys in garlic. Such tidbits, though for many a banquet in themselves, are designed merely to awake the appetite. At three in the afternoon comes the main meal of the day, and in Madrid this must not be missed.

In a country that is not particularly renowned for its cooking (other than for its habit of delicious apéritifs), Madrid has several famous old restaurants, all relatively cheap, that specialize in traditional dishes. One does well if in the first place one knows what to avoid. Spain of the three seas is of course best with its sea food, next with its stews and its treatment of game. Meat other than pig is not good. But in old restaurants such as Lhardy's you will meet memorable dishes that offer the best of regional Spain.

Cocido Madrileño is the city's own. It is a stew for giants, made of chick-peas, potatoes, red and black sausage, fat bacon, chicken and herbs. The Valencian *paella* is another great filler – a pile of saffron-baked rice mixed with chicken and shellfish, such as mussels, small crabs and prawns. Other dishes that will bring you the flavours of coast, of mountain or the hot dry plains are *Langosta a la Catálana* (fried slices of lobster served in saffron sauce with white wine, pimento and parsley); *Bacalao a la Vizcaina*, a north-coast dish of smoked cod, tomato, thyme, red peppers, onions, bay leaf and garlic; *Cochinillo*, from Segovia, a royal platter of suckling pig, usually cooked over a wood fire; and *Fabada*, a stew of fine-chopped haricots, Galician ham, pigs' ears, smoked bacon, fresh bacon, red and black sausage and any vegetables the cook can lay hands on. Such dishes are usually taken with a kilo of bread and a bottle of wine per person.

Naturally the midday meal will knock you clean out and send you crawling to your hotel for sleep. The slumber that follows will be long and dreamless and will carry you on into the late afternoon. When you next sally forth you find the world reborn, with everyone fresh as salads. The siesta habit offers two days in one, and your second day is the evening. All appetites are now renewed and there are many ways in which to use them. First the luxury shops along the Gran Vía or Alcalá, or in the little arcades around the Puerta del Sol. Here you may buy excellent leatherwork and lace and tourist trophies of unforgivable cuteness. If it's high life you want, you can take cocktails at the Ritz or team up with Hollywood at the Castellana Hilton. Or visit the Bar Chicote, of Civil War fame, now living on its past like a garrulous general – its bar stools crowned with failed war correspondents and other bicarbonated copies of Hemingway.

For the tourist, of course, there are the usual attractions: the Sunday bullfight, where you can meet your friends (most Spaniards today prefer football); the tavern of Luis Candelas, in the Arcos de Cuchilleros, whose mild waiters are dressed up as bandits; the 'bullfighters' bars in Núñez de Arce, where they will sell you bulls' ears for fifty pesetas; or the flamenco dives such as La Zambra and El Duende, where you'll see Spanish dancing in its most vigorous decline, with stamping gypsies like glossy black mares dancing to clipped Anglo-Saxon *Olé*'s.

For my part, when I can, I like to go to the old city, the district south of the Puerta del Sol, a shadowy place with sudden outbursts of light – cakeshops, printsellers and the old coaching inns, where carters and truck drivers sit around in the courtyards mending harness and punctures together. Down here at night-time all life is turned outward. Barbers play their guitars between customers. The men are at the bars, the women hang from their windows, the young girls walk up and down, the beautiful children run barefoot till midnight, the old folk doze on the pavements.

From the street peddlers here you can buy a jewelled ring for a few pennies, or camellias and jasmine for a shilling, or a lottery ticket, which is quite worth buying (I have twice won handsome prizes). Just hanging around is a good occupation for the encounters that are likely to occur. Or if feeling more sober you can go to the two national theatres and see Calderón or Lope de Vega. And almost any night, from May to September, there will be a *verbena* in one district or another, a rejoicing in honour of some favourite saint, with dancing, sideshows, balloons and circuses, shooting galleries and African sweetmeats to be washed down with a glass of *anis*.

This, then, is Madrid, the bull's-eye of Spain, stretched high on its sparkling plateau, where duchess and dishwasher speak the same pure Spanish and man is still preferred to the machine, where the days and nights are spent in an electric air and it is almost impossible to be alone.

Fond as I am of this city, however, sooner or later I always turn south. For south is where I most wish to be. South are the cornlands wealed with red poppy, the shipwrecked castles, drunken storks in the vineyards and, on the way, gaunt Toledo, where luminous El Grecos seem to be hanging in every house. Farther south, best of all – beyond the Sierra Morena and the sharp ridge of the Despeñaperros – lies the land of promise, gold Andalusia, tilted towards the sun.

This is the place I feel I know best, to which I return again and again. I came here first as a wandering tramp, long ago, before the Civil War, sleeping each night among the wine-filled fields and playing a violin in the cafés by day. They were the last days of peace and absolute freedom and, spent there, cannot be forgotten.

The Province of Andalusia is the southern edge of Spain, with a coastline some three hundred miles long. It's where the Moorish invasion left its deepest imprint in Europe and was under Islam for seven hundred years. Many of its villages are still severely Arabic, with squat, salt-white houses, heavily barred windows, fortress doors and interior patios. The extreme modesty of the women can only be a relic of purdah; indeed, in some villages they still go veiled.

Almost all that is thought to be most typical of Spain stems from this vivid subtropical region. The cult of the bull – relic of Cretan invaders – has survived here for five thousand years. The modern technique of bullfighting was invented in the hill town of Ronda and most of the best-known toreros of the last hundred years come from two narrow alleys in Cordova. The cult of the horseman, symbol of the Spanish dandy, was born on the bull-herding pastures round Seville. (The American cowboy, curiously enough, was also invented here and imported into the States through Mexico to become the tough-hombre prototype of our TV Quixote with his cut-and dried, black-and-white chivalry.)

Music and dance, the guitar and flamenco, also come from this province, through Africa. The guitar was originally an Arab instrument and the flamenco is clearly Oriental. Some of the most famous Spanish dancers of theatre and cabaret were raised in the gypsy caves of Andalusian Granada or in the gypsy ghettos of Seville. Most of the classical dance forms of the flamenco school – the *Sevillana, Granadina, Malagueña, Fandango de Huelva* – were developed in the hot solitudes of the cities that bear their names. And from the red fields of Jerez, Puerto de Santa Maria and Cordova come the sherries, brandies and amontillados that give the dancers their hysteric powers.

But Andalusia is not just the tourist's dream, the *vida tipica* of the travel poster. It is also the home of starving fishermen and beggar poets, of smugglers, clowns and mad-men, of a people indolent, amiable and vague, mixing cruelty with acts of kindness, and of great religious festivals under whose Christian cloak much older gods are worshipped – Adonis mourned and Osiris buried, Astarte borne in from the sea, the Virgin Earth-Mother praised and prayed to and the corn god resurrected at Easter. . . .

This is an old stretch of land whose signs of occupation go back to the beginnings of man, with rich-painted caves scattered throughout the area – and some of them still inhabited. It is a grape-blue landscape saved from being a desert by the snow waters of the big sierras. Blindfolded mules still draw water from the wells dug by slaves a thousand years back. The earth is rich with quick-growing harvests, with sugar and wheat and olives. In the lives of the farmers, in their tools and techniques, you will see manners unchanged since Homer.

Perhaps the most intimate way to get to know this province

is to travel on the small local buses. One should avoid, if possible, the money-raddled coasts and the well-defined tourists' tracks. Go from city to town, from town to village, make no plans and stop where you will. You will be rewarded by a chain of surprises, and each will be your own discovery.

In Algeçiras, for instance – which the tourist ignores – you can talk to smugglers loaded with watches. Or go to the small local theatre (hard seats, one shilling) and see some of the best strolling players in Spain. In Jerez de la Frontera you can drink sherry from the source and eat free fish just caught from the bay. In Seville, for a pittance, you can learn Spanish dancing in a week and have your name baked and glazed on a tile. In Granada, under the Sierra Nevadas, city of hawks and sadness, you can see the palace of the desert kings, whose lyrical gardens, full of fountains and nightingales, are kept fresh by the mountain springs.

Between cities, take a bus to the cut-off country, to such villages as Medina Sidonia. Bad roads will protect you; there will be only small inns to stay at; but you will be rewarded by a landscape pure as the sea, ancient, wind-ravaged and bare, where storks and vultures circle majestic skies above herds of black fighting bulls. Show that you are in no hurry, that you're ready to let things happen, and the human encounter, which is Spain, will follow. Before you know it you will be invited to a wedding, to a birth or to a pig-killing feast. And if you know a little Spanish everyone will be delighted and will praise you for having taken the trouble.

The great show places are all clearly marked. Follow the first footsore type you see with a camera and he will lead you to them. Meanwhile if you are still restless, feel you haven't seen enough, hire a donkey or mule, leave the main roads altogether and take one of the old drove tracks inland. These are shepherd paths, several thousand years old, and cover most of the wilder country. You will move slowly, in solitude, through steep brooding gorges, over bridges put there by the Romans; you will sleep rough, drink harsh wines, feed on stews of beans or perhaps nothing but bread and olives. But you will be entering a Spain that few have seen, the Spain

of the Middle Ages, passing through silence like an act of
God, into regions of rock and pine, arriving finally at villages
that appear never to have been visited or that seem to have
been waiting for you to come.

Mexico

FLYING in to Mexico on a warm spring night, the only colour I saw was the moon, newly risen and rusty, picking out curves in the Rio Grande. I remember feeling the presence of Mexico even before I could see it: its vibrations seemed to possess the sky; I felt the raw, tense muscles of the sierras below me, the antiquity of buried yet surviving gods.

It is always strange and questioning to arrive at a place at night, especially a place one has long waited to visit, when its features are shadowed and turned away in sleep, and one can only speculate and wait for the morning.

The next morning, in fact, I woke in Mexico City to find a bright sun and the veils drawn away. Here was the beginning, the heart of Mexico, standing on a plateau seven thousand feet high, populated by five million people, and ringed by mountains, and guarded by two great volcanoes. Popocatépetl and Iztaccíhuatl gaze down through perpetual snows, and it is from behind their twin peaks that the sun rises each day, and it was from between them, long ago, that Cortez and his men entered the valley to destroy the Aztecs.

For Mexico is the oldest living city in America. It was built on islands, with gardens anchored in barges, and even today it has a floating air. Its lakes have dried up, but it has a cushiony crust that acts as a shock absorber for earthquakes, and you can still feel a curious dimpling in the ground when a heavy truck goes by.

Today the capital is in a time of building, extending, and changing daily. I saw skyscrapers of glass and mud-baked hovels, colonial churches and Hilton hotels, Parisian-type boulevards and open-drain back streets, blond Americans and obsidian Aztecs. My hotel was Edwardian – full of brass cuspidors, potted palm trees, and whispering bell-boys. While outside there were Indians selling stuffed tamales and corn-cobs to passers-by.

Mexico City, they'd warned me, was pretty strong stuff; I'd been advised to approach it with caution. 'As it's over seven thousand feet up, beware the lack of oxygen; one drink has the strength of three; food's highly spiced, so take it easy; watch out for altitude sickness. . . .' In fact I never felt better, I walked on my toes, the altitude cleared my head, food was various and delicious, and after three quick tequilas I felt I possessed the secrets of the world.

Tequila, the national drink, is made from the heart of a cactus. It is served short and colourless and is taken with fresh sliced lime and a dash of salt on the hand to refresh you. Three, to begin with, is perhaps two too many, but it is exalting without being sinister. For lunch I ate tacos – little rolled-up tortillas stuffed with pork, chili sauce, and raw onion. It is an old Indian dish, enjoyed by Mexicans of all classes, tasty and more comforting than a sandwich.

Walking the sun-warm streets I seemed to see the city close up, lit by sudden flashes of chance. Flowers blew about like coloured wastepaper, and the place was curiously ex-posed with life. I remember a man in a doorway eating fried eggs from his hat, which he'd sprinkled with scarlet peppers. Another, nearby, was selling sauce from a bottle – a penny a shake, if you brought your own food. I saw a boy with a gun carrying two canvas sacks stamped 'Wells Fargo' and jingling with pesos; and a red, racing fire-truck whose bells and sirens said, not 'Look out' nor 'Alas', but 'Hurrah!'

I remember the faces, too – the broad-jowled mestizos, and the occasional steel-grey descendant of Spain; but mostly I remember those far older than Spain, the original soft-footed possessors of the country. What other modern city still has so much of its prehistory walking so vividly about its streets? I saw families of Indians, bare-toed on the pave-ments, bringing in vegetables and pottery from the hills, the men striding ahead as though opening up a jungle, the women and children trotting after. Their dark faces, carved as from volcanic rock, were the faces of Mayan idols – high-cheeked, hawk-nosed, with sharp flaring nostrils, some with slanting Mongolian eyes. Mexico City today may be nudging the future and paving its streets with automobiles, but it can no more shake off these possessors of its past than a tree can shake off its birds.

Later in the day, I drove up the three-mile Reforma to the Zocalo, the old heart of the city. This vast empty square, in the afternoon sun, seemed haunting and far removed from the present. Here stood Montezuma's Palace, and the Temple of the War God – to whom twenty thousand prisoners were once sacrificed in a day. Here the iron hand of Spain slapped down on the Aztecs and reduced a civilization to a mere curiosity. The Halls of Montezuma were replaced by Cortez's Palace, the shrine of the war god by the Spanish cathedral.

Diego Rivera painted his 'History of Mexico' around the main staircase and along the upper gallery of the palace of Cortez – now the National Palace. The work is a brilliant and bigoted masterpiece and offers an explosive introduction to the country. Rising from the roots of the walls on throbbing rainbows of paint, the story unfolds like a proliferating jungle.

One large fresco depicts the old Aztec market. A tall tattooed beauty bears an armful of lilies among human limbs hung up for sale. There are corncobs and beans, fish and wild birds, lizards, frogs and deer; and glittering in the background the silver lake-city of Mexico, with its causeways and floating gardens, its thousand peaked temples, their steps washed with blood, and the walls of the volcanoes behind.

Wherever you look at these murals, the details are compelling, sensational flashes of strife and terror – a red-bearded Spaniard putting an Indian to the sword, a stone knife in a horse's belly, frail bows and arrows pricking at the mouths of cannons, an Aztec temple burning; then rape, torture, the branding of slaves on the face, the chaining of peasants for work in the mines, a fair blue-eyed baby on its Indian mother's back, priests snarling over nuggets of gold. From this grows revolution and its proclamations, rifles and banners in the streets, till the great blood-red face of Mexico's pagan sun is replaced by the pale whiskered moon of Karl Marx.

It is a powerful, naïve, flash-vision of history, seen through the eyes of a man of passion. Distorted though it may be, it has the thrust of life, and could have been painted by no one without blood-roots in Mexico. Its glowing themes and colours, laid on these stern Spanish walls, seemed to me to be a reconquest by the Indians.

Mexico City at night is for self-indulgence. The streets round my hotel – Calle Londres and Hamburgo – were lighted treasure boxes in the early evening. Here was hand-beaten jewellery in gold and silver (chunky-barbaric or fine as an eyelash), blown glass, embroidered blouses, Indian scarves and shawls, and calfskin suits as soft as your cheek. There were also bright precious stones newly dug from the hills – chalcedony, opal, and onyx – and old squat gods still caked with earth, primitive paintings and carved wooden saints.

With a Mexican friend I went to several bars and night-clubs: La Ronda, Jacaranda, Can-Can, El Presidente. We ended up at Mauna Loa, where the dining-room is thatched with bamboo and palm leaves and has a pool full of sleeping flamingos. When dinner began the pool was covered for dancing, and the music woke up the flamingos, who uncoiled their necks and started walking round the tables spiking the food with their long pink beaks.

Later, rather dazed, we walked back to the hotel, and passed a night school where they were learning English. On the blackboard, in chalk, it said: 'Call the Doctor'. A group of Indians stared in through the window. 'Aren't you just flabbergasted by Mexico City?' asked my friend. 'And aren't you flabbergasted that I know the word flabbergast?'

The next day I set off, with a car and driver, on a round trip through Guadalajara, a six-hundred-mile journey through mountains and tableland. I got my first smell of the country coming over a rust-red ridge of volcanic hills into crumbling, dusty farmland. After the glassy brilliance of the capital city, here was the naked flesh of Mexico. Among a scattering of hovels stood neat stacks of maize topped with lucky charms and little crosses of straw. Hens and pigs raced about, and bent low in the fields were those Indians who had always been there.

After a drive of an hour, the country whitened like frost, and we came to Tula, the holy city of the Toltecs. Cement factories nearby chewed the ashen ground, and all the trees were covered with dust. On the top of the hill stood the great stepped temple, the house of the priests and the sacred courts of the ball game.

This was the shrine of Quetzalcoatl, the blond, bearded god, the plumed serpent, said to have come from the east. From this hill his cult spread eight hundred miles south to Yucatan and was also adopted by the conquering Aztecs. Quetzalcoatl, they say, stole the corn from the ants and gave it to the Toltecs to cultivate, and later sailed back east towards the rising sun, promising he would return. Who was he then? Corn god, sun god, or some early visitor from the Mediterranean? Whoever he was, when Cortes landed from Spain the Aztecs thought he was their god returning.

The temple at Tula is one of the most remarkable in Mexico. It is topped by fifteen-foot warriors carved from huge blocks of stone, majestic, silent, and threatening. The lower walls are protected by carved jaguars and eagles – the defensive forces of land and air. A farther wall bears a frieze of the symbol of Quetzalcoatl, plumed serpents disgorging human skeletons. Most sombre of all is a separate stone figure, Chac-Mool, the reclining rain god, who holds on his belly a dish for torn-out human hearts, while turning his head in a blank stare at the horizon.

From Tula we turned eastwards through lion-coloured country, tufted with cactus and wiry mesquite, with a scattering of blue lakes where busy Indian washerwomen were plunging their arms into the reflected mountains. We passed San Juan del Río, a town of pink domes, which seemed to be in the grip of some curious holiday. Most of the men were in the bars, most of the women in the cemeteries, while the rest were out plodding the country roads carrying banners and wheels of fireworks.

Presently we arrived at Querétaro, a town as noble as any

in Castile. It is packed with churches and colonial mansions, and to enter it one drives under a magnificent aqueduct that still brings water six miles from the hills. Streets are paved with flagstones, and the great doorways of the houses are heavy with nails and heraldic devices. Everywhere there is a glitter of glazed tiles and fountains and glimpses of patios full of flowers and birds.

In a back-street workshop I saw a boy polishing opals, another digging them out of lumps of quartz and then throwing them casually into a bucket of water where they sprang alive like instant fire. Down in the market there was a group of Indians who appeared to be eating the heads of wolves. They asked me to join them, but instead I went to a bar, which was full of pictures of dying bullfighters. Two old men were talking, and, as I ordered a beer, I heard one of them say to the other; 'Pedro's so bored he's been out in the country painting faces on all the stones.'

The Covento de la Cruz still dominates Querétaro like a fortress. One small brown friar seemed to be all that was left of that once great brotherhood of Franciscans. He was busy selling thorns from a bush in the garden, picking them carefully and popping them into envelopes. Near the bush was a ladder leading to a small stone tower where the Emperor Maximilian was imprisoned. As we drove from the town we passed the Hill of Bells where the bewildered emperor was shot.

It was now afternoon, and the landscape seemed empty. The light shone in the heat like glass. I saw an Indian family sitting in the shade of a tree like tropical fish hiding under a rock. But nothing else moved save a few flapping vultures and the wild dog that ran beside them.

Then, as it cooled, we came to the edge of a hill and looked down at San Miguel Allende. Trickling in terraces from the hill to the plain, it is a memorably beautiful town, and after Mexico City it was like drinking a fine old wine after excesses of chemical fruit juice.

Almost perfectly preserved, its Spanish-colonial buildings seemed as fine as those of Querétaro. Architecturally, everywhere there was power and grace, lightness as well as strength, and the rose-pink stone gave a warmth and humanity even to its severest religious structures. The walls of the houses were decorated with coloured paper, with silver and copper masks. A delicate-pink light bounced up from the pavement, filling faces with gentle radiance. All was colour – the parish church with its Indo-Gothic tower, a genial fantasy in strawberry stone; young men in broad hats with swinging tassels; donkeys with embroidered harnesses; and girls in blue blouses, red skirts, and black stockings, each with a shower of dark hair to her waist.

San Miguel was one of the cradles of Mexican independence; and I was reminded of this, as we drove out of the town, by the sight of a red-shirted drunk wandering happily round the streets closely followed by two hired musicians.

The sun was going down as we passed Dolores Hidalgo, whose bells signalled the revolution. As colours flared and died, we drove into the forested mountains, home of bee keepers and charcoal burners, and saw the last light fading on curling wood smoke, painted beehives, and almond blossoms. My final glimpse of that day was typically surrealist, the sort of thing one learns to expect – two old men, far out in the country, walking into the sunset, one carrying a cello, the other a huge bass fiddle.

We spent that night in Guanajuato, an old mining town in a gorge, which from the hills, as we approached it in the dark, looked like a vein of silver in a cave. Guanajuato, in fact, had one of the richest silver mines in America, sufficient to refill the coffers of Spain, in the days when Indians worked chained underground and were paid off with lumps of silver.

The mountains that crowd round the town are immense, almost brutal; metallic, turned inside out. But packed in the gorge are great churches and villas – relics of those ancient riches – and beautiful winding streets, wrought-iron balconies, and little squares full of trees and fountains.

Seen from the hills in daylight, the buildings of Guanajuato resemble a crowded library of ancient books, leather-bound, well-thumbed, disordered and overlapping, but each different and irreplaceable. Lyrical as they are, they include some sinister curiosities – the standing dead in the catacombs (preserved by the minerals in the ground), the flooded mines, the abandoned suburbs of Marfil, with their creeper-grown streets, and the iron cages hanging from the walls of the granary which once held the severed heads of the revolutionary leaders.

The next day, at noon, we came to San Juan de los Lagos, and to an occasion I shall never forget. Some sixty thousand pilgrims had come from all over Mexico to honour the feast of the local Virgin. The sight was staggering, not of this age at all; like a mass gathering of Biblical tribes. A thousand white tents, flapping in the hot, dry wind, covered the hillside round the little town, filling the woods and canyons, crowding the banks of the river, even pressing against the walls of the houses. A roar of life rose above the encampments, a mixture of music, laughter, and cries; smoke from a thousand fires filled the sunny air, harnesses and blankets hung from the trees; magnificent horsemen rode among the tent poles and children scooted round their hoofs like turkeys.

The great multitude of pilgrims was a decoration to the landscape; they belonged to these dusty groves; standing, walking, crouching in the shade of trees, or gathered in family groups at their food; but particularly by the lake, where their white and blue figures shone in the distance like quivering irises, and the graceful veiled women came with jars on their heads, pausing awhile above their bright reflections, then knelt to draw water or to wash their brown arms among the muzzles of the drinking horses.

The great local fair was one of the most important in Mexico, and the local Virgin one of the oldest. Down in the town it was almost impossible to move; peddlers, musicians, feather-tufted dancers, jostled each other on every side. Many of the pilgrims had come great distances, whole families spending days on the road. Many had come in answer to a vow, and to some it was a last act of faith: I saw a number of old women, and a man with a boy on his shoulders, coming down the steep cobbled street on their knees, finishing their journey at the point of exhaustion with glazed eyes fixed on the church.

San Juan de los Lagos, on this day of wind and sun, called up prodigious energies of adoration and gaiety. The inside of the church throbbed all day with cries, and people panted to fight their way in. Outside, the dancers, some in animal skins, some in feathers like Aztec priests, cavorted unceasingly in trance-like groups to the music of lute and drum. I saw as many as a dozen groups at once, tossing their heads like shaggy chrysanthemums, while the mirrors stitched to their clothing sent reflections of the sun racing like meteors across the dark walls of the church.

I couldn't bear to leave this rousing multitude and wanted to share in it. I sat in the square to eat my prepacked lunch, and hired a wandering orchestra to play for me. For about fifty pence I got a heart-rending song accompanied by four fiddles, three guitars, and a trumpet. I couldn't eat what the hotel had given me – so I gave the egg to an old lady, the apple to a boy, and the sandwich to a passing horse.

The next day we started back from Guadalajara – a large and sophisticated town. The drive to Mexico City took two fast days and covered some dramatic country. First, red rolling hills, full of solitary horsemen, and occasional herds of long-horned cattle.

We came to Lake Pátzcuaro and Tzintzuntzan – 'the place of the hummingbirds'. (Many old Indian names are onoma-topoeic: Guanajuato, for instance, 'the place of the frogs', has a fine swampy croak about it; and 'Tzintzuntzan' is said softly and evenly, to produce the whispering buzz of wings.) Tzintzuntzan was the great city of the Tarascan Indians and is still dominated by the burial mounds of their kings. It is a small village now and seemed to be full of little girls, who raced around me like humming tops, and sold me some angels made of straw, showed me some old olive trees, and then rang the church bell for me.

We spent a night at Pátzcuaro, and ate whitefish from the lake, and looked at the butterfly fishing boats and the islands. This rose-coloured town, with its large straggling squares, stone arcades, and tall, cool trees, had an air of freshness – part lake and part mountain – that set it apart as a place to return to.

The drive next day – nearly two hundred miles through mountains – was like a shuffling of coloured cards. I remember Morelia; another superb colonial town, with buildings of an extraordinary elegance, and squares of great trees dripping with curtains of bougainvillaea shot through with ice-blue jacaranda. After Morelia came the mountains, climbing to ten thousand feet, through silent and scented forests, and stopping at Mil Cumbres to see a thousand blue peaks, heaped like diamonds, stretching away to the Pacific.

On the last stretch, near Toluca, Indian families were everywhere, swarming in clusters along the sides of the road; the women brilliant in purples, blues, and scarlets, with silver brooches pinned to their hair. Dressed apparently for fiesta, each of their garments was a tradition, scrupulously correct according to tribe. And set against the great hot fields, with the blue volcanoes in the background, it seemed that no people better suited their landscape.

I spent my last days in Mexico at Oaxaca in the south – down where the horn of the country grows narrowest. It stands on a mile-high plateau, completely surrounded by mountains, has houses built of soft, green stone, and nearby are the ruins of two imperial cities, those of Mítla and of Monte Albán.

I arrived on the morning of market day, and Oaxaca market is one of the biggest in the south. Apart from the absence of slaves and human limbs and lizards, it might not have changed for a thousand years. There were stalls of black pottery and terra-cotta animals, delicate basketwork, shawls, and *sarapes*, spiced herbs in sacks, caged birds, live poultry, and enough flowers for the carnival of Nice.

The people were as exotic as the merchandise, especially the women – Mixtecs, Zapotecs, Olmecs from the north, blanket-weavers from Mítla and Tehuantepec, their oyster-coloured veils worn with every variety of grace, sometimes piled on the head like Arabs, sometimes wrapping a child like a leaf round a lily. Some wove coloured ribbon in their plaited hair, while others wore mannish sombreros. One charming sight: a young Otomi mother breast-feeding her infant son, who sucked dreamily away with a small slouch hat tilted jauntily on the back of his head.

The main square of Oaxaca was full of blossoming trees and had a pagoda-like bandstand in the middle. Black squirrels drop suddenly out of the branches to eat lemon peel out of your hand. In the evening the town gathered to listen to the band, arranging themselves in circles, the married with children sitting up near the bandstand, the teen-agers ranging the outside edges. In the shadows old men, with long Mayan faces, sat listening entranced to Strauss, while peddlers went round selling balloons and puppets, trays of jellies and toffeed fruits.

Visiting Monte Albán, once the imperial city of the Zapotecs, I found it less a ruin than a monument to giants. Raised on its hilltop, which is itself an altar, it commands the plain and the glittering ring of mountains, and for its size and mystery, and the natural grandeur of its setting, it seemed as impressive as the Acropolis of Athens. Its buildings, including the two great pyramids, look as solid as they ever were – except for the wandering goats feeding on the steps of the priests and searching for grass around the sacred altars.

Farther south is Mítla, the Mixtec 'City of the Dead', unique for its abstract geometrical mosaics. Shaped columns, huge boulders, delicate tracery of tiles, tricks of perspective, refined weaving in stone – all were cut and fitted without metal tools or mortar and have stood for eight hundred years.

Mítla and Monte Albán, like other old Mexican cities, show the Indians' extraordinary architectural genius. They had a feeling for size, balance, and for Promethean gestures in stone, which could only have sprung from a precise mastery of materials. They were great artists, too, and understood the complexity of the stars, and were sophisticated when most of mankind were savages. Yet everything they did was like a gigantic piling-up of arms against one common enemy – the gods. Their religion and rituals showed them at the mercy of the spirits: they feared nature, time, and fate. Even the best of their art was less praise for life than supplication and bribery. Yet one cannot blame them; all civilizations at some time have fallen into this total terror, when the mystery of life was a kind of panic only to be assuaged by the spilling of blood.

I saw this again, in miniature, at a cock-fight on my last day in Oaxaca – the spectators emotionless, dark as stone, almost dreamlike around the ring; the steel-spurred cocks, feathered like warrior priests, slashing open each other's breasts, and the Indian trainer snatching up his dying bird to suck the blood from its head and eyes.

Then I was flying out of Mexico, looking down at the country and scarcely believing I'd been there, watching the small hot whirlwinds move over the fields, robbing and replenishing the land, the little ghosts of brown dust that gently cover the temples, and fill up the craters of the extinct volcanoes.

A Wake in Warsaw

In the month of their worst weather – and the month also of their most melancholy historical memories – the Poles were paying tribute to Adam Mickiewicz, national poet, patriot, romantic, and a hundred years dead. And in honour of this affair the Polish Government – displaying a romantical-political-mystical view of poetry which I from the West found quite unusual – invited, from all over the world, professors, scholars, and poets to join with them in these celebrations. Five such figures were invited from Great Britain, all expenses paid. But as it turned out, I was the only one able to accept.

The invitation came to me in a warm and frantic voice over the telephone from the Polish authorities in London. It seemed that the other four had already made their apologies. The voice was that of a hostess determined to prevent the wreck of a dinner party. It invited me to fly straightway to Warsaw. But of course I was glad to go.

For what could be more innocent than the celebration of a Byronic poet a hundred years dead? Besides I dearly wished to join the ranks of the behind-the-iron-curtain bores and so be protected from them for ever more. I also wanted to prove whether I could survive the Polish winter. And to find out who Mickiewicz was.

But I decided not to fly. I wanted to taste, at the tempo of the train, the slow approach to Warsaw with all its frontiers. So tickets were provided, and I set off.

On the dawn of the second day I entered Germany, changed trains at Stuttgart, and waited an hour for the Warsaw coach. I had not been to this country before, and I observed with interest the hurrying Germans, so long the bogies of my childhood. Brisk, raincoated, carrying brief-cases like heraldic shields, they emptied themselves from their suburban trains and hastened like lovers to their work. Porters, inspectors, and ticket-collectors were uniformed and swagger as Luftwaffe pilots. Painters, even at that early hour, were painting the station like mad. The obsession seemed to be: never to be caught not working – as curious a conformity as its opposite which prevails elsewhere.

My Warsaw coach, when it arrived, was labelled Second Class and Third Class – and it was explained to me that there was no official First Class, but that Second Class was in fact First Class though formally labelled Second (and, for that matter, Third was also Second). In my comfortable and super-heated compartment, I crossed that daylight Germany, through forests of conifers and hop-poles, across neat and banded landscapes striped like medieval England. Towards Nuremburg the sky darkened and it began to snow. One by one the American Army officers picked up their field-green luggage and left us. The restaurant car was taken off. The carriages on the train grew rapidly fewer. We were approaching Czechoslovakia.

The formalities at Schirnding, the German frontier, were swift and easy. Nobody seemed to care where we were going, or why. There was just time to buy a last German beer. Girls waved from the country platform and shouted jovi-alities. Then the train, so small and quiet now, creaked slowly eastwards through a shallow snow-flecked cutting; the landscape was dark and wet and birchy, and I awaited with excitement the appearance of the Communist frontier. When it came, it did not disappoint.

First, across the cabbagy fields, a broad band of tank-traps came into sight, black as liquorice in the driving sleet. Next, tall wooden watch-towers, with legs astride, stood at stern intervals about the horizon, observing, threatening, keeping their own grim council. Then a dozen soldiers, furry as rabbits, appeared from nowhere and trotted beside the train. With Russian-style hats and quilted coats, they looked as cuddly as children's toys, except for the shining tommy-guns in their hands.

The train halted in a dilapidated station, slate-dark, weedy, like a country halt in Wales. We were in Czechoslovakia. The soldiers took up their positions on either side of the train and watched the windows. In the compartments all was still. There was a great silence, and for a while nothing happened.

While we waited, I peered through the steaming windows to see what I could. Great black engines stood in the sidings, with rusty red stars fixed to their funnels. There were some silent military huts, as scruffy and homeless as anywhere in the world. The platforms were of wet, marshy gravel. There were no kiosks, buffets, paper-sellers, money-changers, or any of the usual business of frontier towns. I saw a troupe of about forty women marching across a muddy field. In the distance a country house, pink, florid, stood in ruins. The only new and polished objects in sight were the bayonets and tommy-guns of the sentinel soldiers.

Suddenly the frontier inspectors arrived, as smart as guard's officers, polite as head waiters, bowing, saluting, and talking all languages. They looked under the seats, took our passports away, and didn't come back for two hours.

At last, in the gathering, vaporous dusk, we moved out of the station. We crossed Czechoslovakia in darkness, and it is the darkness that I chiefly remember. Every so often we stopped at a large town, but the town and the station seemed half-lit and deserted, as though in a state of war.

Towards nine o'clock we arrived in Prague, but the streets were empty, everybody seemed to have gone to bed, and there was nothing to be seen except the stars in the river. We were due for a three-hour wait here, and I was told that an official would meet me and give me dinner.

I stepped from the train, feeling homeless and far away. The platform emptied and I was left alone with one small dark-suited man, who ignored me. We paced up and down for a while, then I heard a gasp: 'But, Mr Lee?' Yes, I said, and the small man whistled with astonishment, then sighed and shook my hand.

We walked to a hotel nearby and had dinner. My companion said he had eaten already, but he had another one all the same. He was a thin young man, seen in the hotel light, with pale eyes and a desperate smile. He seemed very ill at ease, tapping his feet and drumming his fingers continuously. We ate goose, dumplings, and ice-cream, with Pilsen beer. The man, in his tuneless English, struggled hard to talk of culture. Towards the end of the meal I asked him what had become of Jiri Mucha, the Czech poet, who returned to Prague from London some years ago and of whom nothing had been heard since.* At my question the man paused abruptly in his fidgeting and looked at me in expressionless silence for a moment. Then he said, 'Mucha? Mucha?' and drew his fingertip across the tablecloth. 'Do you know, that is very interesting. "Mucha" is our word for "fly".'

I left it at that, and we went back to the station. The Warsaw train was crowded with stalwart young men. I knew I would have to sit up all night, but there was nowhere to sit. 'Do not worry,' said my companion. He threw open a compartment door and in quiet, icy tones, addressed the travellers within. I caught the words 'delegate' and 'poet'. Immediately everyone jumped to their feet. I selected a corner seat and sat down. The displaced person waved cheerily at me, said 'Sleep well, Johnny', in English, and went and sat in the corridor. But I slept badly, for the rest of my fellow travellers, either through habit or by design, ate apples throughout the night.

Poland appeared next day in a grey veil of driving sleet. I had drugged myself, so I didn't see much of it. I remember dimly a deterioration of landscape; flat, soggy fields; dark, wood-walled villages; hovels with thatched, weed-sprouting roofs; peasants on muddy roads, heads down to the weather; steaming horses drawing long four-wheeled wagons; fat, trousered women working the stations and the level-crossings.

Then, after a long, dozing, twilit day, we arrived in Warsaw. I expected ruins; instead I saw a city. The slow approach to the station took us through the rain-drenched suburbs,

* The disappearance was only temporary.

thickly inhabited but curiously unformed. What struck me immediately was the commercial chastity of the place. Factories, blocks of flats, institutes, rose squarely out of the suburban mud. But no hoardings, no shops, no cinemas, petrol stations or cosy cafés. No motor-cars – only wagons and huddled pedestrians about the streets. And at regular intervals along the track, hand-painted slogans on strips of wood, though rather worn and flaking.

At Warsaw station I was received by a delegation of welcome – though we didn't recognise each other immediately. It was rather reminiscent of Prague. The platform emptied and I walked up and down. By the barrier stood four women, plump, in mackintoshes, and wearing what looked like bathing caps on their heads. They fluttered with anxiety and peered around the platform, but when they saw that no one else was getting off the train they decided that I must be the one.

They introduced themselves. Two were official porters, and they seized my bags. One was my interpreter. The older one was a famous Polish writer, chosen to honour me with a personal welcome. She gave me short shrift, however; she told me I was late, drove with me in silence to my hotel, shook hands sharply like a disappointed marriage-broker, then disappeared and I never saw her again.

The biggest hotel in Warsaw had been set aside to house the foreign guests. 'Hotel Bristol' it said in large letters across the front, though I was told the name had since been changed. Flags of all nations fluttered from its shrapnel-pitted façade. Its great hall was dark and full of square, shaggy men in caps and padded coats whom I first took to be spies or secret police but who later turned out to be cab-drivers.

The first thing that I had to do was to sign on at the reception desk of the Mickiewicz Committee. Their welcome was efficient and warm. They gave me a booklet of meal-coupons, to last me a week; an authority to make two free telephone calls to anywhere in the world; a guide to Warsaw; a guide to Mickiewicz, and a discreet white envelope stuffed with *zloty* for me to spend.

But I had been travelling for three days; I was almost

speechless with fatigue, self-pity, and the sense of distance I had come. I didn't want to be just another honoured but self-sufficient visitor, to be ticked off on their list; I wanted to establish some special contact, as one in need of particular care. I was not as robust as I looked, I said. I was, in fact, very delicate, and could be carried off by the slightest breath of cruel air.

The Committee at first looked at me with astonishment. Then they warmed to their responsibilities. Their eyes softened; they began to snap their fingers commandingly at each other. Before I knew what was happening they bore me upstairs, established me in a room next door to the First Aid Dispensary, introduced me to the pretty young nurse, shoved her bed hard against my wall, mine hard against hers, and bid me bang on the wallpaper – at any time – if I ever needed her help. It was an arrangement that worked like a charm and gave me lasting confidence and comfort.

Meanwhile my interpreter, a charming, blue-eyed, but rather prim young woman, had ordered me high tea, and she sat with me while I ate it. During the meal she declared that it would be her happy privilege to remain by my side as long as I was in Warsaw. In fact, she would never leave me; it was her duty and her honour. She smiled brilliantly, and I began to buck up. We looked at one another in silence for a while, each examining the possible implications of her duty. Presently she began to ask questions about my work, taking notes of my replies. She frowned when I said lyric poetry and wrinkled her nose. But she gasped with delight when I said I had written a play about John Ball's Peasant Revolt. 'Is it progressive?' she asked. 'Oh yes,' I said. 'We will have it translated immediately,' she said. Her eyes shone; mine shifted uneasily. I don't suppose we were ever closer to each other than at that moment. Certainly we both soon proved unfaithful. She was disappointed by my liking for vodka and by what she called my 'lack of cultural seriousness'. And I must say that her subsequent passion for a certain sober American professor irritated me no end.

The next morning I breakfasted briskly at nine – pork and two eggs, jam, rolls, and coffee. My interpreter, fresh as a scrubbed lettuce, was at my side. We were joined by her colleague, a young, sadly humorous man who worked in the Palace of Culture. He told me that his favourite reading was Webster's Dictionary, and certainly his English, though fluent, was decorated with much unfamiliar bric-à-brac.

As I sat there, warmed by their undivided attention, I felt again a distinction of strangeness, as one who had penetrated secret Tibetan frontiers and made friends with the monks. The light of the morning snowfall shone through the windows, the whisper and click of the Slav languages being spoken around me rustled like cicadas. I was pleased, after all, at being the unique lone traveller from Britain. Then I had a shock.

Sitting quietly alone at a distant table, reading a propped-up book, and patiently awaiting his breakfast, was Graham Greene.

My heart sank. I asked my hosts to excuse me and went across to speak to him. He received me with a detached warmth as though this place were the Savile Club. He looked ruddy and well. As the private guest of some Polish Catholics he had been given a room in the hotel, but he did not qualify for the meal-tickets accorded to State guests. He had, there-fore, been waiting an hour for his private breakfast, and he didn't think he would get any until we pampered poets had first been served. 'In any case,' he said rather testily, 'shouldn't you all be at meetings or something by now?' As we spoke, his breakfast arrived; a glass of chilled vodka and two rolls. He put the rolls aside and drank the vodka. 'I've lived on nothing else,' he said, 'since I got here.' I was pleased to see him, yet chastened and slightly let down. Here, of all places; and after all the trouble I'd taken. It was like sharing Everest with Tenzing.

That morning there was a great stir in the hotel hall. The interpreter-guides, in their mackintoshes and bathing caps, rushed flush-faced here and there. Poets were being rounded up in their separate language groups – half-dozen of Latin-Americans; half-dozen of East Germans; a brace of Balkans, assorted Nordics, and me. Wonderingly we stood in the dark hall, facing the thick double curtains which separated us from the light and cold of the street. And as one waited for the last late bards to be brought from their beds we asked ourselves which of the two great mysteries would first be revealed to us – Mickiewicz or Warsaw city? It proved to be the latter – the poet for the moment was being kept in cold storage.

A fleet of grey official motor-cars drove us fast through the wide and greasy streets. We were bound for a lecture to be given by city architects. They showed us three great solemn maps: Warsaw as it was in 1939 – a mixed-up mosaic of yellow lozenges; Warsaw in 1945 – total destruction; then Warsaw as it was and would be – the mosaic tidied up in red and sliced through by broad north-south, east-west, boulevards; all, that is, except for one original muddle still remaining towards the north. The woman lecturer, in flowery French, referred to this part last. 'As modern architects, you understand, we wish to build only what is new, contemporary, or supra-contemporary. But we have also found it necessary to make a gesture to nostalgia and the sentiment of the middle-aged by rebuilding exactly part of the Old Town.' And the smile she gave us asked forgiveness.

Later, I drove round the thawing, rain-swept city with my two guides. Moody as ever, they sat in a torpor now, making no comment unless I asked a question. And yet that journey, with the obvious reflections that rose out of it, was my most moving experience in Poland. We drove in weaving circles for about three hours: up the great boulevards, snaking through the new Old Town, crossing the sombre acres of flattened ghetto, and past the vulgar, soaring, Russian-built Palace of Culture and Science. We drove through parks, round factories, past the Party Office; looked at the government paper-mill – as large as Olympia – and visited various monuments. But only slowly did I tune-in through my Western-protected senses to what I was seeing. Naked, prim, unfinished, and dateless in aspect, this city, spreading from horizon to horizon and already the home of a million people, was yet one of the youngest cities in the world. Every building one saw, no matter what the style, was new, and every person in the street – clerk, cab-driver, fat wife, or pretty student – each had a tale to tell so steeped in the experience of horror that to us it is still unimaginable.

There are only two other cities in the world that know what Warsaw knows. The destruction of Hiroshima and Nagasaki, by a triumph of super-gadgetry, lasted only some thirty seconds. Warsaw's fate was more old-fashioned, requiring six years of enemy occupation finally to do the trick. But it was just as complete in the end. Villas, tenements, churches, schools, theatres, palaces, libraries, shops; the baroque, the medieval, the formal, the friendly, the charming, and the poor; by bomb and shell, flame-thrower and dynamite; successively, surely, and not always in the heat of battle, all had been wiped away, and the people shot or removed.

All this is known but all this, in Warsaw today, must be remembered. As must also those late months of 1945 when the people of Warsaw, released from their prison camps, drifted back to reoccupy their city. They looked for Warsaw and they found nothing. Nothing but a drifting wilderness of bricks, smelling rankly of the dead. Perhaps here and there, on the edge, a thin and starving house, like a gob of flesh on a burnt-out skeleton. Otherwise nothing. Nothing that was human or memorable or that could be identified as a city. No roofs or glass, no cloth or fires, no tables, altars, books, or bread, no women, children, horses, or fowls. There were no survivors of this destroyed city. The refugees came back to nothing.

They scratched among the jagged waste of brick and found the streets. They scratched again and found the cellars of the dead. And there, for a while, they set up house.

One of the first things they did, as though to re-establish their identity and the identity of Warsaw, was to reconstruct, in exact detail, the squares and winding lanes of the Old Town. Much of this reconstruction has already been completed and it is a miracle of love and patience – working from old photographs and drawings, several hundred houses have been rebuilt exactly as they stood before the dynamiters blew them to the ground. It is strange to walk through those streets today. The ghosts of the wartime dead, returning now, could find their way intimately among these houses. They glitter again in the frosty sunlight in all the paint and gilding of their seventeenth-century splendour, exact from Flemish roof and gable, down painted walls of grapes, boar-hunts, minstrels, and dancing peasants, to the arched and studded doorways of ancient wood, topped by their wrought-iron lamps. It is an architectural resurrection wrapped in a rare emotional haze – as though we had exactly rebuilt the city of London after the Great Fire, taverns, brothels, and all. It lacks only one thing, some breath of its original human life to animate those faultless walls. For though many of the buildings are lived in, by families of grace and favour, they are cold as museums yet.

The Old Town is a nostalgic pocket, and is only a small part of modern Warsaw. But in much of the rest of the rebuilding an eye has been kept on the past. Successions of broad and formally fronted streets have been re-created, some in a curious Georgian style, others exactly as Canaletto painted them. There is also a certain amount in the non-committal, poker-faced, concrete-and-glass, Great West Road tradition. But on the whole it is nostalgia rather than expediency that has gone into the rebuilding of this city, and Warsaw today, standing upon its ashes – a rolled-out raft of brick and bones which it would have taken too long to remove – cannot be viewed without emotion.

My tour ended on the banks of the Vistula. We sat in the motor-car and gazed across the slow and rain-starred river – not much wider than the Thames at Battersea – and saw the low bank where the Red Army sat quietly through the three-month hell of the Warsaw Insurrection, watching the last of the city die. According to all the known patterns of Hollywood films, Russian films, and the Songs of the Partisans, the Red Army, when it saw the people of Warsaw rise and take arms against their oppressors, should have blazed their way across the river and rescued them. But they didn't. The Warsavians, heartened by the sight of the Russians so near, rose up and fought the Germans with anything they could lay their hands on. The Germans machine-gunned them. The people took to the sewers, were starved out, and machine-gunned again. Meanwhile the remains of their city, street by street, was dynamited. And the Red Army sat and watched across the river.

'What happened?' I asked my guides.

The girl said nothing. The voice of the young man, normally so casual and witty, came to me in a clipped and solemn trance.

'The Warsaw Rising was premature,' he said. 'The leaders were traitors. They gave the signal to rise without consulting the Red Army generals. They gave the signal only because they wished for political leadership after the war. The Polish people despise them as opportunists and career-ists. In any case, the Red Army was helpless – their lines of communication were too far extended.'

'Why was no help flown in?'

'Ah, that was the trouble. The rising was split up – a ring of Poles, a ring of Germans, then Poles, then Germans, and so on. Supplies would have fallen into the arms of the Hitler-ites.' He smiled at me softly. 'No can do, you understand?'

By that evening most of the world-wide guests had been gathered in, and when we sat down to eat we filled a banquet-ing hall. We observed each other closely, as though it was the first night out on a liner. There were poets here of every kind, white-maned Russians, turbanned Pakistanis, bright-bloused Bulgarians, slit-eyed Yugoslavs, prim Dutch, clerkly Swedes, knotty Norwegians; Spaniards speaking French, Hindus speaking German, Americans speaking English and Chinese speaking everything.

At my table I had been joined by two professors from prominent United States universities. They had just arrived on separate aircraft and were delighted, almost hysterical, at meeting each other. Sonya, the interpreter, sat demurely between them and they talked across her. Her dazed blue eyes clicked rhythmically between them as though watching a tennis match.

'Did you get photographed at the airport?' one asked the other. 'Boy, *I* did! Carnations, too. Ha ha! And you'll be speaking on the radio too, you know. Oh, yes. The works. But meantime,' voices were lowered, 'let me tell you about the beds. Let me warn you. The mattresses, for instance. . . .'

After a few days the poets began to stray from their language groups and to mix a little. Our kindly interpreters were like nannies, and it was difficult to slip their clinging hands, but we managed it at last. My first break for freedom took me into the Old Town, in search of a tavern. There weren't any. I had a beer at the counter of a State grocer's shop, but it was as thick and sweet as treacle, and cost seven shillings (official rate of exchange). Finally, in a wine-shop in a side-street, I succeeded in persuading an old lady, by a series of dramatic gestures, to slip me a bottle of vodka in exchange for a small tin of Nescafé. She was pleased by the exchange, and the arrangement preserved itself throughout my stay.

In the course of these excursions I ran into the broad bulk of the Czech poet Nezval and we walked together in the snow, though we had no common language. I also met an Egyptian senator-judge, who was also a CBE and a verse-dramatist (and when I told Sonya, later, all the things he was, she was plainly shocked). I walked and talked with a neat Chinese of the same name as myself, and I exchanged quotations with a Hindu. But my favourites were the Latin-Americans, who never lost their personal sense of celebration. Returning, battered, from a four-hour lecture, they would say to me, 'Come, poet, let's go upstairs and have a concert.' There, round a bottle-laden table, they would fight the cold with Andalusian cries. Neruda, the Chilian, would exclaim '*Pan Tadeusz*!' in helpless amazement, then reverse his jacket for added comfort. The Cuban, Guillen, would sing some Indian songs. Rafael Alberti would fill our notebooks with drawings of fighters in suits of light, and his precocious but beautiful fourteen-year-old daughter, Aitana, would slip me poems in English, complaining: 'I know too much . . . I can talk only with angels.'

I spent much time with this cynical, warm-blooded group, but Sonya, in the end, disapproved of it. 'Wouldn't you like to meet some *Polish* writers?' she asked severely. I said I would, and wrote out a list of names. She tucked them into her bag and said she arrange for a meeting immediately. But not one of them ever turned up.

But Mickiewicz? What can I say about Mickiewicz? When I went to Warsaw I knew nothing about him – at least, nothing about the poet. For a week Mickiewicz was the password of our existence. Our rooms were full of his references. The image of his thin face and flowing hair was plastered about the city. We went to long lectures about him. We attended the official opening of his museum (where a German scholar lost a boot and fell flat on his face before the newsreel cameras). The museum was full of heroic sculptures, paintings, death masks, and first editions in Russian. In the theatre we witnessed his static, five-hour play, *Forefather's Eve*. Finally, in the glittering, iced-cake Assembly Hall of the Palace of Culture, accompanied by all the leaders of the State, we listened to twelve international authorities, in seven languages, deliver addresses in the dead man's honour. He was a patriot, the soul of Poland, a revolutionary socialist, a major statesman, a partisan for freedom, an exile, and a martyr. But I don't remember hearing what kind of poet he was, and I never succeeded in finding out.

Yet sitting there, spot-lit on the brocaded seats of honour, in the great hall, with the official mighty, and surrounded by several thousand breathless citizens, young and old, I could not help feeling stirred and amazed, as the hours went by, that such reverence and such a national pause should be devoted to the memory of a poet, no matter how dead or good he was. I began to compare this august ceremony with those major literary occasions we sometimes enjoy in Britain – the Foyle's Luncheon, the PEN Club Dinner, the Annual General Meeting of the Royal Society of Literature, and the furtive annual opening, by a speechless mayor, of the Shakespeare Memorial Festival. Here in Warsaw's Palace of Culture, large and holy as a cathedral, I looked about me, took a deep breath, and inflated myself. The Secretary of the Party, the Prime Minister, all the country's great, sat dumb and enslaved, gazing up at the fifty-foot portrait of the poet and at the bright-pated literary figures who sat like gods on the high platform. We had been fetched from the world's ends for this moment, all expenses paid; we had been lodged in pomp, cossetted, flattered, and treated with awe. We were the possessors of powerful secrets, each one a kin to Mickiewicz's immortality. Surely, I thought, here, if nowhere else, the pen has inherited the earth.

It was not till the lights were turned down, and the newsreel cameras had departed, and the week-long celebrations were ending that I began to discover a reason for all this. I may be wrong, but it seemed simple enough. Was it not that Poland, whose identity has always been threatened with evaporation by hot blasts of power either from Germany or from Russia, was seeking a major figure, a national myth; and one, moreover, who, though in every sense a Pole, had for much of his life been nourished and sheltered by that part of the Western world to which their emotions naturally turn? The shadow of Russia had always been close and heavy. Someone must be found who was innocently free from this. So Mickiewicz, exile and mystical patriot, romantic poet, longtime dead, Moscow-persecuted and Paris-protected, was their natural choice. And to the founding of this man as State-god, forefather Adam, we from around the world had been bidden as witnesses. It might have been worse, I suppose. It might have been a general.

On my last day, with the celebrations slowing down, a free-for-all had been arranged at the University during which the visiting poets were invited to read from their works.

The assembly hall was packed with students of both sexes, their faces shining with welcome and youthful grease. Amid thunderous clapping a dozen of us filed towards the platform while girls ran forward and showered us with winter flowers. We sat on the platform grinning amongst these blooms, while a sea of blue eyes sparkled expectantly below us. I had never, in the name of poetry, seen so many listeners gathered together before, and again that drunken feeling welled within me.

Then, one by one, in our several languages, we read a poem each. And almost all made the same mistake. Assuming that every word would be intimately understood, most poets read in that scared, inhibited voice which seems part and package of the modern style. I was lucky because I came last on the list, and it soon occurred to me that what the students really wanted, in default of sense, was passion and noise. (This was proved by the success of the Cuban, Guillen, who read a poem in a dialect so springing and rhythmical that you could have danced to it.)

Then – worse still – a tweedy, dapper, Dutch poet got up and announced a poem in English – which I thought was my province. 'This poem is about Poland,' he said, 'and in it I have developed the charming idea of referring to Poland as a woman.' Low-voiced and deferential, he then read a poem of straightforward, though scarcely top-grade, pornography – 'your lips, your eyes, your hips, your thighs' – ending as an afterthought, 'Poland shall never die!' I was outraged. Who did he think he was fooling?

As I followed this man I thought, we must do better than that. My poem, sense or no, was really going to sound like something. I gripped the lectern with both hands and bawled my head off. I made more noise than all the rest of the poets put together and ended up shaking all over. I don't suppose I was ever so moved in my life.

It was noon, and time to leave for England, and I was ready to go. On this day, and on two others in the week, a sleeping-car ran straight from Warsaw to Paris. My ticket was bought and I looked forward to a comfortable journey. Then, on my return from the University, I was met by long faces in the hotel. 'We have bad news for you,' they said. 'You cannot leave from Warsaw. The sleeping-wagon is broken.'

The winter blizzards were really beginning to blow that day. 'There must be *some* train out of Warsaw,' I said. 'I'll take anything.' 'You will?' They opened their eyes in astonishment and went away to confer. Presently the Celebration Officials approached me, jaunty and jovial 'Ah, Mr Lee,' they said. 'We hear you are going to Paris the sporting way. Ha ha!' And they shook hands with generous relief.

The journey proved to be more sporting than even they

had imagined – fifty hours, five changes, three frontiers, and no porters. To make matters worse, I was loaded with a three-day hamper in a loose cardboard box and a half-hundredweight of Polish books tied up with string. The hamper contained a goose, a pound of ham, six pickled gherkins, butter, cheese, three bottles of pop, and two dozen big red apples. Across the face of Europe, scrambling in and out of trains, in snow and rain, in mist and darkness, I fought a losing battle with these things. At every station the hamper burst and apples and gherkins went bouncing away beneath the cider-pressing feet of Poles and Czechs and Germans. Then, as the wolves of exhaustion began to catch up on me, I selected and abandoned, one by one, the thick black books my Polish hosts had given me. A five-volume collection of the poems of 'X' (in Polish) was donated anonymously to the station-master at Prague. Ten volumes of literary criticism went through a lavatory window near Petrovice. The collected reflections of the Slavophil 'Y' I dropped into some passing goods-wagons just outside Nuremburg. As for the collected works of Adam Mickiewicz: fifteen volumes, in brown, gold-embossed leather; I stuck to them through thick and thin. It seemed the least I could do.

There is a little more that I would add. Among the unsorted odds and ends that still remain with me I remember the thin, plain maid in the hotel, who asked me to send her as many copies of *Vogue* as I could lay my hands on. The Rumanian poet who had a brainstorm and left the hotel, screaming. The pale, sick face of the English ex-patriot, late of the British Council, who is now a Polish subject, successful and despised. The cabaret that made us laugh so with its attacks on queues, transport, and the Palace of Culture. The Polish poet who is just bringing out, with official backing, a two-volume, *de luxe* translation of the works of Lord Byron.

Two more things. For much of my journey back across Europe I was accompanied by a young German wife and her child. She was married to a Pole in Cracow and was on her way to visit her Stuttgart mother, whom she had not seen for nine years. At Cheb, on the Czechoslovakian frontier, I saw a hundred elderly, silent Germans, with pink, pinched faces, in new overcoats and boots, line up to board the train. They were political prisoners being repatriated. For twenty hours the Polish-German wife made small talk with me; then, when we arrived at last in Germany, she wept as I have never seen anyone weep. The hundred elderly Germans, received at their home-stations with bands, flowers, press photographers, and crumpling-faced wives, turned away from their welcome, one by one, and leaned against the hoardings, weeping like found children.

Having been able to compare, even so briefly, the two worlds that make up our world; having sensed the solemn, passionate, puritan purpose of the one; the brassy, busy, bosomy, every-man-for-himself cosiness of the other, I am in no doubt now which one I must choose. But I am not at all sure that, in the long run, it will be the one that history chooses.

Ibiza High Fifties

You got there by a slow boat, full of beatniks and Germans; and unless you were lucky you sat on the engine from which a reek of hot grease, coughed up by the pistons, accompanied the wallowing journey. It was six hours from Mallorca, empty sea all the way, and you dozed on a bed of rivets. That's how we got there anyway, knowing no other method. (They in fact built an airstrip during the course of our journey, but nobody told us about it.) So we idled all day across the hundred mile sea, playing dice and drinking bad wine, and when the island appeared at last in the twilight we felt we'd come to the end of the world.

I had no notion what to expect, I knew nothing about Ibiza and the young gentlemen from Palma in their blue dacron suits had coughed when I asked them about it. 'Very rough and brutish,' they said, 'very backward. No cars and no society.' And now it approached us – a red rock like a shell splinter, bare headlands like a new kind of metal, with a few bone-white temples standing on the empty shore among which a dark group of figures watched us.

It looked like a place no one else had visited, something waiting unused for this evening, the shade of some long-preserved netherworld even older than the Mediterranean. Who were these watchers among their temples? What were their clothes? their gods? We sidled nearer towards the quay-side. Details grew steadily clearer. Revealing the watchers to be boys in more blue dacron suits, the temples new holiday bungalows; and we couldn't land till a French actress on board had been filmed disembarking three times. . . .

The port of Ibiza, the main town in the island, has a

commanding but scratch-me-down look – a broody old citadel squatting plumply on a rock and trailing feather-white slums in the water. Save for occasional sea-mists it has extraordinary clarity and if Greek would be hymned for its light. Politically Spanish, emotionally Catalan, and pagan-Catholic by nature, it is otherwise nothing but itself – which is something history has never defined. Long successions of occupiers have set it apart like a dungeon in which to develop their private excesses – it was a Roman jail, an Egyptian lust-pot, an Arabic treasury, a hide-out for pirates, a nip-and-run depôt for the fleets of Napoleon, and during the Spanish Civil War a brief theatre for murder. In the intervals it was usually abandoned or ransomed, having little but isolation to offer. And even today when no ships come, or are delayed through storm and sloth, there are times when the streets grow suddenly silent, and the town sits and stares at the sea, and temporarily lowers its prices, and drinks an absinthe too many, and wonders if it's not been forgotten again.

It's never forgotten for long however. It has what we runaways want. Heat, sunshine, the antiseptic sea, iced drinks, and the cheap peseta. Also that flattering air of the Latin retainer which makes every bum-poet feel a Byron. If you're a tax-refugee you'll feel easy here, as you will if you have nuclearophobia. For the British tourist there are brand-new hotels where the waiters are reassuringly insolent. For retired colonials there are echoes of the Pacific, with the natives to deplore at sundown. And for painters and writers, idleness without guilt, and more light and more drink at less cost, and the feeling of being recharged with important experiences.

It was some time since I'd been on Spanish soil, and never before on a Spanish island. We found a cheap *fonda* down by the harbour and then went to look at the town. Night had fallen and we had no guide, but we instantly felt at home. By air and by sea we had come a thousand miles, but we were still in SW3. For the Mediterranean image – Chelsea/King's Road version – had been snugly re-imported, a reassurance, to avoid disappointment, that local folk-lore was still in flower. In the Bagatelle night-club, done in bamboo and fish-nets, two blondes called Pam were embracing. On the floor with his head in a champagne bucket was Ronnie, dressed Capri à la Simpson. 'I'm Giles Stoke-Manderville, the brass-arsed Crusader,' he mumbled, and invited us to take a rubbing. From farther up the street came sounds of wild clapping mixed with Anglo-Andalucian cries -- and there, sure enough, was a *Casa Pepe*, with a guitarist, and several Susans in prints. The guitarist, a hollow-eyed man from the mainland, played flamenco with a livid sneer, while the nordic girls crouched round him, sweating gently, sipping brandy, and bawling *Olé*!

Where were the inhabitants of Ibiza this night? I fancy they were cowering indoors. This was not Ibiza nor anywhere on earth, but something we'd packed like a picnic, an idea we'd brought with us to ensure local colour in case the natives should turn out untypical. This night-life in fact, apart from the price of the brandy and the casual licensing hours, could have been anywhere in Central London. (Indeed, most of the management came from there; you could even pay for it beforehand in Regent Street.) Down the road, just as jealously, was a cave run by Germans, reflecting their version of Spain. And I suppose this is now what tourism has become, what it had to become in the end. For the more one travels the more one seeks home (or to have one's home prejudices confirmed). Certain cyphers may remain – busbies, post-marks, ruins, kilts, funny money, and subsidised ceremonial. But travel is little more than a round-about way now of collecting postcards and stamps; for the rest one seeks continual reassurances – one's native language, home cooking and drink (beer in Jerez, gin and lime in Gerona, ham and eggs in Assisi, Coca-Cola in the Loire), familiar plumbing, air-mailed newspapers, and Thomas Cook's guaranteed return.

Did we once naïvely believe tourism would make us cosmopolitans? We find we don't travel for that. Tourism is fast creating a third world, one that is neither home nor abroad, a never-land of posturing fishermen, of scrubbed peasants from a Museum of Folklore, of pre-fabbed hand-crafts and papier-maché charm, of dirt and poverty bleached off the streets, of booming Shakespeare in indifferent Stratfords, holy shrines with the cocktail annexe, and bullfights run for Anglo-Saxon kicks while the Spaniard surreptitiously plays football. Tourism is to many countries an alternative agriculture which can turn even the bad lands green. The haycocks are hollow, the milkmaids of wax, the flowers everlasting, of plastic – but the paying crop is national self-consciousness, served with salads of dollars and pounds, sprayed artificially to tickle the nose and air-brushed for Kodachrome. Who's to blame for all this? Should anyone be blamed? Client and pandar have worked it together. The tourist, revealed as essentially a home-bird, prefers to see the world in his image. And as tourism develops and grows ever more easy it offers this paradox – that we are able to feel at home over wider stretches of earth, while we learn less and less of the world.

Ibiza, even so, is not yet quite obliterated; it still maintains an underground life. Our quayside *fonda* was bare and obliging, with a back door open all night. One climbed the steep stairs as a test of sobriety to an irregular room with two beds. The room was white-washed, plain, and monkish, but scarcely designed for rest. There was no glass in the windows and mosquitos came in, also moths the size of newspapers. The electric light had an invisible switch and so burnt all night long as in prison. Through the open windows came the sounds of the night; constant, various, and arresting. From a nearby house a man howled for two hours; a child went 'er-ha, er-ha'; someone started to practise a hunting horn, the cockerels to twang and cackle. At dawn a sea mist came up from the harbour and wrapped us in hacking coughs, and the damp rolled off our eyebrows. When I got up at last I had to iron my notebooks and put my cigarettes on the windows to dry, while the moths and mosquitoes, now waterlogged themselves, splashed down round the floor like tears.

The boat from the mainland was due at dawn, so we watched the preparations. An old man with a broom first swept the harbour. Then a dog fell in the water. Beachcombers gathered to watch it drown. The waiters set out their tables. Facing the sea like theatre boxes the harbour cafés rapidly filled. It was 6 a.m., so we went down and joined them and ordered our coffee and coñac. Around us were mothers with ribboned daughters, boarding-house keepers and priests, officers in pyjamas, gaunt models with hangovers, and local beat-boys waiting for money.

We sat there, not speaking, in the early sun, watching the sea like a letter-box. Then at last round the lighthouse slid a cat's-cradle of rigging, and the boat moved into the quayside, and towered above us, flat and emotional, like the troopship in *Cavalcade*. No wonder we all rise at dawn to meet it; everything that is not Ibiza is here. Everything that is not of this ground nor of this shallow sea, that is not wood, clay, straw, or crude alcohol -- every ounce of petrol and necessary metal, every pound of rubber and nylon, every bottled brandy and aspirin, plastic cup and ballpoint pen, everything that makes this place tolerable for us exiles must be brought in at dawn like this. New mistress, rival, the draw, the discard, the boat bringeth and the boat taketh away. . . . It is not that we seriously wished to run away at all, and we're down here each dawn to prove it.

The morning's arrivals, the new blood of the island, are viewed first with a gingerly suspicion. A party of Lancashire dads, with their print-frocked women, are packed in coaches to their pre-booked hotel. Then the Left-bank Messiahs disembark one by one, bearded, with Parisian pallor, uniform in unisex jeans, carrying chess sets and guitars, trailing their uniform twin-sister girl-friends. They are soon absorbed by the local colony, and new chess games are quickly in motion. The pool of beatniks is thus replenished, with scarcely a ripple, hardly a word. Threadbare and silent, this brotherhood moves not, but sticks closely to the harbour cafés. Members are casual, bronze, and sad, and few either work or spend. So they shuffle and cut, and deal each other like cards, and change their rooms and their bed-mates weekly. Yet most of the men are quite solemn and moral, believing non-involvement to be a state of grace. Silence is the Word;

conversation is vulgar, show-off, the lush affectation. Communion, if any, is by pre-set phrases, telegraphic and agreed beforehand. The Brotherhood consists mostly of poets and painters, but activity in either art is frowned on. Pure creation lies in inspired inertia, the controlled passivity of the pole-squatter – any physical statement, either in word or paint, merely blurs and diminishes the Image. Sterility is fecundity; least said furthest sent; pure silence and balance is all.

Even so there exists a kind of domestic life, a relentless second force, which writes out its own loud separate pattern like flowers nibbling round a tomb. Willy-nilly, these fakirs have fathered a swarm of children – those noisy, golden, bell-haired angels one sees bouncing around the town. These Nordic imps create a counterpoint to the silence, as do their open-bloused, sunburned mothers – each of whom seems to be called either 'Heidi' or 'Trude', and are as alike as a row of Dutch cheeses.

These girls – all beautiful, young, and low-heeled – play the patient rôle of salvation. They set out the chessmen, cushion the theories, glide dutifully from market to bed. Their huge empty eyes reflect the unsized canvases and unwritten poems of their men; meanwhile they guarantee sanity, as did Mrs Blake, by sitting naked and making no noise.

The importance of the girls, and their likely history on the island, can be illustrated by the case of Heidi the Fleming, who had just recently come to Ibiza. One saw her often about the harbour, lacey and slender – even more beautiful than the others – trailing some morose and crop-pated Buddhist. This violet-eyed, loose-haired, decolleté love-knot seemed to glow like a public street lamp, and to have no will or purpose other that that necessary acquiescence – shared by her sisters – to the man with the lighter. Typically enough she had been brought to the island by a rich button-maker from Hamburg, who had established her in one of the harbour hotels and there planned an unhurried seduction. He was romantic, noisy, carnal, and plush, but he misinterpreted the girl's morality. Quite shocked by his tastes she had locked herself in the lavatory, where she found a poor sleeping Swede. They had passed the night there, then he gave her to a friend, who bequeathed her, when he left, to a Dane. Since when she had passed formally from hand to hand like a soothing bubble-pipe.

As for the men of the group, who were they, where did they come from, what sent them, and why were they here? Unanswerable questions, most of these, except for their points of origin. More various than their girls, they were yet alike in habit, each sharing a similar ennui. Their numbers included some stranded Fulbrights, a Mexican pundit, a Lapp, a Bill-of-Rights painter, a Fulham Road ditto, and several classless stateless Australians. Perhaps the most vocal were the two Dutch outsiders, who each worked several hours every day. I remember the first of these taking me aside and confessing that he was 'the only Dutchman to have read the whole of Louis MacNiece's study of William Butler Yeats in English'. He then broke down completely, admitted that he just finished a 200,000-word novel, adding unhappily, 'I am not very quiet about it.' The second Dutch scribe wrote for strip-cartoons, about which he was much more brazen. 'If this must be boring,' he boomed, 'then I am telling them in what way it shall be boring. If bad, from what direction its badness. . . .' And finally there was he whose type had never before walked mortal earth, the miracle Quiz-King from Brooklyn, a plump youth of twenty, already bald, who having won a small fortune on the television networks had got out of America for good. In all, this company are the gypsies of tourism, inbred and vastly conventional, exotic only in a professional way, forming no part of the land they live on.

This symphonic seaport of Ibiza soon palls, and in spite of our affection for its ragged bustle we decided to move on else-where. The season was early so we found a house without trouble – a concrete villa in a small sea-village standing at the mouth of the island's one river This ugly box, which we shared with two friends, had five rooms and a shower, a charcoal-fired kitchen, was furnished, and cost £6 a month.

Perched on a hill, beneath a fortress-like church, it over-looked farms and the sea, with the village itself – scarcely more than a street – lying some distance below to the left.

We liked it here: the roads were bad, and a wooden bus ran but rarely. There was nothing to do except work, drink and swim; nothing to look at but fields and the ocean. Some-times a four-masted schooner, carrying salt to the Peninsula, spent the morning working up the horizon; or a cart climbed the hill with a barrel of water; or someone beat down the fruit of a carob tree. It was otherwise a landscape of slow, clean stillness which is the bonus of bad roads yet. Anywhere in the world, if you want longer days, or to taste the cream of old speech and actions, it's not craft-guilds, national parks, or medieval mummery you need, merely a generous allowance of potholes. Here, for instance, only a few miles from San Antonio, where speedboats and charabancs roared, bad communications left time in the air, a floating bubble of unrippled reflections. Little girls and old crones sat all day in the fields, watching the family's pig or goat; a man opened a water sluice, went to sleep for three hours, then woke up again and closed it; a straw-hatted girl hung her babe in a tree and started to sickle some grass; three boys walked the hill sucking sugar canes; the blacksmith hammered a wheel. . . . The most violent shock any newcomer might suffer would come from the wild Ibicencan hounds – pale rib-thin beasts with mad slanting eyes who ran on the slopes like cheetahs, and would suddenly spring on you from behind a rock, fawning for bread and fish-bones.

All was easy and indolent here; there were no hours, even in business – where you could unlock the post-office, buy stamps on credit, even recall a rash letter once posted. An impudent dignity informed one's relations with tradesmen and other commercials – you were told what to buy, you didn't choose, you also learned to accept their charity. For instance I'd been in the village two weeks, and hadn't bothered to shave, when a man came up to me in a bar: 'I encounter your beard very ugly,' he said. 'To me I find it most bad.' 'Who are you?' I snapped. 'The barber,' he answered, 'Francisco Juan Tur, your servant.' It was after midnight; he led me firmly to his shop, unlocked it, and shaved me for nothing.

I had come to Ibiza to finish a book, because I write on wine, and it's cheaper. The days were so hot, I worked in a shuttered room, with my bottle in a bucket of water. By late afternoon the words were running with sweat, so I'd bathe and then go to the cafés. The evening drink, which was *palo* or absinthe, together with the measureless life one led, created for me a set of new dimensions by which to observe the world. In the rose-hot twilight under the café trees it was the minute in scale that absorbed me. There was a cactus nearby in which a colony of spiders shared a vast dusty web between them. Motionless for an hour I'd watch a solitary earwig, each foot on a separate strand, go waltzing across the throbbing cotton while the spiders recoiled in nausea. For a while that web could fill the whole sky, become the ladder and plains of Babel, a hideous progress up which the earwig marched, beset, on his way to paradise. Next I might watch a small hole in a wall disgorge a winged troupe of nuptial ants. Their pale silver wings gave them the frock-coated appearance of fashionable bloods at a St Margaret's wedding; some would take off and go spiralling into the heavens, but others just lounged round the nest – till savage little pages, wearing mobile shears, came and snipped off the laggards' wings. Last of all were the flies, who were legion here, so that one swatted a dozen a minute. I'd swat several more, watch them roll on the ground, and again feel that dislocation of scale. . . . Who knows, I'd think heavily, their last slow hours, their immense capacity for dying, that they lie all night among boulders of sand, or among lacerating brambles of floor-dust, broken, panting, cracked with thirst, despairing of aid or rescue, with dying shades of bliss and terror running across their million eyes?

Weekends in this village would not be so strange; they could be lifted from my village in Gloucestershire – take off twenty years, add ten degrees heat, and serve with oil instead of boiled water. What happened was this, here's a typical one;

no wonder I felt at home.

At Saturday noon, from ancient habit, I stopped work and put it away. Then left the house and went down to the river, to the pool they called the 'sweet water'. Here were two cool bridges and a ledge of blue rock down which the river trickled like milk. The pool was deep and the colour of moonlight, with sleepy blue trout down under. I lay with my head half under the water, listening to the nightingales, who sang all day in the riverside bushes as they rested on their journey from Africa.

Presently girls from the village, in crisply ironed dresses, began creeping among the reeds. For an indolent hour they would play whispering games, eat nuts, or doze, and wait – waiting for the boys to come and dive off the bridges, to swim round the pool and excite them. The boys kept to the water, the girls kept to the bushes, calling ritual obscenities to each other, croaking away through the long afternoon their slogans of difference.

At five o'clock was the futbol match, played on a pitch of bare earth near the sea. Tough and bounding, in sexy white shorts, each player played a game on his own. Whoever got the ball shot immediately at goal, be it never so far and wide. Explosions of dust billowed up from the field, the football was fetched from the sea, blows were exchanged, men were carried off insensible to cries of 'Conair!' 'Offsigh!' and 'Goll!' The first side to score could be relied on to win, for the other despaired very readily. It was the local side, this time, who went under first, and were soon playing blinded with tears. The last goal was scored in a deathly silence. . . . The villagers walked white-faced away.

After the game, exhausted by emotion, I went off to seek some rest. I found a rocky wilderness above the village and lay down on a large flat stone. I closed my eyes, smelt sharp herbs and dung, and heard all the sounds of the valley – cuckoos, nightingales, crickets, flies, donkeys, goats, and cockerels, the creak of a cart, a gossip's voice, the fish-seller's trumpet below. As I lay on my peaceful sunset stone a flock of sheep drove over me, followed by a man on a horse, a crone with a goat, then several gaunt figures in black. I was faintly surprised at being so disturbed in such a secluded place, less so when I got to my feet at last, to find I'd been lying in the middle of a road.

Going back to the village I called in at the graveyard which was walled like a Moorish fort. Wreaths of coloured tin marked a new-filled grave, together with a black-edged card on a post. Round the graveyard walls stood more permanent sepulchres, and several pits full of bones. The names on the tombs, some of which I remember, showed the local in-bred variations – Vicente Juan Tur, Vicente Juan Guasch, Catalina Guasch Tur, Vicente Tur Guasch, Catalina Tur Tur, Juanita Guasch Guasch, Tur Vicente Guasch Tur, Guasch Tur Guasch Guasch . . .

One might have expected this island, or at least this village, to have escaped Franco's Civil War, that it must have proved too distant and intractable to bother with. But this was not so indeed. The War festered here as violently as anywhere – perhaps more so in its isolation – and though twenty-odd years had passed since that time, the village still smarted with it, and people still told you about it, though with lowered voices, as though of a relation who had had 'the Disease'. It was the luckiest ones whose voices were lowest, those who had backed the right side and won.

Doña Rosa, for instance, who now owned great properties but would still cook a meal for a tourist – first her brother had been shot, and then her son, who were both Civil Guards, and hated. After Franco's men came, the island was starved. But not Rosa. . . . She spoke in a whisper. 'Food was rationed to nothing, but we did well. There was no oil, but we had abundance. My husband cooked banquets for the captains and colonels; of course we had what we wished – tins of butter, ham, and milk, German sausages, wine, and brandy. You'd see starving girls fall down in the street – sometimes I'd give them a slither of bread. The poor children were as white and thin as bones, having nothing at all they needed. There was murder, yes; prisoners were shot; there were many thrown over the cliffs. A few escaped with crippled limbs – you'll still see them about today. . . .'

In fact the conquerors didn't really want Ibiza; it was punished and then ignored. Even now, should a general be disgraced in Madrid, he will be posted here to cool off. It is an island for exiles, not for permanent life, and refugees abound – conducted tourists, international crooks, assassins, film-stars, lovers, they come here for sun-tan, to get lost, to repent, or to drink themselves cheaply mad.

So now to Ibiza (as to the poor Spanish mainland – like fish-picking Malaga and the once-starved Costa Brava, where earth, Church, and State were but the peremptory buriers of a wasting and hopeless people) something resembling a miracle has happened. Without labour or seed, floating harvests of wealth now fall on the sterile island. The visitors come, asking only for charm, sunlight, and nostalgia confirmed. The island cushions them readily, like a sun-warmed lilo, quickly regaining its shape when they've gone. It provides the hideout, charges a modest fee, but is neither amused nor corrupted. Since the day of the Phoenicians it has been regularly visited by such waves of foreign restlessness. All the same, it considers these times unique, they are boom times by its reckoning. Only a few years ago its people were dying in the street, now everyone is plump and busy. How this could have happened, how long it may last, are things too uneasy to ask. . . . For the first time in a history of countless invasions Ibiza is being occupied, not by arms, but by money.

A Festive Occasion

I CAME down to Cannes in a four-berth couchette with a Parisian clerk, an Algerian widow, a club-footed grandma, and a dog. At some point during the night the clerk bit the widow, the dog bit the clerk, and the ancient club-booted me in the shins for trying to turn the light on. We entered the dawn in a state of watchfulness, while the clerk licked his wounds and muttered low, 'What a pretty pet. What agreeable companions.'

Two hours from Marseilles rose the Mediterranean Sea, as smoothly lecherous as ever, silkily tonguing its tiny red-rock coves. And again I was struck by the power of this water – oily with rainbows of morning sun – to shrive as always my nordic nerves and to say, 'Forget: indulge!'

It was the opening day of the Festival of Film, and the gate at Cannes station was crowded. Crew-cut newsmen, with cameras charged, had gathered to meet the train. They were pale-drawn and petulant; they stamped up and down, and gazed glumly through all the barriers. 'Who's coming, for goodness sake?' they asked. A Festival Officer fussed around them. 'Well. For instance. Eddie is coming. Eddie Constantine is. For instance. . . .' There were howls and groans and a spit on the floor. But not even he came. Nobody came. Save me, and the club-footed woman.

The Hall of Festival was facing the sea, shining, splendid and rich. Its façade was dressed in the flags of all nations that stirred to a north-east wind. Inside were pressmen of all the nations, dressed in American coloured shirts, stirring each other for stories. But we were all too early. No names had come. All was chaos and nothing was ready. The publicity booths were only half built; and even our press cards were lost. A wet-faced woman, with white-cropped hair, met us with soothing moans. 'Patience, messieurs. Your cards will soon come. Meanwhile Eddie Constantine is here. . . .' More gloom and groans while we kicked our heels. Then we were shown to the press room; and sure enough Eddie Constantine *was* there, in a yachting cap, lonely and worried. We ignored him, and smoked, and looked out at the sea – which was slicing up now into mint-green blocks well-sugared by whipping winds. Eddie C. was too early. We were all too early. There was nothing to do but wait.

Then I heard that someone was handing out tickets for the Gala Premiere that night: *Around the World in Eighty Days*, by bounty of Michael Todd. I went to the press desk and stood in line very ready for anything free. But admission it seemed was by invitation only. 'You are not on the list, Monsieur.' 'Scandal!' I cried, without emotion, and wandered back to the press room.

A flashing of cameras greeted me there. Eddie C. had been launched, on a flood of ennui. They had found him a girl – white-shorted, cream-haired – and posed her at one of the typewriters. He leaned on the desk and leered hysterically. The girl fluttered, typed, and looked into his face. Eddie looked into the cameras. The cameras looked into her blouse. There were professional cries of joy and encouragement. Someone undid some more buttons. The girl re-settled her corn-brown legs, the star re-settled his yachting cap, a few extra bulbs were sacrificed, and the party broke up well pleased.

But I was entranced by the ritual; and as the tiny starlet sidled away I watched her bare heels with interest. Plant-like, crisp, and exquisitely portable, she was the first of the crop I had seen. Who was she, I wondered? From what fresh field had she sprung? Her typewriter, deserted now, still held a piece of paper in it; inscribed no doubt with her secrets. Stealthily, then, I whipped it out; on the crumpled sheaf I read:

'Mi chiamo Grazia uf e sono a Cannes per fare un prov di

v nostro f f a ho remi f chiamo Grazia e sof a Cann edmo koi s dmmila anos fr sino non . . .'

A cry of near-wordless ecstasy. Alas, I never saw her again.

In the afternoon I collected my press card, together with publicity material weighing one and a half kilos. It was to be, it seemed, a very Olympiad of Films, with entries from thirty countries. The major powers had booths in the Festival Hall; the minor ones worked from the bars. Most of the iron-screened countries were represented, as were the obvious free States, and such unknown starters as Tunisia, Ceylon, and the Lebanon. There would be four films a day for the next two weeks. Meanwhile the curtain had not yet risen, and there was little to be witnessed save the pasting of posters that were going up all over the town.

These posters, bright as heraldic shields, seemed part of a private battle. Those of Britain, it's true, were remote and exclusive. They showed white waves breaking on rocky cliffs, or over the bows of destroyers, or against the stern British chin of Mr Richard Todd. They properly told our rough island story and seemed to claim to have invented the sea. But the other big countries mixed the battle more closely. Hollywood led with a girl in black tights. Italy countered with a girl in brown tights; even younger, and with a doll. Japan from Italy reclaimed her rice-fields with a young girl knee-deep in a bog. And Russia, astonishingly, moved right in on Hollywood with two lovers embracing in water.

With a book of free tickets stuffed into my pocket, and no films to be seen till the morrow, I walked up the sunlit, windy front, thinking how lucky I was. A mile of white poles were set out like standards, each bearing its propaganda. And my country was not at all backward here, for every fourth pole bore a well-known likeness, each done in that malted-milk tradition so suggestive of homely night-caps. The cosy pantheon of Pinewood stars – brother, sister, scout-leader, and nurse – they gazed reassuringly down upon me alone in that sinful crowd.

Further up was the Carlton, sugar-white and beflagged, holding the Festival's flesh and blood. In the street outside a crowd of witnesses had gathered. Butter-faced schoolgirls with autograph books were waving at a porter in an attic window. The porter waved back – it was Eddie Constantine. I continued my walk and came back an hour later. The girls had all gone, but Eddie C. was still there, drumming his fingers on the window sill. The crowd had moved to stare at the beach, where a large gas-balloon was swelling. As the balloon inflated, so Eddie wilted, but bravely he stuck to his post. The air-bag was one of Mike Todd's devices and a squad of police were on guard. I approached one of these and showed him my card. '*A quelle heure partir le ballon?*' I asked. The official turned crimson and could not speak. But an older, more sober comrade answered, 'It departs, Monsieur, at eight o'clock – but only to fifteen metres.'

I sat down at a beach-bar and ordered a drink. It was that lambent half-hour, before the setting of the sun, when the light of this coast works miracles with one's self-esteem. The wind had dropped and the world seemed transfigured. Never had mankind looked so well. A coral glow embossed the crowds with a rich and magnificent carnality. Old women passing by looked flushed as flowers, old men as noble as Aztec gods; lovers went wrapped in immortal hues; and little pink girls ran over the sands with bare feet trailing pink powdery clouds. There were smells in the air of wine and pine, scorched leaves and sun-festering lilies. For a long, slow instant this minor Babylon hung up gardens of seven wonders. Then the sun sank at last, the cold wind rose, our cheeks turned grey; and the neon lights took over. . . .

That opening night was America-Night, thanks to Todd and his Jules Verne Colossus. With a series of exclamation marks, nicely chosen, he dominated the town. First came the balloon, a corking stunt: precisely at eight, as the policeman said, it rose floodlit over the sea. And there it swung, at fifteen metres, like a tethered planet or lantern. Two gum-chewing boys, in Victorian dress, hung precarious in its basket. From time to time they doffed their toppers, released more sand, snatched wildly at ropes, looked sick, and cried out through their megaphones. An attempt by ruffians to cut them adrift was beaten off by the police.

Next came the showing of the film – a mink and tiara job. A magnificent squadron of mobile police – the Household Cavalry of Dough – in rampant uniform, with motor-bikes couchant, had been hired to line the approaches. A hundred more, armed with sticks and revolvers, hid in side-streets behind the Hall. Fish-finned cars slid up to the entrance dispensing blonde girls like eggs. Mr Todd and his wife arrived at last – he biting his lip like a worried schoolboy, she moist as a bunch of violets. Up the carpeted steps he shielded her, scowling most stern and proud. Then the Hall of Festival shut firmly down for the three and a half hours of the film.

Later, at midnight, came the Casino Party, with champagne and caged lions and lobsters. The invitation list of course was limited; but such was Mike Todd's popularity that we all wished to do him honour. Two hundred cards, stolen beforehand, were sold in the streets and bars. Then as the guests arrived, their cards were collared and whipped back to the streets again. The whole of Cannes was at the party; it was the greatest party of all. Mr Todd, with his missile in the sky; and Todd A-O, the ultimate detergent, had together captured the Festival.

I didn't see Todd's film that night; instead I went to a cinema in the town where an unofficial film was showing – *L'Empire du Soleil*, a blazing trail of the Andes, made by the makers of *The Lost Continent*. How contrived it is I cannot say, but I watched it with drunken pleasure. It is a visual bombardment by a world unknown: a vast cinescope of thunderous mountains; there are Peruvian Indians dressed like straw dolls of harvest; dances, festivals, work, and love. There is a woman in labour hanging from a tree; a vulture riding a fighting bull; clouds of black cormorants bombing the sea; surprise, amazement, and poetry. . . .

Dazed by, and dreaming of, this film, I went next morning to see Mike Todd's – which was being shown again for the peasantry. Vigorously conceived, superbly made, and acted with immaculate polish, it sets a girdle round the earth in eighty clichés. (I know where I'm going, and I know what they'll show me. . . .) France? – there was Paris and a post-card chateau. Spain had its bullfight and gypsy dance. ('For the bulls get the best, what's-his-name? Dominguin; for the gypsy dancer that guy José Greco.') Then India, yes, a pretty big place. We'll have rope-tricks and elephants and sacred cows, suttee, a Princess, and Colonel Blimp. Siam is easy; it's King and I. For the old USA, the old-time works: democratic elections, saloon-bar molls, a free-lunch counter, a Kentucky crook, the railroad spanning the Middle West, a Red Indian raid, and some buffaloes. England, of course, is club-life and cabs, a hint of Royalty, and incipient decline. . . . It was jolly, bounding fun all round; but as globe-circling Fogg neared the shores of Britain (sailing mysteriously into a westering sun) I felt the merriment pale a little. It was like being dragged, at once, through a Baedeker dream-book and an international casting-directory (starred pages only). Nothing was spared to us except surprise.

From *Around the World* I came out to the sun, blinded as by a sea of milk. When my sight returned I looked about me. A noonday party was in full swing on the beach, watched by a solemn crowd. I flashed my card and joined the revellers and a drink was thrust into my hand. It was one of those gilded anonymous gatherings which seemed to spring up instantly whenever there was a patch of sun. Fat, busy film-men, their backs to the wind, sold projectors one to another. Long-haired girls languored here and there in stately Borzoi silences. Cameramen clicked and crawled and hunted, selecting and rejecting the girls. They posed a red-head with a rubber horse; she flashed frantic smiles, they flashed their bulbs, and the glaring old sun was ignored. A tasty morsel in a raffia skirt watched glumly for a while. Presently the cameras turned upon her. She dilated, and stripped in the gritty wind, and took up a hundred postures. She writhed on the sands, nubile and shiny, knotting and unknotting her limbs. The cameras sought her, circling slowly. Their long phallic lenses pried and prodded; and she opened generously to them all, fondling with every gesture her idea of the knowledge they had of her.

The power of the levelled camera on a girl. A moment ago she was a dull-faced bun; now her flesh seemed to burn like an electric fire, and her long green eyes, turning restlessly upon us, sparked with voluptuous longings. I couldn't bear it a minute longer: with my small cheap camera swinging between my legs I waded into the fray.

'It's no good wearing *that*,' said a voice. 'These girls are experts; they demand *equipment*. Anything less than a Rolliflex and they'll book you for indecent exposure.'

The sage who spoke, a pink, Sunday columnist, was squatting at ease on the sand.

'And it's no good looking at her either. That little number is fiendishly faithful. She's got eyes for no one but her girlfriend Lola. Why did you come? This place is a wash-out. There's no love, but *no love* at all. All the girls are on yachts, or are queer as nutmegs. And look at the weather – like a Trades Union Congress. I think I'll go back to Twickenham.'

We lunched together in the strong east wind, with the table-cloth nailed to the table. Other gossip-men joined us, wailing, wailing. What are we going to send home? No personalities, no griff, no stories. Princess Grace won't play, I've tried her. Ex-King Peter? No good; only wants puffs for his book. Do you know Somerset Maugham? Well, I've got Dorothy Dandridge. How about getting them together? I'd pay you, you know. A pity. If only Eva Bartok would come. . . .

We drank Calvados through the long afternoon, then drove to the hills for a party. It was given in a villa of rich Baroque icing, commanding a magnificent view. Our host was a painter whose pink-lipped nudes had made him a considerable fortune. There was champagne in the garden, and a swimming pool; the wind had turned soft, and the evening was the colour of peacocks. All the guests began to appear very familiar to me. There were the cameramen from the beach party. There were the two cropped boys from the balloon. And there was Mr Eddie Constantine. When I left at last, the desperate newsmen were trying to get him to jump in the pool. . . .

That night they were showing *Celui Qui Doit Mourir*, Jules Dassin's long-looked-for adaptation of Nikos Kazantzakis' *Le Christ Récrucifié*. Alas, I never got to see it. Instead, I ran full-tilt into an unexpected taboo. At least, it was a surprise to me.

Having arrived at the theatre and shown my card to the flunkey, he suddenly barred my path. 'But Monsieur is not wearing his "smoking",' he said. 'Then, *alors*, he cannot pass.' I stood perplexed in the flower-banked foyer. 'Who said anything about "smoking"?' I asked. The big man shrugged. 'For the evening, it is obliged,' he said. I was cross: I said I had come a thousand miles; I said I had no 'smoking'; I even said I was a poet. Streams of black ties were flowing past us. The doorman sent for his superior. 'He says he's a poet and has no "smoking".' 'Throw him out,' rapped the chief. So they did.

I went off to a café and worked up indignation. Capitalist dummies and dolls! Was I really going to stand for this? Would Stephen Spender stand for it? Very well, neither would I. I sat down at a table called for paper and ink, and wrote off a note to Jean Cocteau.

'Cher Maître,' I began (in so many words). 'This night I was ejected from the Hall of Festival because I wore no "smoking". I have no smoking. I come from England to see the films of the world and not to attend a parade. May I, with all the admiration I cherish for you – you who have broken every rule to achieve the supreme law of your own genius – protest against this sartorial dictatorship?' The note had the right Gallic flourish, I thought. The next day, his reply: 'You should make as I do,' he wrote, in French. 'Go to bed at night – and so avoid the necessity of the "smoking". But failing this, I enclose a note to help you – though my wishes do not necessarily correspond with my authority.' The note he enclosed was sharp as a lance. 'To whom it may concern,' it ran. 'M. Laurie Lee has come to Cannes without his "smoking" – *mais avec son coeur*! Please be kind enough to receive him *in the manner which he merits*. Signed: Jean Cocteau. President du Festival de Cannes.'

Armed with this note I returned the next night. 'But Monsieur is without his "smoking",' droned the flunkey. 'He cannot pass.' 'But, look,' I exclaimed, 'regard this paper.' Slowly, mumbling, he did so. 'Please be kind enough to receive him in the manner which he merits,' he read. . . . So they threw me out again.

I stood in the street, dazed and nonplussed, as though a cheque had bounced hard in my face. Then I gathered myself and fought my way back. I found the superior and rubbed the note in his face. 'Read it,' I cried. 'These are not idle words.' He read it twice, and slumped and bit his lip. 'All right,' he sighed wearily. 'I suppose you must pass. But not till the lights go down.'

In fact, from then on, I was admitted, *sans smoking*, to soirées of every description.

Cannes Film Festival is a great Spring Fair which caters for all lines of business. Nationalism offers its barking side-shows and distributes free dollops of snake-oil. Film-renters meet to buy and exchange – job lots, shockers, new or old, a Sofia Loren for two Monroes – according to the state of the market. Famous screen shadows incarnate themselves, can be seen on the beaches and touched in the bars. Girls, with new lines in thighs or eyebrows, offer themselves here for discovery. Newspaper-gossips, their ears in the sand, hatch the rumours their readers know. Everyone lives on expenses and bluff, Cannes takes its cut; and the films themselves, chosen for showing, are inclined to come last on the list.

But the glue that binds this Fair together is mixed by the parties that everyone gives. According to the geography of our particular hosts, we lived in Cannes on champagne and nuts, champagne and vodka, champagne and schnapps, champagne and saké, champagne and gin. Every morning we wore, like a national decoration, a different species of hangover. And although every party had a separate point of departure, each achieved common ground in the end.

I go to the Carlton, the Casino, the Martinez; I go to the Whisky à Gogo. The hosts that receive me are from all over the forest; the resulting scrum is the same. A fight at the bar formally opens the ball. Contemptuous waiters, stern and forbidding, ladle drinks like free soup for the poor. The champagne flows, or trickles, or dries, in controlled and strategic tides. I am rubbing elbows now with a lifetime of film-going. Little did I think, I say. Once cherished faces, the sex-symbols of my youth, swim fading before my eyes. Vivian Romance leans near and asks for a light (her shape on that Naples bed!). And there's Lilian Harvey – with whose image I once climbed a beech-tree. . . . Both comfy now, like my Aunt Alice. Maria Schell embraces me, smiling bright: 'Dear poet,' she sighs, 'we must meet again.' She turns to the arms of her co-star, Curt Jurgens. Photographers gather; lights flash; they cling together. But not for long, alas. A carbon-eyed girl slides into the picture, grabs Curt's other arm and stays put. 'My very best husband,' she breathes in his ear. Her cat-like body strokes him slowly, her inked face purrs and glows. Who is this? Eva Bartok! A happy sensation. Miss Maria Schell looks grave, Miss Bartok looks legal, Herr Jurgens a double-head winner.

So the parties sparkle, and spill, and flatten. There is Ram Gopal, in an astrakhan hat, leaning beautifully against a pillar. And a Russian star, with a water-scrubbed face – Strict Baptist Chapel, she. The Japanese soirée meets all our wishes. Lanterns surround us. Little men bow. Their girls have piled hair, kimonos, and clogs, and pretty print parachutes at the rear. Recorded music comes out of the walls – the drums and plucked strings and pipes. 'What music is this?' I ask a small doll. She drops her slant-eyes, bobs her bobbin-filled hair: 'It is very provincial,' she says. 'It does not signify.' 'Your kimono is beautiful.' 'It's the first time I wear one. I live in South Kensington, see.' Rice-chicken and saké are served until two – then the lights are switched off like a pub.

But the party I remember best of all was the luncheon served up by the French. We were piled into coaches and driven from Cannes as though in full flight from the plague. At a handsome auberge, alone by the sea, the hors d'oeuvres lasted two hours. Food, and flowers, and wine, and girls, entirely surround us there. And the girls, printed on my eyes by that hot afternoon sun, are those I remember now.

There was Jackie, a cool, blue, straw-hatted beauty who smiled blindly at the call of her name. There was a barefooted Tahitian who sang love songs to a guitar, then covered her face in confusion. There was a young French actress, schooled at Gerrards Cross, who spoke fondly of hockey and rissoles. There was a tumbled, teen-age apparition, with wide, crushed, elderberry eyes set in a cream-white face, who looked vague, dreamy, and ready for bed. And there was Eva Bartok. There was another with long hair, and violet eyes, and tight check trousers buttoned down the back. And there was Eva Bartok. There was the kitten with fringe, exhausted childish face, and chemical yellow lips. And a tiny Italian scampi scampering among her lovers. And again there was Eva B. . . .

But such are the flesh of the cinema, the figured flames through which it projects itself. Britain, it's true, seems to get on pretty well without them, relying for the main burden of its message on the shutter-lipped hero and the family joke – with the girls, at most, their stooges and waiting wives. Hollywood has built up the lactic, ageless Mom, sterile by rule, but whose lovers become her sons. But here and there, on the fringes of France and Italy, the White Goddess of cinema is still a force. One saw her in Cannes again and again – liveblooded, hare-brained, earthy-beautiful – her very vagueness itself a vessel of truth, her figure a legend-bearer. Such girls, mysterious in origin, renew themselves each year, bringing skins of light and names of poetry – Nicole, Mylene, Ma-Ea-Fior. As they pass from darkness into darkness their motions, shapes, and unstoried faces are the camera's ideal reflectors. They are the divine animators of the cinema dream, and can endure in that priceless purpose. So long as they are loved, encouraged in mystery, kept womanly raw, and told nothing.

As for the films themselves: my stay was limited, I saw about half, but these included some of the most notorious. One could not believe that all were their country's best; their selection at times was inscrutably unexplained; pains had been taken that no one should be offended; but almost all of them shared one quality. Blatant or implied, according to origin, most films enshrined some large or tiny lie without which they would not have been made. The high cost and corporate talent involved in modern film-making depends for its existence on sponsorship. And every sponsor – be he political, moral, or plain money-grubbing – demands the transmission of some particular illusion. Even so, we saw much to arrest us; spotting the angle was part of the fun.

The Festival was already half-way through when my time for departure arrived. Cruel winds whipped the sea and chilled all spirits. The US 6th Fleet was away off Jordan. HMS *Birmingham* arrived to see Todd down the Yangtse. Pressmen packed up and pursued scandals to Rome. Most stars had long fled – even Eddie Constantine was gone.

So I looked my last at carnal Cannes, and drank milky Pastis and studied the crowds. The locals already seemed back to normal. Moneyed widows with huskies swept by in flash cars. Old ladies tottered off to the Tables. There was a beach-girl in briefs parading around with a trade name lip-sticked on her bottom. And every so often a honey-locked boy, handsome, tight-trousered, with matted chest, walked up and down, and up and down – a dream of hairy with the light brown jeans.

Hazily I tried to sum up the films I had seen while television in the bar behind me snared the old fishermen's eyes. My mind clicked with images and I started a poem. But for whom? The printed word was out of date, old and gone as the clay tablets of Ur. Instruction now was for medieval peasants, a shade on a wall, and a preaching voice. 'One picture,' they say, 'is worth a thousand words; and a moving picture a library.' I wrote no more, but watched the sun go down. Then I looked through a telescope at the crisp half-moon and at Jupiter spinning its balls.

Finally, I took the night train to Paris, and slept, and had a dream. I dreamed I walked with the Queen of Festival, a pocket-sized beauty in white. Her Grecian dress was too big for her. So I gathered it up and fastened it with a brooch, which I'd swiped from a suicide's body. 'You're the prettiest desiccated man I know; the fastest one without feet,' she said. We walked hand in hand through the crowded town. Nobody saw or cheered.

Gift from the Sea

HOLLAND is like no other place on earth; it is a gift from the sea, Atlantis in reverse, a nation hauled from the waves by the Dutch. A thousand years ago half the land lay submerged, as it had been since the days of the Ice Age; and it was the dyke-digging, dam-building, busy-beavering Hollanders who dried it out and gave it back to the world.

Holland, perhaps, is a miracle of salvage. Originally it was less a country than a deposit of debris dropped in the sea by three of Europe's great rivers, the scourings of the hinterland borne on the foaming floods of the Schelde, the Maas and the Rhine. The first settlers, so they say, came to these marshy lowlands by swimming down the Rhine on tree-trunks, finding little to welcome them save a few blown sand dunes, the salt lakes, and the creeping tides. From this half-drowned bog lying between France and Denmark, constantly gnawed by invading floods, the Dutch rolled back the sea like a dirty blind to reveal a rich new land, a land rich in soil, in history and humanity, whose way of life has helped to fertilize the world.

The sea-faring Dutch, long the traditional rivals of Britain, have always haunted the horizons of my country; and as a boy they also haunted my history books and the envious edges of my curiosity. So recently I made my first trip to the country, an hour's flight across the grey North Sea, to try to discover at last what lay behind the legendary nation that had both disturbed and enriched our past. My journey, starting from Amsterdam, was a grand circle round most of the regions, during which I found less of those things I'd been led to expect, and more beauty than I'd bargained for.

Dutch bulbs, Dutch barns, canals and windmills, jolly clowns in pantaloons and clogs, raw rosy faces scrubbed with carbolic soap and a landscape flat as a defeated *soufflé*: such images, ready-packed in the traveller's luggage, can be thrown away at the start. The reality to these was but a distant kin, as it is to most preconceptions, and had a vibrant, factual quality of its own, far more startling and various.

My first impression of Holland was of a victorious battle-field, a defiant frontier between sea and sky; it was a shining horizontal, all light and water, racing clouds and immense reflections. Folded so delicately between the dykes and the sea, its fields seemed as fragile as petals – an illusion of impermanence that was almost poignant, as of something floating and vulnerable. All day, as I listened, I seemed to hear the pulsing of pumps, balancing the waters and keeping the land alive. But the intricate structure of the sea defences have the strength of centuries of tough experience, behind which the farming Dutch, with the threatening sea always in their nostrils, live out their lives with the cool confidence of sailors.

Schipol Airport, near Amsterdam, is thirteen feet below sea level, and the name means 'a refuge for ships'. There is a smell of salt breezes, osiers and leeks; and water is everywhere, like holes in a planet. Amsterdam itself is the beginning and the end of the Netherlands, and it is where I started and finished my trip. It is as gay as Paris, as free-going as London, and as beautiful (I think) as Venice. Like Venice, it was also built in the sea (but, unlike Venice, has not become a fossil for tourism). Its main streets are water, with fifty canals linked by over 400 bridges. Riding the canals you see the city best – the fortifications, secret arches, watch-towers, warehouses, and the wealth of tur-reted seventeenth-century mansions. Almost unbelievable in this age of concrete replacements, these old houses are the treasure of Amsterdam, lining the curved canals in their mellow rows, narrow-fronted, high-gabled, serene, each differing in its eloquent notes of detail but all joined in one harmony of style. The delicate gables by day quiver with watery light, at sundown turn to beaten bronze, and at night become cameos of antique silver lit by the flood-lamps hung in the trees.

This is a keen modern city that still inhabits by choice the romantic props of its past – the mansions and storehouses of the merchant adventurers who once made it the richest port in Europe. Walking the crowded quays, with their nail-studded doorways and worn steps leading down to the water, it isn't difficult to imagine having just come ashore after a journey to some sweltering spice-island.

It is also a city for the young; you will see them everywhere, students from all over the world, sitting in cafés, walking hand in hand, reading their books under bridges, or piling their bicycles against the university buildings like herds of silver-antlered deer. One could write a love-song to Amsterdam for its honest reality, its fine balance between work and pleasure, and for the warmth of touch that laid out this city around its human quays and waterways.

Briefly, I remember not only its diamonds and liqueurs, but the little shops down its narrow alleys, shops selling birds' eggs, butterflies, telescopes, tarred ropes and medieval maps. Also the cheap students' food-bars, like *Brootje van Kootje*, where you could lunch on thick sandwiches of meat or crab. And the many Indonesian restaurants whose multi-plattered suppers might well fill you up for a week.

I hope I can also preserve, in some visual corner of my brain, a few of the paintings I saw in the Rijksmuseum – the golden canvasses of Rembrandt, who was born in Amsterdam, together with over five centuries of the country's art. Here, trancelike as dreams, were early visions of the scriptures, cool Dutch virgins becalmed by faith; affectionate winter land-scapes full of gay skating peasants, scarlet-clothed, bright as birds in the snow; sensuous studies of flowers (a drop of dew on a petal mirroring a minute but infinite summer); drinkers and lute-players lit by wine and music; a crucifixion like frozen moonlight; and cryptic portraits of widows hugging bags of gold and top-hatted merchants counting their profits. From the Middle Ages and the Renaissance to the golden age of Rembrandt, this collection reveals one of Holland's most

GIFT FROM THE SEA

astonishing achievements, a continuous flowering of art, supported by the church, then by commerce – with perhaps the artist getting the last sly word.

Work, relaxation, and a tingling sensation of the mind ventilated by casual friendships and the reflective canals – this is the particular make-up of Amsterdam. And here, as in most other countries in the world, you get the quick feel of a city in its bars. In Hoppe's, for instance – a place of tropical wine casks labelled Port à Port, Crème de Cacao, Curaçao – I found commerce and culture mixing as close as clubmen, briefcases among the beards. It was evening, and there was a buzz like a Spanish tavern coming from bargees, bankers and burgomasters. There were also lean working artists still wet with paint, a few jazzmen getting stoked for the night, students hungry with visions, lovers floating in corners, and a young girl wearing jeans and a tiara. . . .

Another bar, the Scheltema, lying close to the post office, was really a snug working beer-hall for writers. Here was a long plain room with an iron stove in the middle, wooden tables, writing desks and newspapers, pools of silence and animation, a journalist reading his proofs, a wordy scribe talking wastefully to his girl, and, head down in the corner, with a jug of wine and a book, a poet actually on the job.

Holland is a consolidation of rich dry land imposed against the will of the sea. But it remains a seaman's country, a nation of mariners, and wherever you go you can't forget it; even the inland farmers walk with a kind of sailor's roll, as though not quite sure of the solidity of the ground. The cities are like seaports, no matter how far they lie from the coast, their houses hugged by canals and ships. They are not copies of Amsterdam, being provincial and distinct, though most of them have something of its open charity. I went to two of these cities: 's-Hertogenbosch in the south and Groningen in the far north-east.

Groningen is in one of the older parts of Holland, east of Friesland, on the north road to Germany – a region not visited by many outsiders, lying somewhat out of range of the obvious. It surprised me when I came to it, rising from fields of burnt wheat like an egg-cup in a well-baked tart, and I liked it so much for its unexpectedness that I couldn't pass it by.

Groningen is sugar, corn, flowers, tobacco, ship-building, and learning. Canals like tree-rings radiate round its centre, marking the 1,000-year growth of the city. It is provincial yet worldly, land-locked yet nautical, and its university is old and famous. My first memory is of the Vismarket with its Parisian chestnut trees, its pavements covered with buckets of roses, and the girls round the flowers like golden bees – Nordic students with pollen-dusted skins. There was also the Grotemarket nearby, in the town's main square, tented with stalls like a Mongol village, where I bought clogs and honey, and some thin smoked eels – the finest I have ever tasted. The eels come from Kampen, on the old Zuyder Zee, and are best the size of the little finger. The black silken skin comes off like a stocking, leaving the flesh faintly touched with pink; and nibbling at these as I walked round the market I seemed to be enjoying the rarest refinements of cannibalism.

My hours in the Grotemarket were musically quartered by the bells of Martini Tower, whose feathery harmonies came floating through the air as though borne in the beaks of pigeons. This 300-year-old carillon is the pride of the city, and the makers' descendants are still in the business. 'At their factory,' I was told, 'you'll see nothing much – just shabby people messing about with sand.' But these Dutch bells are famous; they seem to gild the air, and the Hollanders love to ring them.

On the canals of this town ancient barges from Amsterdam moved as slow as the shadows of sundials; in its museums were relics of Bronze Age tombs mixed up with wicked little Roman gods; I saw a church stuffed with carvings of Hebrew sacrifice – bearded prophets and bleeding rams, and a medieval poorhouse inscribed over the door: 'Do not mock. No one knows his fate.'

Most of the bars in Groningen seemed to be run by sailors taking a rest between trips round the world. Their conversation was burred with the slang of ten languages, and their recollections were gaudy as parrots. The bars at night were crowded with students playing dice or talking of destiny, and wearing red college caps stitched with long brilliant feathers that seemed to grow straight out of their brains.

Almost everyone in the city spoke fluent English, for the Dutch have the gift of tongues; yet it was English with a difference, with capricious inflections, so that you never quite knew where you were. I remember one student describing the liberation of Groningen, after the siege of 1672: 'We were attacked by persons from all the world,' he said, 'but by God, you know, we beat it!' Another invited me home, and described the way – or perhaps it was some private dream of his own. 'There are three large blocks of flats,' he said, 'and I am in the first.' I went, and there were four, and they were rather small, and he was in the third.

But my biggest surprise in this provincial town was the sophistication of its food. Most British hotels (out of London anyway) offer lugubrious dishes cooked in railway steam and served in the spirit of family prayers. But for dinner here I had *gigot d'agneau à la Provençale*, wild duck 'in the Chinese Fashion', and a white Rhine wine (Deidesheimer Hengottsacker) as clear and cold as dew from a grotto. The head waiter received my praise with modesty, his mind clearly on other things. 'I am serving two lobsters for Mr X,' he said, 'a very particular man.' Mr X was in charge of a local shipyard which was building a yacht for the Prince of Monaco. Eating my ripe wild duck, and watching the Prince's man at his lobsters, I felt Groningen to be a versatile town.

Unpronounceable 's-Hertogenbosch, lying south near the Maas, offered another variation of provincial life. Its name, in English, means 'The Wood of the Duke', and I found it medieval, ornate and lively. This is a Catholic city, with the gay, sumptuous bars which seem often to go with the faith. (Is the stand-up, sink-it-quick, hang-your-head type of bar entirely a nonconformist invention, I wonder?) I spent an evening here in a rousing café singing songs to a mechanical organ – a relic of Can-Can Paris, magnificently decorated and covered with life-sized goddesses in wax. Here I drank local gin, which tastes like a mad relation of Calvados but which insidiously captures the palate. For late dinner I had trout, and the local richly-stewed 'hunting-dish' (designed to be

I CAN'T STAY LONG

eaten from the back of a horse), followed by the town's own brandy, mixed with cooking sugar, and Bossche Koek (or gingerbread) with coffee.

's-Hertogenbosch is no tourist town, but has mysterious beauties of its own, where motionless canals, full of silver light, lap the houses like baths of mercury, and rooftops carry creepers whose wing-pointed leaves resemble the devils of Hieronymus Bosch. This fifteenth-century surrealist was, in fact, born in the city, and some of his work can be found in the cathedral. The cathedral, they say, is the best in Holland, and its carillon the finest in Europe; recitals on its bells are given every Wednesday morning, during which the cafés switch off their mechanical organs.

Holland is one of those small coastal countries which have made a big noise in the world, the sea carrying its reverberations. It lies coiled on itself like a North Sea prawn, clasping the Ijssel Lake to its heart, and poking a bent antenna of sandy islands in the direction of Scandinavia. Its web of waterways is what holds it together, and its towns are the knots in the system. But between the canals lies the rich green farmlands, many of them below sea level. And everywhere I went on my circular trip I was met by that stamp and diversity of coast and landscape which is the unique hand-print of the Dutch on Europe.

First, the wind-torn sand dunes north of The Hague, which seem in summer to be entirely inhabited by children – brown-legged and handsome, with mysterious ice-blue eyes and blond hair cut in ragged cups. They raced round the sand as though spawned by the waves, shouting sea cries at one another, and in their faces one saw the origins of both English and Americans, for these were first-base Anglo-Saxons.

These sand dunes ran north for some seventy miles, covered with gun-sites and tangled grass, one of the original sea-walls behind which the mediaeval Dutch began to dry out and consolidate their nation. Here was Oude Holland, a north-pointing thumb wearing cities like garnet rings, with such quantities of sky that the roads shone like water and the cars seemed to ride on air. The reclaimed fields stood at different levels (the oldest having sunk the lowest) with canals running past at roof-top height and ships sailing among the chimneys. Trees leaned one way, bent by winds, but the fields were apple-green. Foals stood in the grass licking each other's shoulders; there were windmills like great stopped clocks; boys were fishing in ditches full of water-lilies, watched by cows from the tops of the dykes. It was somewhere around here that Sir Philip Sydney, tired of summer and the Lowland Wars, threw off a poem like a short sharp cry, one of the truest war-cries of them all:

> Oh, western wind, when wilt thou blow,
> That the small rain down may rain?
> Christ! that my love were in my arms
> And I in my bed again . . .

North of this ancient battlefield there is new-found land, only recently raised from the sea, great plains of ripe wheat rolling in heavy waves as though the sea was still there, but edible. Then there is the twenty-mile dam across the Zuyder Zee, a narrow chalk line ruled on open water, which only recently has changed the whole geography of the country, turning a sea into a placid lake. Over the dam, in Friesland, is old land again, some of it dyked in the Middle Ages, where the rolling blond farmers speak a language of their own, being unaccustomed to visitors, and raise their black and white cattle – which on the vivid green turf look like negatives stuck to landscapes of Kodachrome.

Spinning between the towns one is constantly bruised by the light, as though everything had been torn from a rain-washed sky. But there is a stillness about the country places, slow movements of men and grass, steady rhythms of barges and solid horses drawing cargoes over fields and water. South of Friesland the villages stand grouped like paintings, so perfect you scarcely dare go into them; and along the spacious basin of the three great rivers all is so quiet you can hear the fish. Crossing the Maas by ferry I remember coming to a small river town which seemed never to have been visited before. Had I had an accident? they asked. Was I looking for someone? Should they fetch the pastor and show me the graveyard? They gave me a drink in the beautiful square, deserted save for playing children, who themselves were beautiful – a mixture of butter-gold blonds streaked with something dark from the Indies. . . .

This curiously vivid intimacy, as of something seen under glass, is one of the most haunting qualities of Holland – old barns with thatched roofs streaked with brilliant mosses; old farmers wearing embroidered skull-caps; old women on bicycles, their heads down to the wind, their skirts ballooning like pirates' sails; the flat, pressed fields as neat as card tables; vivid streaks of garden flowers; and the bright-backed cows standing along the dykes like old china arranged on shelves.

One Dutchman who never forgot this original light of his homeland was Van Gogh, in spite of his years of exile. In a wood north of Arnhem (Hooge Veluwe by name) you'll find one of the finest collections of his work in the world. Over two hundred canvasses, covering the whole of his life, hang in a gallery set among the trees. Here are the gold-spinning sunflowers (the cottage flower of Holland); the rhythms of wind in the clouds and fields; the brilliant Delft-blue paint; the darker blue of Dutch clay; and those weather-knotted portraits lit by a still green glow as though reflecting the old canals. Van Gogh, the master, over-towered the dykes and was less national than most Dutch painters. But a visit to Holland helps you to see with his eyes, where simple objects – a chair, a table, a jug – seem double-lit, raised up from their background. He gave such objects identity, yet enlarged their meaning, fusing them with the whole, so that his sunflower is life, his chair a portrait of solitude, his last landscapes the tortured whorls of creation. I particularly remember one of his earliest studies, that of a family of peasants eating; their clay-furrowed faces seemed forked from the earth, and they were eating with hands like roots. . . .

In spite of the sophistication of the cities, of Rotterdam and the Hague, this peasant structure is still the reality of Holland. It exists on all sides, in habits and dress, in traditions, in work and leisure. I remember coming by chance on a pony market, in the village of Bemmel, near Nijmegen. It was a market holiday, the surrounding fields were empty. Little girls were carrying bridles and a year's supply of whips; sturdy young

farm boys, dressed in suits of velvet, were tapping their clogs
with malacca canes. There were tents of gold cloth, like a
mediaeval tournament, where the boys and their girls were
dancing, or were sitting on barrels drinking beer and flirting
– and this at ten o'clock in the morning. Under the trees by
the tents were gathered several hundred ponies, bushy-tailed
and golden-maned, over which farmers were bargaining by
slapping each others' hands, petulantly, in the traditional
manner.

This was a straight village market, compact and oblivious,
making no concessions to tourists or visitors. Another village,
even more mysterious in its self-containment, was Staphorst,
on the road from Groningen, where only recently a local
adulterer had been put in a cart and dragged round the streets
in shame. Here was a puritan society, based on fifteenth-
century morality; they wore traditional dress, and hated
cameras.

It was Sunday morning when I came to Staphorst, and I
found the village deserted. I walked slowly the length of the
empty street, eyes front, showing my empty hands. Every
window shuttered, either with heavy dark curtains or with little
screens of opaque blue glass. I saw nothing, heard nothing; I
came to the end of the street and began to retrace my steps.
Then gradually I was aware of a twitching of curtains, of
faces hovering behind the geraniums. I was the tourist, but
Staphorst was indoors, and Staphorst was watching me.

It was like being in a forest full of invisible life, conscious
only of eyes in the undergrowth. Then – perhaps because I
was alone, or because my eyes got used to it – I noticed a
slow relaxation of nerves. A tiny figure in the distance suddenly scampered across the road, followed by another going
in the opposite direction. Next, I saw a child, quite close,
standing in a full skirt and bonnet, watching me gravely, like
an old-fashioned painting. One by one, other shades began
to appear, wearing clothes of another century – a mother and
child dressed austerely alike, a boy in velvet leaning against
an apple tree, and four young girls, dark as a Grecian chorus,
grouped silently around a well. The girls particularly were
like apparitions, dressed from head to toe in black – black

shawls, long skirts, and silver-buckled shoes, with black bonnets tied under their chins. I left them there in their watchful silence, their faces white against all that darkness, standing in the Sunday garden, born for the boys in velvet, born to this village and perhaps never to leave it.

Staphorst in most ways was a private world, resembling a page from an early Bible; but I found that traditional dress in Holland comes in two varieties: the true and the tongue-in-cheek. In Staphorst it is the garb of a religious conviction, but in some of the show-towns, like Marken and Volendam, it is worn to put more colour into the tourist's camera. Down in Zeeland, however – those four delta-islands groping like fingers in the North Sea's mouth – isolation has preserved a number of genuine old styles, still worn by the wives of farmers and fishermen. You see them hurrying by, carrying buckets of fish to the market, dressed as richly as Stuart queens; puff-shoulders, lace veils, embroidered shawls, coral chokers, a dazzling rattle of heavy gold jewellery – all containing ornate yet subtle variations, and all eye-catchers against modern drab. The starched lace headdresses may be plump as pumpkins or tall and narrow as sticks of celery; and the gold head-ornaments rise like spiral horns, or frame the face like barbaric horse-blinkers. This weight of real gold, worn daily to market, may be worth several thousand pounds; it is often indeed the wearer's dowry, which she may carry until she dies. But such glories are passing, the wearers are growing older, and you must hurry if you wish to see them. For these rare birds of an often puritan paradise will soon be as extinct as the Madagascar roc.

Zeeland, like many other parts of Holland, has learned to live on the edge of disaster. Its only security is the dykes, 'the dreamers and watchers', the first and second sea defences, as strong as the hands and the faith that built them, but still vulnerable to treachery and fate. Twice in the last twenty years, first by war and then by storm, the dykes were broken and the islands drowned. It meant wilderness and death when the sea came back; then the slow rebuilding of dykes. Now giant new works are planned to join the islands to the mainland and to block off the sea arms for ever; another of those promethean gestures made by a patient people who have never considered the sea unconquerable.

Maybe it isn't; but part of the quality of the Dutch is their knowledge of its power, and their passion for a soil they cannot take for granted, and for their towns and fields which, precious and threatened, they hold together by love and nerve. On my journey round Holland I was constantly reminded of this, and it gave an extra value to all I saw.

My last night in Amsterdam was spent in a small students' bar papered with manifestoes on the meaning of life. Here I talked until dawn with a tall thin undergraduate and his short and fat companion. For several hours they addressed and questioned me, debated jazz and the finer points of philosophy. The lean Quixote explained that they were from the city's two universities; 'One material, the other spirit.' The nodding Sancho agreed, admiring the tall one, especially his final question: 'How can you prove to a Dutchman the existence of doubt, when doubt has no dimensions? . . .'

That was Holland; a country washed bright by water, luminous as a stained-glass window, through which one could see a drowned land live, knowing no dimension of doubt, holding the flood at its arm's length and beating the sea wolf back from the dykes. It is also a country whose people, on the practical side, used the sea to extend the world; who founded New York, bought Manhattan from the Indians, gave Brooklyn and Harlem their names, who pioneered Australia and the Pacific Indies – and are even said to have invented golf.

Their other talent is clarity; clarity of courage in action, the clarity of their light and art; a country of radiant simplicity where more things can be seen against the sky than anywhere else on earth. In the store of its past and in its present vigour it offers example without aggression. What it gives to the world it gives with two hands – 'material and spirit', as the students said.

The Sugar Islands

I ARRIVED in the Caribbean – my first visit to these regions – in the middle of an act of piracy. Off the shores of Trinidad, the Portuguese *Santa Maria* had been seized by a rebel crew, was even then dodging among the many islands trying to escape from law and vengeance. In the Port of Spain taverns, sailors debated her chances and drew maps on tables with their rum-wet fingers. The sympathy of centuries was with the outlaw ship, for these were the buccaneer islands of Henry Morgan and his Brethren of the Coast, of ravaged galleons and the lost treasure of kings. Outside the bay the reefs seethed and bubbled as though hot swords were cooling in water. I was more than content to have arrived at that time; it all seemed perfectly natural.

I had flown out from London overnight, yet felt it improper to have reached Trinidad so easily. This steamy, two-horned, bull-headed island nudges the coast óf the South American continent. To my ancestors, who were sailors, this would have meant a six-months' journey, sailing with salt-meat and possibly scurvy, to find a spot on the map that was not even certain and of which little was expected save hardship. Now one steps casually from the plane in a clean, cool suit, after four thousand miles of sky, to a rattle of iced drinks and familiar English on an island only a day's journey away.

I found Trinidad less pampered, less conventionally picturesque than I'd been led to expect by the brochures – its variety of landscape and mixture of races offer the traveller a more satisfying brew. Continents tend to congeal and stale, but islands ferment and quicken; it is the history of Trinidad and the fiery mixture of its blood that give it its rousing life.

Trinidad is the crucible of Caribbean culture, feeding its spirit to the other islands, so that almost everything we think of as 'typical' – music, dress, and behaviour – originated here. Like the United States, it stirred many races into one stockpot to create something new. Take the calypso, for instance: it has a wide range of essences. The aboriginal precisions of Carib and Arawak, the semi-Arabic string-music of Spain, English court dances, Irish jig, Scottish reel, Portuguese *fado*, the erotic display of the French, the subtler elements of Chinese and East Indian, and finally North American jazz – all these have been taken by the West African Negro and beaten into something both beefy and rare. It was the African slave and his free descendants who made one of these many cultures. Possessed of a lively sense of imitation and invention together with an original genius for rhythm, the African was taught something else by centuries of oppression – consolation through parody and wit.

It was this mixed face of Trinidad that first enthralled me on landing from the damps of London. What had appeared from the air to be green English grass sprouted into sugar cane eight feet high. A brisk shower of rain blew in from the mountains but nobody put up umbrellas. Driving in from the airport, I saw landscapes like Gauguins – red hills rising from South Sea palms, young Hindu girls bathing in vivid saris, and water buffalo wading in reeds. I smelled sugar cane burning – half the sweet smell of herbs, half the aroma of boiling toffee. There were cabins on stilts, to keep them cool and dry; elegant walkers with pails on their heads; and rising above them the cranes and scaffolding of a new luxury hotel by Hilton.

It was the hottest hour of the afternoon. I went exploring through Port of Spain. In the bay there were barques and banana boats, sloops and cutters and dugout canoes, all riding at ease in a tin-blue haze under the shadow of a great Cunarder. The town looked scruffy but was indolently alive, wooden shacks mixed with concrete stores. Lithe chestnut-cheeked girls in brilliant frocks walked coolly in the shade of verandas. Handsome, slender boys with smoky eyes draped the doorways in classic postures. I saw Chinese, Hindus, nobly bearded Yorubas, Anglo-Saxons, and Venezuelan Indians. There were beautiful Creoles with delicate shoulders, whiskered Spaniards and magnificent Negroes; black hair, blond hair, curly and straight, and every skin colour from high noon to midnight. But the mixture made one; this was a single community flowing together in a languid stream and chattering away in the musical dialect that proclaims the born Trinidadian.

This sound warmed me. It had echoes of home, yet was fresh like an inventive child's. It greeted me freely as I walked by the docks. 'You from *Santa Maria*, maybe?' 'It's a too long damn time we not go to Tipperary!' 'You French or Spanish gentleman, man?' Snatches of argument would come from a bar: 'That is not mathematical, sah. You doan need hab Solomon a-tell you that. That a fair and just remark. . . .' More off-beat still were the signs on some shop fronts: 'Holsum Bakery', 'De Rite Shoe Shop', 'Sincere Company Limited', 'Mon Repos Grocery', 'Sea View Bar (Mr Chin-a-Fat, Manager)'. I saw an Indian restaurant advertising *Paella Valenciana* to the music of Greek *bouzoukia*, and a man wearing a shirt showing an old English stagecoach driving up the slopes of Fujiyama.

Just before nightfall, I wandered out of the town towards the shoreside swamps and suburbs. Here was shanty town, near East Dry River, a place of almost apocalyptic strangeness. It was overcrowded, yet bare, smoking with rubbishy fires, a red desert of cabins and water. Huts were propped in the swamps on the old legs of tables up which naked children were scrambling. Little boys by the roadside offered swamp-fish for sale in black bunches like bicycle tires. In the setting sun the swamps were all red and the fires burned brilliantly; vultures walked stiffly along the shore, wind-ruffled, aloof, and funereal.

The next morning I drove to the beach at Maracas Bay, ten miles north of Port of Spain. I was driven by Pierre, a country boy from near Toco, who swung me rhythmically up the mountain road. The road was a new one, built during the last world war, and the jungle still fights with it. Fallen rocks, landslides, and the roots of trees stroked our wheels as we zig-zagged among them.

Pierre was glad to be out of the city, back in the cool hills where he was born. Taking our time and stopping often, he showed me the details of the forest, the nests of the tree ants, the strangling vines, the lairs of bushmasters and basking scorpions. Pierre had five scorpion bites as a boy, he said, but scorpions didn't hurt him now. He liked to catch them alive and roast them for supper – they had a delicate taste, like shrimps. Pierre also showed me the jungle trees: the red-flowering immortelle, the wild tobacco with its soft white blossom, and the wild coffee, which he gave me to chew. I saw a cannon-ball tree hanging with great black shot; the clacking bean of the 'woman's tongue'; and two short papayas, a male and a female, posed stiffly like a wedding photograph.

Maracas is a bay of almost perfect proportions, a curve of sand like a giant shell, with tall, leaning palms, and Negro boys turning cartwheels in the waves. The fresh, light trade-winds cooled the bay's noon sun and bent the palms into fans. We drank a beer on the beach, then swam in a sea that was as warm and clear as the air.

Driving back, Pierre told me about his boyhood in the hills away east by the Galera lighthouse. A good life, poor, but with the free food of the forest; all that was necessary, it seemed, for the taking. There were nutmeg, cocoa, coffee, and breadfruit, golden apples, bananas and mangoes. With his brothers, he went hunting for armadillo, caught tree ants to fatten the chickens, stole coconuts for milk and sweet cane for sugar, crushed cocoa for cooking oil. The days were fat, and the cabin nights cosy, an oiled rag in a bottle for light, with his father busy fermenting rum, and a salt pig in the smoke of the fire. . . .

The next day I flew to nearby Tobago, which some call Crusoe's Island. With its white-coral beaches and goats and coconuts, it would certainly have suited him. It is a honeymoon island, compact as a nut, and it repays the trouble of getting there. In the morning I walked round Milford Bay, a long sweep like an ivory horn. A lean black dog, with the bright eyes of a hermit, appeared from nowhere and walked beside me. For two or three hours we seemed alone on that island – its ingredients were those of a dream. The immaculate white sands, laundered by wave and wind, bore no footprints save mine and dog-Friday's. Fresh clouds meandered round the hot, blue sky, spilling rain briefly like sips of spring water. I let the silence, the summer warmth, and the vivid images of the bay sink slowly into my body and mind. Heavy black pelicans lumbered over the sea, or dived swiftly with swept-back wings. Or there were sudden, hysterical flashes of light as flying fish ripped out of the water, skidding like pebbles over the indolent surface and exploding in brilliant spray.

A few steps from the beach and its almost snow-blind sands, and one entered another world and season – the green, towering forest of coconut palms, dripping coolly with collected rain; and a white goat tethered in the steaming undergrowth, and a small thatched hut, deserted. No sound but slow raindrops and the wet wings of birds swooping in vivid streaks through the air. For the crowded northerner, as for the ship-wrecked sailor, it still seemed an unexpected sanctuary.

No more than twenty-five miles long, and at the most seven miles wide, Tobago is a get-away island. Once a floating fortress off the Spanish Main, for two centuries it was furiously fought over. Some of its capes are still studded with cannon, but for almost a century and a half it has been an island of peace, slumberously contained in its coconut shores. Its reefs are alive with dazzling fish, its sands have great shells like orchids, its lambent nights are full of phosphorescence and stars, and close at hand there are birds of paradise.

I flew back from Tobago for my last day in Trinidad. A quivering rainbow impaled the island. Oily black streams oozed out of the hills and there was a miasma over the swamps. It is easy to forget this other wealth of Trinidad – the fat pitch lake under its skin.

Port of Spain was as hot and active as ever. I went for a final look at the market. There were fruit of all colours, fish and meat, tables of spices and curious tree bark. Blue crabs, wrapped in fibre, lay knotted together like fragments of electrical equipment. A customer examined some tied-up chickens, feeling feathers, looking behind the wings, while the tousled birds lay with gaping beaks like a collection of second-hand handbags. Another customer was bargaining with a sharp-tongued stall-holder: 'You wanna be a robber all your life?' Such markets are the visible heartbeats of cities, while the well-ordered supermarket is the heart in deep-freeze.

Trinidad Carnival was only a few weeks away, and Port of Spain was preparing. The shops were full of silks and muslins, gold-threaded with stars for the girls. Grandstands were rising in the Savannah, and steel bands were tuning up. In every town and village the calypso poets were testing new songs for the golden crown.

I spent my last night at a 'calypso tent' in a great, bare hall in Duke Street. No tourist stunt this, but a hot-spiced meal of music and satire for the islanders. Mighty Sparrow, Lord Melody, and other exotics tried their latest inventions on the faithful. The hall, packed full, rocked like a field of black beans to the intricate wit and wordplay, while out in the street several hundred more drank in their share through the open windows.

The calypso has been exploited, degutted and emasculated to suit the more timorous ears of the north. But in the 'tents' of Trinidad it remains untamed, is still as tangy as a ranging cheetah, has teeth and claws – and a kind of furry tenderness at times – that is the true voice of this mix-blooded island.

Imagine a pear-drop floating in water, or a glass goblet as green as Ireland. That's how Barbados appeared in the tropic sea after my hour-and-a-half flight from Trinidad. It seemed gentler, more pastoral, than that other island and was certainly more of a piece. The English settlers who came here more than three centuries ago had left a clear stamp upon it. They were gentlemen farmers and had used white labour to clear the aboriginal forests. After planting tobacco, they then switched to sugar, which is when they brought in the African slaves. You can still see the great country houses set deep in their fields of cane, with elegant drives leading through the avenues of mahogany – a tropical parody of the Englishman's ideal.

But other influences have enlivened that temperate design; the jaunty streak of the African is everywhere, as are the brilliant outbursts of vegetation – the Caribbean jungle hitting back. The green Nordic island, as seen from the air, looks different indeed from ground level. Where the sugar cane ends, the wild island begins, washed by a tidal rim of flowers. Flamboyants, jacaranda, hibiscus, and oleander, the butter-gold pride of India, the African tulip, and delicate frangipani all burn like the bush of Moses. This is an island, too, of darting hummingbirds, jack-spaniards, and turtle-doves; of mongoose, monkey, and the whistling frog who sings like a bird in the moonlight.

I was shown round Barbados by an Old Negro called Ennis, whose accent seemed Cornish or Cotswold. 'Waat we lookin' far today?' he'd ask me each morning. He reminded me of my Gloucestershire uncles. His accent, I found, was typical of Barbados and could have descended from West of England settlers. Ennis showed me the island, its curious cliffs and subsidences, its coral ridges and deep, wooded gullies, from which springs of sweet water (most rare in these latitudes) issue sparkling from underground lakes. He showed me the haunts of the monkey, the flying fish of Bathsheba, the cliff caves of the Arawak Indians, fed me on fruits (some wild) that he plucked from the trees, and grumbled continuously about the pain in his back.

With Ennis, I saw an island of curious mementos, a kind of dusty album of relics – gusty landscapes of cane and ruined windmills, worn pathways where camels once walked, and slave-built 'castles', once the homes of tyrants, now hotels of quiet comfort. I saw place names, too, that spoke strange juxtapositions, part history and part emotion – Indian Ground, Mount Misery, Strong Hope and Graveyard, Sweet Bottom, and Prerogative Prospect. Particularly haunting were the village churches, stone-spired and sleepily rural, whose tombs bore inscriptions to faithful slaves, or to girls who died young of the fever.

These churches, though as English as tea and biscuits, become something quite different on Sundays. Then they burst at the seams with Negro choirs who bring to their worship an entirely African passion. Sunday in Barbados is a thing I remember, a day of holiday and lively devotion. No tight-lipped, hangdog, puritan mourning this, but a day to be treated like carnival. Exquisite black children, white-gloved and beribboned, wearing fresh-starched flouncy frocks, appear crisp to the eye as candied-chocolate, are like flowers blowing along the road. Dandy fathers and brothers, and straw-bonneted mothers, shepherd the dazzling children to church, which in a while breaks forth with such beats of song you might think the occasion a wedding.

While with Ennis, I saw the cane harvest begin, the climax of the Barbadian year. Shining young giants with flashing machetes hacked their way through the canes like demons. 'He cuts the kens by the tahn,' said Ennis. 'Some can cut 'im ten tahns a day. Teks the trash ter the animals. Sheep an' pigs. Cane meat. The poor man's bank.' Sugar cane, to old Ennis, was still the life of Barbados, still sacred, the green thumb of God. 'Ketch a ken-burner,' he muttered. 'Better kill a man dead. Much better to what we do t'im. . . .'

Evening, the short sundown, while driving back from the country, was for me the most opulent time. A half hour of light rich as melting butter anointing the village cabins, sparking the flowers and the petticoats spread on the bushes with its final golden glow. Groups of men would be sitting in the middle of the road, playing draughts, drinking cane juice, or talking – talking with that curious jerk of the arm as though throwing their words at the listener. In a doorway, a couple of bonneted aunts, holding hands, would gossip more secretly. In the thoughtful face of a resting Negro, one might glimpse the pallor of a long-dead Englishman. Even stranger, like apparitions among the cabins, a sudden scattering of gold-haired children – the descendants of the 'red-legs', the early white labourers, many of whom were political rebels, who were transported from England several centuries ago and have kept themselves separate ever since.

My memories tend to concentrate on the interior of the island because it was a place that drew me. The beaches and hotels are the lazy playgrounds to which one can always readily return. Among the towns, I liked Bridgetown,

especially at night, for the tattered life of its streets. But even
by day it has a miniature charm, still bearing the thumb-
notes of history. It has a statue of the sea-god, Horatio
Nelson; George Washington was once stationed here; and the
arcaded barracks of the old British garrison are still the
handsomest buildings in the town. Fire, volcanic ash, civil
war and plague have each in turn possessed it. Meanwhile,
for almost three hundred years, it has remained a wellhead
for shipments of sugar and rum.

Barbados is rich in soil and sun, in flavour of fruit and
flower, in the taste of home dishes (pepper pot, puddin' and
souse, suckling pig, flying fish, and jug-jug), in the white-
coral mansions along the coast of St James where millionaires
have made their homes, in the sheet-smooth beaches and
their rippling reefs and the brown hours spent beside them,
in the work songs of the people (the diggers and barrel-
makers, fishers and banana-boat loaders), and especially in
the islanders' elegance, warmth and vividness, their proud
and argumentative wit. Barbados still bears the print of
apartness, coral-coasted and country-wild, with an air as
delicate, I sometimes thought, and as heady as its rum. There
is a hypnotic blur about the place that can steal one's
memory of elsewhere. It is some eight hours from New York
by air – another world only a short sleep away.

The last place I visited on my Caribbean whip-round was the
northern island of Jamaica. Over one thousand miles from
Trinidad, and the largest island in the West Indies, it is in
many ways the most mixed-up – a neon-lit play-coast of five-
star sophistication surrounding an interior almost as wild as
Africa.

I arrived in the evening, after the day's flight from
Barbados, and landed at Montego Bay – the holiday centre
on the island's north coast facing Cuba and Florida. We were
greeted at the airport with free rum punch: 'With the
compliments of the Tourist Board.' On the roof of my hotel –
the country house of Blairgowrie – several roosting buzzards
were waiting. I sat on the terrace, an iced drink to my lips,
looking at the bay and its mangrove islands. I repeated

'Jamaica' several times to myself and still couldn't quite believe I was here. Then a steel band played, a great moon rose, the bay lit up like a tray full of diamonds, while over the sea I saw my plane heading northward to New York and a raging blizzard.

The next morning I woke to a midsummer dawn, the sky a hot brick-red. The birds were a chorus of unrecognizable noises – whirring sewing machines, clocks running down, disapproving elders going 'tch-tch-tch', tearing cloth, and chipping marble. I find birds more emotive than food or music, proving whether one is at home or in exile.

Having had a glimpse of Jamaica's interior wilderness in my flight over the island the previous night, I thought I'd go back and have another quick look at it, so I took the small rail-car to Appleton. Almost immediately we were climbing the backwood gullies through country no motor road knows. The rail tracks were old, laid on hand-axed sleepers through which grass and wild flowers were growing. We met women and children and small black pigs walking the track on their way to market. This was their road, they scarcely bothered to step aside, the wooden crossties shone smooth from their feet. It was like a country lane, and to enter the tunnels one burrowed through tendrils of dripping fern.

On our journey we passed forests of bamboo and satin-wood, crossed a plateau of palm-shaded cattle, threaded remote-looking valleys where the women covered their faces and naked children scampered up trees. We stopped at hill towns that appeared quite large on the map but in reality were just five or six cabins. In the one street of Cambridge I read a bill on a door asking questions that would have worried the Sphinx: 'Who was not born and never died? Whose bones resurrected the living?' In Catadupa it turned out to be 'killing day': fresh meat hung on wires from the trees, a butcher was measuring out strips of mutton, and a sign said: 'Cooking Done Here.' Near Ipswich we visited a limestone cave; 'Hot as cotton in thar,' said a Negro. In Maggotty the track was covered with coconuts that had to be cleared before we could pass.

At the end of the line, in mid-island Appleton, it was

payday, and there was an open-air market. Bright clothing and saucepans hung on lines in the sun, painted china, straw hats, and baskets: there were pig meat and fruit, corn on the cob, wild honey, and coconut water. Cool in the shade, old hags puffed at pipes, jalopies were tethered to trees, donkeys and goats wandered hazily about, beer and syrups were ladled from buckets. I bought some cigars from a girl with a basket. She had 'penny-ones', 'chup-pennies' and 'chix-pennies'. Then we all returned to the waiting train and started back with a deafening whistle.

We had been to the edge of the Cockpit Country, those wild and mysterious highlands, where the Maroons, the descendants of African slaves, had taken refuge when they escaped from the Spaniards. For three hundred years they have defended their liberty and are a separate race in the heart of Jamaica. The Cockpit is clearly a mountain island, and most roads stop short at its frontiers. But several Maroons came to peep at our train: one saw their faces peering out from the forest, weathered, black, like pickled walnuts. They are Jamaica's oldest and proudest Africans.

'Jamaica' is Arawak for 'land of wood and water' – symbols of plenty to the early Indians. Later, more brutish settlers from Spain left the names of similar gratitude: Rio Bueno and Ocho Rios, Oracabessa and Montego Bay – the last two corruptions of 'head of gold' and 'pig lard'. But the peaceful Arawak, whom the Spaniards destroyed, cared less for gold than water. Jamaica helps the wound-up northerner wind down; it is vague and easygoing. Though my time there was short, and I had to compress much into it, I was left with a coloured stack of impressions: I remember a journey in a motor-car that would only go in reverse (of all places to 'The Land of Look-Behind'); the phosphorescent bay along the north coast near Falmouth, which at night was like swimming in mercury: Discovery Bay, placid and deserted, where Christopher Columbus first landed; and Seville nearby, site of the first Spanish town, now as desolate as Nineveh or Troy. I remember the four-mile Fern Gully leading to Ocho Rios, a deep canyon of matted trees, with the sun cut off and night coming early, full of shoals of dazzling fireflies; the slow talk

of the Jamaicans and their grape-blue skins, the supreme
grace of their walking and standing, their tales of duppies and
spidergods, the pure beat of their musical phrasing.

I remember rum and coconut drinks from hollowed-out
pineapples; swimming at Doctor's Cave, the water so clear
one seemed to float on nothing save one's shadow on the floor
of the sea; the proliferating golf courses and great hotels
spreading like gold leaf along the north shore – Half Moon
Hotel, home of tycoons and film stars, whose tables were
decorated with white plastic orchids (and this in a land of
flowers); Eaton Hall, too, run by a retired British tea-planter
(curry lunch with 'southern Indian accompaniments'); and
Ridgley's Steak House, in Montego Bay, where the steaks
weigh several pounds, so thick and sizzling and juicily tender
I had to wrap up half of mine for next day. I remember a
brief flight to Kingston and a bloody fight in the street; the
violent smell of a true seaport; Spanish Town from the air,
bone-white and deserted, a delicate cameo discarded by
history; boys bending to drink from a village tap, their
cupped hands like ebony goblets; children gleaning the
fields after sugar harvest, sucking cane or carrying it home
to make juice.

For those with the time and the will to spend, there is
everything to do in Jamaica. You can fly-fish for mullet in the
mountain streams or troll the deep sea for marlin; you can
raft from Blue Mountain down the Rio Grande, through
canyons of bird and jungle, or hunt for crocodiles in the
swamps of Black River, or sail round the buccaneer coves.
There are night clubs, floor shows, banquets, and dances
along a sea-coast as luxurious as Cannes. Or inland, an
unvisited world as mysterious as the Mountains of the Moon.

Trinidad, Tobago, Barbados, Jamaica: these are but four
of the Caribbean cycle. Each one is different, but the rhythm
is the same, the shared beat of the West Indian sun. High
season is winter, when the rich and the weary fly down to
these refuge islands. Life is not cheap, but if you go there in
summer almost everything is half-price. 'Summer', in the
Caribbean, lasts the year round anyway, with an average
temperature of eighty degrees. The islands are spread over a

vast warm sea, but the air makes them stepping-stones. Bottled within them, behind their glassy-blue shores, you will find an eccentric brew preserved. Gold-obsessed Spaniard, hedonist Frenchman, trading Dutch, and piratical English – they have all left their touch on landscape and manners, on language, religion and blood. Yet of all the many elements that make up the Caribbean, the Negro is the catalyst. More than anything else, the colour and effervescence of these islands remain a tribute to the vitality of Africa.

Voices of Ireland

IRELAND, for me, started at London Airport, with flights of
nuns floating heavenward on escalators. All the names on the
loudspeakers began with the rhetorical O, and Irish eyes
were everywhere. The trim girls of Aer Lingus may have
over-tinted their hair, but they couldn't dye the deep blue of
their eyes. Cloth-capped gents in the plane were reading the
racing pages ('Two-Year-Old Greengage Worth a Nibble'),
and the captain's announcements were in Gaelic – but
sufficiently familiar in cadence to allow me to read into them
my usual flying anxieties.

The flight to Shannon was stormy, the cloud wiped away
only at the last moment, when came my first sudden view of
Ireland – a rush of old green fields quartered with ragged
hedges, cattle like bones on a sliding cloth, narrow lanes, bent
trees, and seething elderbushes swept by a streaming Atlantic
gale.

Fresh from tidied-up England, with its stockbroker farmers,
this seemed the kind of landscape I'd not seen since childhood
– rambling, shaggy, wild but intimate, a place not yet
bleached and neutralized by the machine. I'd come to western
Ireland, to the edge of Clare, to part of the saw-tooth Atlantic
coastline; and although I was English, and it was my first
visit to the country, I was made welcome like a returning
prince.

Clare is a country of castles, and I'd not been there long
before I'd seen the insides of two of them – 'Dromoland'
Castle, where I stayed the first night, and 'Bunratty', where
I was invited to a banquet. Both castles were strongholds of
the warring O'Briens, descendants of the first King of Ireland:

'Dromoland', now a dreamy luxury hotel set in 1,500 acres of wooded parkland; and 'Bunratty', a tower of rose-coloured stone recently re-roofed.

The 'Bunratty' banquet was a conscious charade, served by wenches in fifteenth-century velvet, a feast of medieval dishes eaten with sharpened daggers to the accompaniment of mead and the music of minstrels. The storm had blown itself out as I drove to the castle and even the landscape itself looked medieval – golden fields full of rushes, a cloaked girl herding cows, a horse cropping salt grass by the river. . . .

At the castle I was honoured by being made earl for the night, and set at the head of the banqueting hall, with my own butlers and food-tasters, power to command the minstrels, to distribute tidbits to my friends, and to condemn rowdies to short spells in the dungeons.

There were some two hundred guests in the candle-lit hall, and every dish was served first to me. We ate, I remember, such things as stuffed boar's head, pull'd fowl, and petty toes in gellye, washed by flagons of claret to follow up the mead, and ending with everlasting syllabubs.

A 'medieval banquet' may sound rather an arch proceeding, but this one was saved by its vitality and wit. Perhaps no one but the Irish could have got away with it, but it was a pleasure to be taken in. The Irish are all of them actors, and love a performance, can slip back into history as readily as into a favourite old coat, and possess, moreover, a sense of delicate self-parody, which protects them from the corruptions of tourism.

It wasn't, after all, such a bad introduction to Ireland. We were fooled with both style and grace. And somewhere buried deep in the whole friendly imposture was the reality on which it was based. The O'Briens were still alive in the hulking stones of the castle, the food was a genuine re-creation, and when the minstrels and the serving girls played and sang, we were carried away with them as they, too, were carried, for they were singing of what they knew. . . .

Ireland begins with the land, the first and last thing here – a glacially scarred old beauty full of poverty and grandeur, mossily green as a holy well. It is an abode of old heroes, a sounding board for legend, a place where nothing has been forgotten. It is also a land of voices that talk of nothing but Ireland, of its history and the men it has made. The human voice, unelectrified, is still the most subtle power in the land, and nothing can hush it, in spite of its softness. The voices of the women are even softer than the men's, round and gentle as furry bells (except perhaps when they laugh, when they give the wild pagan shriek of surprised women anywhere). To travel about Ireland is to be continuously accompanied by these voices, always remembering, telling the country's story.

Perhaps the first thing that strikes one is the uncluttered bareness of the place. It shows little of the affluent litter of Europe. It is still for the most part what it always was: bog, rock, crisp grass and forest, dominated by the elements, the Atlantic wind and rain, the light of the sun and moon.

Poverty, perhaps, has always been the abiding thing in Ireland, but the Irish are still the princes of imagination and language. Possessions can often reduce the native poetry in a people, gadgets switch them into gaping silence, while as their landscapes fill up with roadways and powerlines so the gods of distance and mystery die. The Irish to date have been kept pretty free of possessions; their native wit has also stayed free.

When I set out to discover some of Western Ireland, my companion, an O'Connell (nicknamed 'The Liberator' by his friends), was another Irishman who had forgotten nothing. It seemed he had a tale for every stone and tree, details of the generations of every cottager. 'There's a fine salmon fall here along,' he'd say. Or, 'That's where the last of the O'Flahertys died.' He filled up my days with a bardic continuity of conversation which never lapsed into triviality or dullness.

With The Liberator I saw much of the best of the west – the coasts of Clare and Galway, the heart of Connemara, the rocky thrust of the Kerry peninsula – the teeth and tusks of the west-facing island, the talking mouth of its history, where, since pre-Christian days, when men first appeared on the headlands, most of what was important to Ireland has happened.

I remember the coast of Clare, a mild wet headland cosseted by currents from the Mexican Gulf: deep lanes banked with honeysuckle and purple-speared foxgloves, rocking moon daisies bruised by the sea. Spanish Point, where a ship of the Armada foundered, with a thousand dead still lying under the dunes. And the small spoiled farms scattering the empty land, with an occasional goose, head down to the wind.

This was a place of steep cliffs and little golden beaches washed by waves milky-blue like moonlight, yet dispossessed of visitors even this summer day, with only birds on the sun-beaten sands of Liscannor, and only two horses in the town of Lahinch.

Northern Clare towards Galway was coastal mountain and plain, sharp descents, changing levels and distances; a country of rocks and caves, little shrines and hayfields, or of lush grassy inlets lorded by Tennysonian castles and floating with waxen swans. The long, curling roads for the most part were empty; few people seemed to be going anywhere. To meet traffic was an occasion, when the clear, slanting light outlined the oncomer with classical brilliance. A flock of sheep perhaps, driven by a grave young girl wearing her brother's long coat and boots. Or a cart stuffed with children like a basket of figs. Or a caravan of red-haired gypsies.

Before dropping down into Galway Bay, one enters the moonscape they called 'The Burren', a district whose fields appeared to be picked to the bone, leaving long, splintered ribs of rock. Here was a graveyard of history, littered with massive boulders, stone forts and sixth-century churches, where 3,000-year-old legends grow like lichen on the rocks, and a dog may scratch up the crowns of kings.

Galway Bay, I remember, was a long dagger of water stabbing into the heart of the land, polished and gleaming the day I saw it, and studded with the three blurred Aran Islands. Galway town, itself, had a chartreuse-green river full of shadowy, weaving salmon, and un-Irish names written over the shops, relics of Anglo-Norman invasion. Best of all round

the bay were the country places, where the finger of time had
fumbled, and the small hunched farms, ingrown like tree
roots, seemed to ask no more than a horse in the field, a
hound, a goose, and a rose bush.

North of Galway was the sweep of Connemara, a place it
is vulgar to try to paint or describe. To see it is to taste the
ultimate essence, a drop of locality distilled from all others.
It is the hard stuff of Ireland, not a pampered paradise like
Killarney, but a gulf of silence scooped from the lap of
mountains, a place of sovereign remoteness and self-containment that almost steals away one's identity. The saw-peaks
of Twelve Bens fill half one sky, the brooding hulk of Maam-
turk the other, while cloud shadows run slowly across their
emotionless crevices like silk scarves drawn over the faces of
gods.

'If you were to suddenly wake up here, you wouldn't know
where you were,' said The Liberator. 'An Arab or Indian
would think he was home.'

Connemara is the Gaelic 'hound of the sea', and is almost
an island, moated by lochs. It is Irish-speaking, a place of
shepherds, turf-cutters, fishermen and wandering tinkers. The
sheep are like stars on the vast blue slopes, the tinkers dwarfed
in the long mountain passes, glossy Connemara ponies browse
round the shores of the lakes, and the lakes are full of lilies.

The Irish Sunday was the day for talk, the voices coming out
of the fields and houses, gathering in groups with a long easy
breath to see that no man should suffer for silence. Rows of
up-ended carts surrounded the village church, horses grazing
while the folk heard Mass. Then there was a parade of small
girls in lace frocks and straw bonnets, while the men side-
stepped to the pubs.

With Sean, a young friend, I followed them. Talk in the
bar was being dealt like cards. 'Tom Burke, the healer? I
knew him well. He's dead and gone to his people.' Creamy
pints of stout, blackcurrant-coloured, stood in each fist like a
miner's lamp. 'Not a cow in the country he couldn't heal
with his hand.' 'Could heal an elephant, let alone a cow.'
'Knew a man's broken bone by the look on his face. Do you

believe me now?' 'I do.' 'A great shoulder-alterer he was, to
be sure . . . straightened half the cripples in Clare. . . .'

With Sean I drove off to another village. He was wanting
to buy a horse. It was afternoon now. A group of lads watched
the river. A girl in the meadow twisted grass round her
fingers.

'You wanted a horse?' Chickens were brushed from the
stable and the two horse-dealers settled their caps. They were
brothers, middle-aged, with the fine hungry faces of men of
the old-time frontiers. Sheamus, the elder, took charge of the
matter. Yes, he'd a fine mare down in the field. 'She's in foal
I saw, but even if she were going to have a jackass, a terrible
great horse it was going to be. . . .' She was bred by his
father. 'He fell dead off a stallion and is gone where comfort
is.'

Sheamus trotted the mare up and down the lane, running
like a frisky boy beside her. She was not right for Sean, but
the brothers were not dismayed. They knew of another
farther along the cliffs. 'I didn't see him move, but I saw him
standing by the sea with his head up and a great star on his
forehead. A terrible great horse he looked to be. I'd be
ashamed not to tell you the truth.'

They said they'd take us to see him. We drove off up the
cliff with Sheamus' bicycle on the hood of the car. The
brothers in the back shouted, 'Lovely! Lovely!' Then the car
broke down in the bog.

We abandoned the thing and took to our legs, an hour's
walk above Galway Bay, the brothers waving their arms and
rolling about the rocks, intoxicated by the wind and by
Sunday leisure. Ringing political arguments began to rise
between them, debating the worth of old Irish leaders. 'He
was the man of his time. I tell you true. All the great men now
are dead.' 'But when the blaze came to his bottom he minded
himself.' 'Hold away now! Have ye finished? Listen! . . .'
They roared at each other like a couple of seals, building up
passions of rhetorical insult. They jumped up and down, and
threw their caps in the mud. Agreement would have murdered the afternoon.

We found the horse on the cliff edge – a mighty wind-blown beast with the whole of Connemara framed by his legs. But the farmer's price was too stiff, so, not to waste the day, Sheamus started bidding for a couple of heifers. The ritual of bargaining was long and elaborate; there was still half Sunday left to use. Sheamus offered a price. The farmer wouldn't think of it, the heifers were not for sale. 'Forty-one, I'm offering.' 'Forty-five wouldn't buy them.' They used the whole landscape to stamp away from each other. We fetched them back. 'Are they my heifers now?' 'They are – at forty-five.' An hour later we were still at it, tramping up and down the cliff, supporting the struggling pair. Neither would yield, and no deal was made, but the negotiations had been fine and subtle.

It was the brothers at last who pulled the car from the bog and dragged it lifeless back to the village. They sent out their daughters to find a man to repair it and steered us away for some evening drinking. Sheamus' face was now red as a Bengal cock. His eyes clouded and shone with the past. Remembering the horses he's known, and his poor old father, and the hungry times they'd had, cutting a winter's peat for thirty shillings and eating bread dipped in river water. And the best day of his life – watching a twelve-year-old girl jumping one of his unbroken Galway hunters, taking it over the wall like a flying lion: 'The tears laid on my eyes to see her.'

We'd arrived as strangers, but we'd developed the day with the brothers, and they were now proud and protective with us. They pointed to Sean: 'Look at the arms upon him.' I, too, was Irish; it was running out of my ears. And had we ever in our lives seen a bay like Galway? – 'And the sun there, dropping, dropping. . . .'

The pub in Ireland is still a kind of chapel of ease and shows the Irishman on top of his time. The television, for instance, will usually be kept in a small back room and will be killed when a man is talking. The pub is no place for lone drinking, or solitary introspection, but a public chamber in which to make yourself heard.

I remember a particular night, in Hogan's Bar, Ennis, a

few doorways from The Old Ground Hotel. There was a squat, nimble fiddler from the Spancehill horse fair and a pale piper as thin as his flute. It was early, but already, behind their long black pints, the men of Clare were clearing their throats. What followed was typical of other bars I went to, up in Galway, down in Kerry and Cork – something halfway between a wake and a wedding, half celebration, half common grief.

The fiddler began with some horse-fair reels, then the piper took his turn. 'A sad gigue,' he announced, 'to banish misfortune'; and his little flute made the cries of sea birds. Then one by one, as the finger pointed, each man in the bar sang a ballad: old men, with the slurred incantations of bards, young men with hot fruity tenors, each singing, eyes closed, reaching back in his mind, songs which smelt of the very skin of Ireland.

This was not the boozy wail of the usual pub singsong, but a haunting restatement of identity. 'The ballads of Ireland,' said someone, 'tell the whole of its history. They are the jigsaw of three thousand years.' The songs I heard that night were heard in silence, or with little murmurs of approval. And they were almost all of them cries of loss – lost love, a lost cause, the loss of Ireland itself, parting, departure, death. To be born was to die, but the Irish died twice, for exile was another death. 'The Last Rose of Summer', 'Fare Thee Well, Enniskillen', 'Spanish Lady', 'Raise the Gallows High'; they had that bite and melancholy at the heart of all folk song, celebrating a beauty too brief to bear.

The night was long and deep; everyone took his turn; and not even I, the stranger, was spared. A fiddle was put in my hand, I leaned against the bar and played the only Irish lament I knew. The old fiddle was the sweetest I'd ever touched, and my performance was airborne with whisky. When I finished, an old man struck the bar with his cap. 'Englishman,' he said, 'we forgive you.'

There is small distance in Ireland between the cultural classes, between the pub and the National Library. Irish literature is less for the sit-down man than for the stand-up singer and actor. Yeats, Oscar Wilde, George Bernard Shaw, O'Casey, wrote their best for the living voice.

I met a man in Kerry who keeps a small-town pub and is now one of the best playwrights in Ireland. J. B. Keane succeeds Behan, but with less of his one-man violence, and perhaps less of his self-destruction. I found him sharp as a gypsy, and without self-grandeur, and with a sly love for his Kerry countrymen.

Keane sent me to Cork to see his play, *The Highest House on the Mountain*, performed by a small local company with a large reputation, in a church hall, down a narrow side street. The night was pelting with rain, and the theatre packed, and the play a swinging flight of wit and compassion. Irish as the hills, and full of cavernous undertones, it rocked halfway between the bogs and heaven. The production was on a level with those of The Abbey, Dublin – though Dublin may not admit it.

As for Cork itself, it is bright and alive, full of bridges and branching rivers, provincial, yet open to the airs of the world, its waters haunted by Atlantic liners. The deep-wooded creeks round Cobh and Kinsale are whitened by yachts and herons, and the green hills above them were often the last sight of Ireland for exiles bound for America.

From Cork I took a fast new train through the country to wind up my trip in Dublin. Dublin is as Irish as New York is America, and has been called the most beautiful city in Europe. Largely built by the English as a place of privilege and grace, it is a city of elegant squares and terraces, houses of toast-warm brick, set with exquisite doors and balconies, recalling the Georgian grandeurs of Bath and Cheltenham. For nearly two hundred years it was a coiled jewel on the Liffey – but the new builders have come at last, and what they are doing to the terraces is like replacing pearls in a necklace with a succession of iron bolts.

Dublin, even so, is still a meeting place, and a town where there is place to talk. I spent two hot days in the company of Dubliner poets, riding their verbal streams; listening to the ballad singers of Howth, keening through stout and tobacco smoke; to tragi-comical tales of The Troubles; being led over bridges from bar to bar, where every 'snug' had a literary memory, and the last words of heroes hung like bells in the air, and every drinker straightened up to ring them.

Dublin struck me as a neutral drug-city for exiles, where dreamers gather to remember Ireland. And it was only here, gazing down into the slow brown Liffey, that I was able to look back on my own short journey.

I had travelled eight counties, and stayed in every kind of hotel, from princely 'Dromoland' to a hovel in Dingle. I remembered sea trout in Cork, sprawling over my plate, as huge as a boxer's arm; homemade bread up in Galway, light as a honeycomb; fat Dublin Bay prawns at Jammet's. . . . But I was remembering, too, the great hills in the west, where man seemed only a tenant. The long, stone fields, the cottages like hives, the old tombs of kings by the sea. And the green of the country, 'the forty kinds of green', fired or damped by every shade of weather, from an electric brilliance to something deep and cold as the eyes of a witch's cat.

I recalled the long, empty roads, a man and a horse upon them; the tinkers with hair like thistles; the sound of carts in the villages – the rattle of wheel and harness; the smell of rain on the burning turf. There were the old men on donkeys with the faces of American senators, others looking like New York cops.

This was a country of horses, of blacksmiths hammering, working dogs, children getting in the hay; of pink-cheeked young priests walking alone by the rivers, unwed girls staring across the fields. And ruins everywhere: great abbeys, castles, cottages abandoned, the black thumb of Cromwell – the marginal brandmarks of the country's history, worn like wounds, and never forgotten.

Ireland is constant, but the Irish move; they have put no great mark on their land. They seem to inhabit its surfaces as birds ride on the sea, coming and going with wind-blown cries. As near to it in heart as any men to their birthplace, perhaps they are more conscious of their hopeless impermanence. Meanwhile, they fill it with their voices, and keep its memory green, singing their farewells up and down its valleys.

Arrack and Astarte

I was in Beirut, briefly, once before, when I landed on a flight from Cairo to Cyprus, in May 1945. A sad mechanic walked across the scrubby air-strip and waited as we refuelled. Then he said to the pilot: 'Bring me back a bride, will you?' and handed him a bunch of bananas through the open cockpit.

Cyprus – seventy miles westward over the edge of the sea – was long famed for the beauty and compliance of its women: since classical times it had been the sacred island of love, the birthplace of Venus rising from the dawn-pink sea.

Venus in fact, was an early immigrant to Cyprus. The original love-goddess, under her various names, had her home in the hill-caves of Syria and the Lebanon. Did the forlorn Beirut mechanic, in those hard end-of-the-war days, feel his city and land deprived of its pagan birthright?

He need not have worried. When I returned, years later, to booming Beirut, I found it transformed, magnificently re-risen from the sea, and splendidly balanced on its old trident of wealth, pleasure and sensuality.

Beirut, packed tight on its western-facing peninsula, has been a trading sea-port for some five thousand years. 'A sore thumb sticking out in the wrong direction,' is also what some cynical desert-Arabs call it. Nevertheless it must be unique in its throbbing energy, in its concentration of diverse faiths and cultures, moreover in its unusual achievement of general tolerance which makes it one of the most successfully Western cities of the Middle East.

It is also very rich. Flying in through the gold-mist of sunset, you suddenly see below you, crowding the peninsula and round the bay, gold slabs of apartments, offices and new hotels – a kind of Fort Knox of well-stacked affluence. It is saved, perhaps, from the total hell of urbanization, by the villas that trail away steeply to the clouded mountains. One soon learns to enjoy the shades of difference between Beirut and its environs – the public, money-making, pleasure-domed city, and the quiet villas on the hills, their terraced arches clotted with the reflections of sunsets, turning them the colour of old Syrian glass.

Beirut is not, as one might expect, an oriental city. Although ridden for centuries by Muslim invaders, by the Ottoman Empire and the Mamelukes, it is predominantly Western in wit, social styles, material success, and in its guiltless pursuit of pleasure.

Perhaps this had to be so. For since its beginnings, Beirut has stood in the centre of a narrow strip of land running north-south between sea and mountains – a trampling ground for the armies of clashing civilizations: Egyptian, Persian, Greek, Macedonian, Roman, Mongol and Turk.

No doubt it was the early presence of Greek and Roman, tempered later by that of the easy-going Muslim, which developed Beirut's partiality for humanism and law. Equally, it must have been its position as a trade centre, beach-head between Asia and the West, temporary territory for advancing and fleeing armies, which taught its diverse peoples, many of them permanently displaced by events, to settle and live peacefully together.

For scattered throughout the city, and scrupulously represented in the legislature of the country, are almost a dozen different faiths, including Maronite Christians, Armenian Orthodox, Armenian Catholics, Greek Orthodox, Greek Catholics, Sunni Muslims, Shi'ite Muslims, Protestants, Presbyterians, and the Druzes. The Maronites – the majority – are the survivors of an eighth-century heresy; the faith of the indiginous Druzes is tribal and secret.

Clearly, this boiling diversity of peoples is one of the sources of Beirut's effervescence, and you get the feel of this as soon as you arrive. Driving in from the airfield, for instance, my progress was intermittently arrested, not only by the taxi-

driver's personal eccentricities, but severally by an 80-mile-
an-hour motor rally, a parade of nuns, a television crew
filming a mid-street commercial, a marching brass band, a
concentration of football fans, and a friendly riot round the
flower-decked car of a newly-elected deputy who was celebrating with a bleeding nose.

My hotel, The Mayflower, was one of modest luxury, with
a relaxed and civilized atmosphere. The proprietor, a handsome Anglicized Lebanese, loved the British way of life without being too rigid about it. Not only, for instance, could one
have a lush English breakfast in the morning, one could also
have a hot meal in one's room at midnight. Built into the
hotel, there is also The Duke of Wellington – the proprietor's
dream of an English pub. The barmen wear bow-ties and
tartan jackets. British-brewed beer cost about 40p a pint.

The Mayflower stands in the Ras Beirut, a mainly English-
speaking area, American-educated, brashly commercial, and
much of it newly built. Flats, shops and cinemas, hotels and
banks, even an outbreak of sidewalk cafés, all stand jumbled
together like a millionaire's playbox. The hundred-year-old
American University lies aloofly to the north.

I stepped out of The Mayflower, on my first evening there,
and breathed a temperature 30 degrees warmer than London. The narrow streets were full of hoots, squeals, thumps
and bangs as motor-cars bounced off each other. Some cut
across pavements as they took the short way round corners.
Bluff and quick-thinking sustained the anarchic flow. There
seemed to be few pedestrians abroad, except in the wider
boulevards; you travelled by motor-car as the only means of
protection. For visitors, in any case, getting a taxi was no
problem; you simply took one or two steps along the pavement and one pulled up silently beside you.

A system of 'service' taxis criss-cross Beirut and are the best
and cheapest way of getting around. They follow a fixed
route, charge a flat rate, and can be hailed like a bus. You
take an ordinary taxi for a private journey, and the fare must
be arranged in advance. But once you've agreed on a price
you get something extra – a multilingual driver who becomes
your guide, confessor, body-guard and initiator; one who will

suggest where you should go but will not insist; who will follow your whims to the end, will protect you from false temptations and all the perils of the night, and will even see you home safely to bed.

Whether I wished, that first evening, to walk or to hire a taxi, was a decision that was quickly taken for me. I had scarcely left my hotel when I was aware of a fellow walking beside me, his hand buried deep in my jacket pocket. No threats. Perfectly friendly. Just: 'Whayawant, mistah? Boy? – girl? Gimme a beer. I take you.' I double-shuffled in reverse. A taxi slid to my elbow. I jumped in, closed the door, and escaped.

The driver introduced himself as 'Jack,' sang in Arabic as we drove, cursed other drivers in American, and asked me my wishes in French. To taste the edge of sin in my district we dipped into several second-grade Hambra night-clubs, but it was too early and nothing much was happening. A bottle of beer at the bar cost about 75p, but one was not compelled to drink alone. Each club had on offer a range of spectacular girls whose company and conversation were available at champagne prices. They all seemed to be called Trudi, Heidi, or Judy. I met none who was Lebanese.

It soon becomes clear to the visitor that the attitude of the citizens of Beirut to their city is a peculiarly schizoid one. It is their pleasure-ground and their source of wealth; with one hand they caress it, with the other mutilate it for gain. During the First World War the Turks destroyed much of old Beirut; after which many new town-houses were erected bearing a kind of French-Lebanese imprint – lightly arcaded, cool and charming. Throughout the past ten years – with the coming of the land-developer's high crane and excavator – most of these eggshell structures have been systematically crushed to make room for the international concrete block. Most rich families in the Lebanon own some such new property in Beirut, not necessarily to live in – mainly for speculation. Perhaps they boast one of the city's three hundred hotels, or one or two of the seventy-odd banks; or, if really chic, a block of high-rise flats. As the city has spread, you see these bright new apartment houses standing marooned on bits of waste ground. From the air they look rudimentary, like gold-miners' stakes. A number of them are empty, some built by oil-sheiks from the Gulf largely as funk-holes set against times of trouble. Not all the latter are entirely empty, however; in the echoing edifices of some an oil-sheik will have installed a blonde 'Doris' from Leeds, or an even blonder 'Ingrid' from Malmö, to whom he and his brothers, arriving in their private jets, will pay regular and attentive visits.

Beirut is where the money is – banking, import, export – but the dealers no longer have to live on the job. After work, in half an hour, they can escape to their villas in the hills and look down on their many-storied wealth – which may explain, in part, their guilty love of their city and also their physical abuse of it.

I was shown two instances of this attitude: the destruction of a square of exceptionally fine villas to make room for a parking-lot and go-cart race-track. The other, more tragic; the ravaging of the classical old town, the main traces of which are being lost for ever. This was the site of the original Roman city, Berythus, famous for its law school, and favoured by retired Roman captains. Naturally, rebuilding has been going on for two thousand years, the new gently overlaying the old. Most of the Roman city had long since been lost to sight, surviving only in folk memory and civic myth.

Following the Turkish destruction of this area, the lay-out of French-Lebanese shops and buildings achieved a distinctive and civilized style. Now that ultimate destroyer, the modern excavator, has moved in with bizarre and final results. Ploughing far deeper than the labourer's traditional pick and shovel, it uncovered large areas of the lost Roman city – splendidly preserved columns and tessellated pavements buried as much as twenty feet underground. The developers' economics left no room either to rebury or preserve them – apart from one minor token ringed by 'municipal' railings. The glories of Roman Berythus were revealed again only briefly, then smashed for ever beneath the basements of supermarkets and offices.

Beirut is a racial club-sandwich – as is New York – and it balances its variety of factions with ease. It also displays a paradox of tolerance and intrigue. In the old commercial quarter of Bab Edriss, for instance, some ten thousand Jews carry on a busy, healthy and unharrassed existence in spite of the Republic's deep enmity with neighbouring Israel. The rest of the city has its distinct ethnic quarters, but they lie comfortably against each other

Early one morning I went to visit the old town *zouks* – those crowded, coffee-drinking Arab street-markets which have scarcely changed since the birth of the Prophet. Apparently still untouched, with hardly a plastic container in sight, they snuggle together close to the harbour, and I was taken there by a pretty Lebanese girl who, though perfectly happy to show me around, said she wouldn't dream of going there alone. 'A good place for shopping for old women and servants,' she said, 'but if I go by myself, they joke of me in Arabic, and it is not nice that I understand.'

Here it all was: the narrow noisy lanes heaped with wet fruit and vegetables; streets of tin-smiths mending kettles and slavering over old Ford radiators; streets hung with bunches of plucked chickens still indignantly alive (kept alive so they'd stay fresh in the heat); streets of caged birds, tame pigeons and grounded ducks, of bleating kids and lambs waiting for the knife, of ropes of red meat hung up like silken scarves, fat men in cubicles propping up bags of beans, shouting porters and beggars, boys scampering around with coffee, tailors sitting cross-legged on platforms, heads down, stitching madly. . . . I'd seen it all before, two thousand miles to the west, in the *zouks* of Fez, Tetuan and Tangier, all part of that Arab civilization which still has no great wish for change, which remains traditional, self-nourishing, enclosed.

'A pity,' said my guide. 'When I was just a little girl, I came here every day with the cook. Everything we bought was fresh and cheap. Now I am grown and respectable and cannot shop here no more. I must buy my grocery frozen and wrapped in the supermarket.'

She took me on to the 'gold *zouk*' – much grander, of course, but still intimate, with all the suave dealers related. Here was much displaying of bangles, bracelets, rings and coins, rapid mental calculations in the world's various currencies, lots of running in and out to fetch cups of coffee or tempting trinklets from neighbouring booths; but no bargaining – this was fixed-price, genuine gold.

I ended that particular morning with a visit to a respected 'dealer in antiquities', recommended as expensive, but honest. The place was a treasure house, and no sooner had I been introduced than a young expert snatched the signet ring off my finger, placed it under a powerful glass, and pronounced the stone to be Roman (*circa* Caesar Augustus).

I was encouraged by this beginning, having had the thing for years and always thought it was Tottenham Court Road (*circa* George VI). Clearly the shop knew its business – the Lebanon, with much of the Middle East, being one of the most valuable archeological mine-fields in the world. Apart from being the cradle of the Phoenicians, the world's first international traders, every other local civilization had left something buried here. Dug up through the years, by peasant's plough or prospector, funnelled into the National Museum or through the hands of private dealers, Beirut has collared most of the region's portable prizes of the past – and quite a lot of it was in this shop. I saw exquisite Syrian drinking glasses (3rd century AD) the colour of orange sunsets, the dry soil still on them. There were Roman necklaces and ear-rings, gold and silver coins, clay masks of remote Assyrian goddesses. And a bronze figurine, Greco-Roman, classical, standing in a posture of innocent nakedness, image of that earth-mother who once ruled this world – Astarte, Aphrodite, Venus.

There was little in the shop dated later than the 4th century AD, and prices were naturally high. I thought at least I might haggle for a few old coins. 'A London dealer was here just a moment ago,' they said. 'He left with a hatbox full.'

In the bar of a nearby hotel I thanked my guide for her patience. She raised her white wine to the wine-dark sea. Relaxed now, she began chattering in her French-accented English, showing every so often her bronzed Assyrian profile. 'D'you believe in these love-goddesses of yours?' I asked waggishly. Her large dark eyes gazed back at me. 'Of course not. They were a myth.' 'The Virgin Mary, then?' 'But naturally.' 'Weren't they all the same?' 'No, only the Virgin existed in truth.'

My guide was a Maronite Catholic. Her grandfather fought the Druzes. She was French-influenced, innocently bigotted. She gave me a slow, indulgent Jesuitical smile. Her face was the glowing ghost of Astarte.

As I was not in Beirut for oil, banking, or property development, I devoted myself to its other rewards – to its first breath of spring, its night life, food, and the hospitable vitality of its people. No matter who they are, or what racket they are in, they seem to take from their city an easy-going urbanity. You are unlikely to get the best of a Lebanese in a deal, but you will not be cheated – merely out-smarted. Business aside, you are met with generosity and warmth, and this is one of the memorable charms of the place.

On the strength of a single introduction to a young professional couple I was immediately invited to an intimate family celebration. The occasion was the first communion of their ten-year-old son, and I was collected early from my hotel and driven out through the spring-flowering hills to a shining new church, built to serve a Jesuit college. The church filled up rapidly with friends and relations flashing gold teeth and Japanese cameras. The young mothers wore French frocks, the grandmothers tribal black, the menfolk Douglas Fairbanks moustaches. Then to a wail of liturgical treble, the first communion boys processed slowly towards the altar, each one habited in white, a Dominican mini-monk, each holding a fluttering vestal candle.

Afterwards, outside, there was more photographing of the boys, grouped with their fathers, spiritual and temporal. French small-talk skipped and bounced as we regained our parked cars standing in rows under the flowering trees. Only the distant mist-covered mountains suggested the existence of rougher, unconverted and older tribes, still grinding away at their mysteries.

With all colour-film exposed and celebration cards exchanged, my friends rushed me back to their Beirut apartment. Gracefully Lebanese in style (albeit five floors above ground) it still preserved the lineaments of local tradition: a large central room set with slender pillars and arches, kitchen and bedrooms leading off all round. One could imagine vines climbing up the pillars, the ceiling open to the sky, a well of sweet water in the middle of the room – the cool domestic design, the inward-looking refuge, that once marked the Arab world from Spain to Damascus.

Together with her many relations, the mother of the first communion boy had prepared a large meal in his honour. There were crates of wine and *arrack*, French and Lebanese dishes, mountains of sweets and ice-coated cakes. It was an immensely long but light-hearted meal, interspersed with songs, recitations and speeches. I was perhaps the only guest present who was not a member of the family, but this was in no way held against me. Though general conversation was in Arabic and French, an old gentleman sitting opposite described the ingredients of what I was eating and also gave me a detailed run-down on the Republic's constitution. I was provided with a flute to blow, a tambourine to bang on my knee, and I was asked to sing a song. Then an Arab-speaking youth on my right suddenly switched to English and apologized for leaving the banquet so early (it was five o'clock). He was an undertaker, he said, and he had to dispose of three corpses that afternoon – each one of a different religion. 'Some of the rituals are more implicated than others, y'know. I expect you'll not see me again.'

Among the variety of restaurants on offer in Beirut, Dimitri's is probably the most individual and eccentric. The grey-haired, charming, but unpredictable proprietor will sometimes close shop when he sees guests coming. He'll simply hide away in one of the many shady rooms and not bother to answer the door. I'd invited two Lebanese friends for lunch, and when we arrived at Dimitri's we found the place barred and shuttered. We stubbornly rang the bell and waited five minutes. Finally there was an unrattling of chains, and Dimitri appeared. 'Of course I open. Come in, come in!' The smile on his face shone like a fresh meringue. Doubtless he had vetted us through a spy-hole.

Dimitri's is a series of dark intimate little rooms, each with a fireplace, the brown walls covered with nudes and proverbs. One of the last genuine old houses left in Beirut (and soon coming down to make room for a ring-road). It was one of Kim Philby's hide-outs, and as I sat in the smoke-darkened bar I could imagine him crouching there and drinking his way out of his labyrinth. One understands that it is not done to mention Philby here. Instead, Dimitri beams and talks of other things. 'I came here from Constantinople, forty-seven years ago. Before then this house belonged to a very rich merchant. He kept his women over that room. Kept his uniques here. Now you come out and see the garden.'

Old, ripe, screened with laocoöns of vines and bougainvillia branches, the garden was a series of bosky little enclaves, each designed, one could imagine, for secret meetings and intrigues, each separate like the rooms of the house. Dimitri's restaurant is old-fashioned, irreplaceable and doomed, peeling with an atmosphere of out-dated wickedness – pre-electronic, operatic, cast with Faustian shadows, where characters actually arrived in cloaks, sat down, and really ate with daggers.

The restaurants of Beirut seem to offer something of everything; French, Italian, Greek, Russian, Spanish, Chinese, Japanese, American – and best of all Lebanese. I remember visiting three of these last, two with friends, one alone, each meal a variation and a surprise. First I dined at the Yildizlar, on the Rouche, having driven there in a hurry and getting the car-door slammed on my thumb. However, the throbbing pain and quickly blackening nail was soon anaesthetized by the restaurant's *mezzeh* and *arrack*. *Arrack* is pure grape alcohol flavoured with anise, a colourless spirit which clouds white with water and has the impact of smashing into an iceberg. *Mezzeh* consists of up to forty-odd separate dishes, to be savoured slowly to the accompaniment of the wit of your friends. Originally intended, no doubt, as a mere appetizer to an orgy, my first *mezzeh* took about two hours to get through. Among its delicacies I noted sheeps' brains, chicken livers, asparagus, Russian salad, dried fish, chickens' legs, sheeps' tongue, sour plums with salt, pancakes of fish mixed with onions, almonds, and chopped, spiced lamb.

After demolishing these forty dishes (with *arrack*), one can, if one is able, move on to one or more of the specialities of the house: *Kibeh Nayeh* – strips of fresh raw meat pounded with coarsely ground wheat and seasoned with onion and pepper; or *Shawarma and Hommos* – lamb cooked on a spit and eaten with a paste of chick-peas flavoured with garlic and sesame.

You can round the whole thing off with some of the sweet-meats of Lebanon, of which few in the east are sweeter, such as a plate of Tripoli cream, chopped nuts, topped with mountain-honey syrups and sprinklings of crystallized orange blossom.

Next day, I went to the Bahri, where the meal was even more formidable – largely because I was accompanied by a Lebanese artist who knew what he wanted. He bullied the waiters with a kind of grandiose bonhomie and we were served with a *mezzeh* on a lavish scale. His eyes then scoured the dishes, and if he saw anything missing he demanded it with a ringing shout. Replenishments, extensions, exotic variations, were produced and popped into my mouth. The Bahri overlooked the old harbour, and vines growing across the ceiling quivered with light from the sea. Four half-bottles of *arrack*, with the *mezzeh*, took us long into the blue-green afternoon, and we finished with a baked dish of *loup de mer*.

Beirut's many restaurants are not only places in which to eat, they are places in which to be seen eating expensively and well. Apart from a rash of Wimpy and Hamburger joints, aimed at the Americanized young, the Beirut restaurant is a temple of unblushing hedonism. Here it is the thing to display publicly your gastronomic lusts, to exhibit an almost erotic self-indulgence for food. You don't eat alone, or snatch a snack, or gobble the cheap *plat de jour* behind a crumpled newspaper. Rather you book a large table and eat your way leisurely through the menu surrounded by your whole family and all their collateral tribes.

My third Lebanese restaurant was not as lush as the others, but it had its own, rather dotty charm. I'd booked a table and was expected, but no one spoke adequate English or knew quite what to do with me. 'Welcome, Mister Laurie!' beamed the proprietor and his brother. I was shown to a table and given *hors d'oeuvres*. Nuts and sliced carrots were apparently on the house. The head-waiter's napkin dusted me down. When I referred to the menu, he cried, 'Mister Laurie, yes, welcome!' More raw carrots were pressed upon me. Then another plate of nuts. Then a dish of cold sliced lamb. Try as I would, I could get nothing else. Large families around me were eating whole beasts from a spit. The succulent aromas were too much to bear. I shook the head waiter by the hand and said I must go about my father's business. 'Yes, welcome, Mister Laurie!' he cried.

I suppose I reached my epicurean peak when I lunched at the Hotel St George, which looks, and is, the most distinguished hostelry anywhere in the Middle East. Standing on St George's Bay, it commands a panorama of the city, the haze of the hills, and the pine-topped mountains. Not only is the hotel of Edwardian elegance, the cuisine reputed to be the best 'east of Suez', the service of an almost nostalgic, sychophantic smoothness; it is also the key place to go in the city, the place to be seen, the place to look and listen and enquire. Especially at lunchtime, it is Beirut's centre of business and rumour, of brief encounters and social display. Oilmen, government officials, the rich and the lonely, con-men and journalists of all nations – all gather here at midday to taste the special quality of the place, the food, the drink, and the pregnant proximity of those who run the city, or are simply passing through.

My table was in the window – pink roses, pink cloth, and an intricate arrangement of 'gold-chased' plates. Asparagus, local fish served hot and boned, and a local white wine labelled '*Caves de Ksara*'.

Apart from the sharp-eyed gossip-writers exchanging notes, most of the diners around me spoke deep throaty French. Big business was being done, opportunities probed, boardroom and bedroom liaisons established, each table piled with the paraphernalia of five-star eating, each diner holding his cards to his chest. Heavy, dark-suited men; wise silver-haired politicos; opulent, well-sprung, musk-scented ladies.

Taking lunch at the St George gave me, more than anywhere else, a sense of Beirut's simmering sense of *affaires*.

Nubile, bikini-wrapped oil-girls, with figures like greyhounds and waists as pliant as a bundle of banknotes, inhaled and exhaled their exquisite physical presences up and down the sun-spotted terraces. At one stage I saw a trim little warship peek into the bay, turn and hesitate, and then race out again. A passing Canadian oil-driller put his hand on my shoulder and complained that last night he'd been stood up by a whore. And a Greek one at that. You wouldn't expect it would you? He was led away by a friend.

My last memory of St George was that of the single table nearby, its occupant clearly identifiable by her voice and style – one of the modern world's wanderers, desolate in her well-heeled pain, a temporarily shocked casualty of American divorce. Tense, attractive, in her early thirties, but too young to be just a jolly widow, she sat staring across her coffee at the sea.

Apart from the usual concentration of clip-joints and high-priced bars, there is also a new fashionable growth of 'British Pubs'. They come in an assortment of styles – plastic Tudor beams and dartboards – and some of them nearly get it right. The Duke of Wellington, already mentioned, serves fine English beer, but to an accompaniment of raw carrot, which I found set my teeth sideways. The Pickwick Inn, just up the road, was rather nearer the mark – run by a whiskered Battle of Britain pilot and a barmaid from Liverpool (or nearby), who had a sharp but forgiving tongue. The Rose and Crown, just off the Hambra, didn't quite hit it off, I thought – the wrong kind of dartboard, and again too many carrots.

These pubs offered another angle on Beirut – hustlers, drug-pushers, and girl-friends of pushers; exiled British journalists longing for home, stringers sitting on their golden expense accounts and courteously borrowing words from each other (that week it was 'tendacious' and 'pusillanimous').

They were also the refuge of visiting blonde English actresses. 'Trev, darling, can't stand another three weeks of this. Fly out Daphne and I'll even play her mum'. International airline crews, too. (A pilot bought three of my paperbacks on tick. His stewardess was rather more critical. 'Didn't like your last one, to be honest – not as much as the first.' 'All right, you don't have to say it three times.') Also mysterious French-Canadians pressing into one's hand crumpled visiting cards each bearing different addresses. And fruity flutters of matrons on a cruise from Massachusetts, enquiring if there was a local *guru*. And especially I remember that lone, ex-Army businessman from Tunbridge Wells who wanted to line up the TUC and shoot the buggers down.

The great, Parisian, Place-Pigalle, pseudo centre of Beirut's night-life is, of course, the Casino du Liban. It stands on a sharp cliff-edge about fourteen miles north of the city and is well understood to be an imperative for tourists. It is a mythical projection, tinged with Orient wealth and wicked-ness, offering the twin attractions of gambling and women. It is not as sinful as it sounds. Gambling is a State monopoly and to enter the gaming rooms one must show one's passport. The main cabaret, held in the Salles des Ambassadeurs, struck me as being brave but derivative – scenes echoing *Tannhäuser*, Hollywood in the 'thirties, the Lido in Paris, and the Ziegfield Follies; gorgeous girls whizzing up and down in golden cages, cascading waterfalls and dissolving stages. . . .

I found a place more to my liking in the somewhat shabby Fontana – sited incongruously opposite the American Embassy. This is considered by some to be a 'working-class' night-club: bare floorboards, plastic decorations, sagging balloons, and a wooden platform at the end of the room. It struck me as pleasantly sinister, down-at-heel and invigorat-ing. You could sit at your table all night for the price of a bottle of beer. On the stage a small orchestra, dressed in European clothes, played excellent Arab music. There were two virtuoso violinists, lute, pipe, drum and cymbal, and a male singer dressed like a gas-meter reader. He was later followed by a full-figured beauty who poured passionately into the microphone husky throatfuls of desert desire and madness.

These popular songs quickly heated up the audience, which was mostly noisily male. One or two glowing bubble-pipes were handed round to the customers. The night blew thick and scented from the sea. Nearby, two old tribesmen, in-flamed by the beer and the music, were rapidly going off their heads, thumping the floor, whinnying and whistling, and flashing delighted teeth. A young hostess by the door sat with her dark head in her hands, waiting for something to happen to her. A giggling crone, in a shawl, slowly circled the room selling bunches of jaded flowers.

Just before midnight, the orchestra built up to an orgasmic crescendo, and the belly dancer strode on to the stage. She had all that the audience could wish for – the cool face of a twelve-year-old, the broad beam of a tribal mother, a belly fruitfully rounded and erotically pitted, and a waist as loose and vibrant as a virgin's.

The girl wore a brief shiny garment of gold-tasselled blue, reminiscent of a Harrod's lamp-shade. And young as she obviously was, I was fascinated by her expertise, her knowing air of carnal remoteness. Physically she was superb, her richly shaped body the result of generations of deliberate desert breeding. Technically her dance was as traditional as her body: the face blank and receptive, the shoulders steady and broad, and below them the loins presenting such a hypnotic offering of herself that the old tribesmen behind me were soon howling like dogs.

Beirut is a good place to visit, and a sybaritic place to enjoy; but beneath its almost frantic vitality, its meeting ground between East and West, its neutrality and tolerance, the worm of intrigue grows fat.

The day after I arrived in the city, a Sabena aircraft was held to ransom in Israel by members of the Popular Front for the Liberation of Palestine. By guile and gunplay, the Israelis wiped out the hijackers in the plane – the only way to deal with them, they said. 'Manic,' said Beirut journalists. 'They gambled the lives of a hundred innocent passengers.'

A week in Beirut was long enough to meet members of the PFLP, whose headquarters are in the Lebanon. Sympathizers drifted in and out from all parts of the world. Weird 'training' routines were being carried out in the mountains.

It was the day after I flew back to London that three young Japanese gunmen massacred sixty-eight air-travellers in the customs hall at Lydda. A reprisal, it was announced, for the earlier killing of the Palestine guerillas. The surprising thing was that everyone was surprised.

Concorde 002

WHEN I left home in my youth it took me two years of foot-slogging and scheming to get from Gloucestershire to the north of Spain. The other day I travelled practically the whole of that distance – and back – in one hour and forty-five minutes.

I did this in the Concorde 002, flying from its Cotswold test-base near Fairford; and although it meant reaching heights and speeds to which my senses had never before been subjected, my most tangible memories are still more of the take-off and landing than the supersonic part, which remains little more than an airy nothing.

To be ready and early for the trip, we put up the previous evening at a comfortably coal-fired Fairford hotel. The night was wild and howling with Shakespearian augurs, and next morning we found windows blown in and chimney-pots scattered – not from sonic booms but from a Force 8 gale.

'Never ever known no wind ever blow like it never,' said the chambermaid. 'Not never in all my days.'

In the distance, as from the sky, I could hear a thin ghostly wail. Perhaps the flight would be cancelled? My spirits rose.

'Oh, no, he'll fly,' said the girl. 'Or so I expect. They bin warmin' 'im up since seven.'

We drove out to the base, which is speculatively shared between the RAF and BAC. Typical airfield, typical cold slap of upper Cotswolds, typical petulant winter's day – water-tanks on stilts, huts roofed with bent iron, wet concrete, birds flying backwards.

A handful of security police filtered us through to the Press Centre building, where we found we'd arrived too soon. A girl asked us to sign something, probably a disclaimer. Then a young man called Peter bustled in and took charge.

'I only just heard,' he said. 'So I popped over from Filton by Dakota.' He shook the rain from his hair like a terrier.

Would we fly? Yes, he thought so. There was low cloud, strong head-winds, but the Concorde was still warming up outside.

Ever since breakfast we'd been aware of it; a presence, not an intrusion, a continuous sound in the air. A relaxed, high-pitched purring of steady power, the Concorde waiting, the breath of the dragon at rest.

Peter from Filton suggested we went out for a look. They were towing the plane back from the end of the runway. It approached us side-on, gliding slowly past, and I remember writing pompously in my notebook: 'The long silver line of aerospacial truth, stamped with its trade-name, like a plastic container.' Sideways, in fact, it looks rather neuter, suburban – a classy, high-speed capsule dotted with tiny commuter windows and carried on wheels on long thin stalks. It is only when it turns towards you that you see its new beauty – the high questing head, the delicate neck, finally the wide-swept snowgoose wings.

I went forward with Peter, saw the forty-foot-high tail, the four under-slung jet-vents as black as tar-barrels. The service trucks were plugging in wires and tubes, air-conditioning, battery charging. I noticed long strips of paint flaking off from beneath the wings. I asked: 'Was that meteorites? Or did you hit some birds?'

'No. When we first painted the job, we got the undercoat wrong. We'll get it right next time.'

I retreated out of the wind behind the Concorde's hangar – a curve-roofed building half the size of Paddington Station. One vast wall was open on to a measureless interior peopled by distant tiny mechanics. As I stood there, an old bent man went past in the rain carrying a small yellow cranking handle. This he stuck into a hole and started to turn it and groan; and slowly, majestically, the gigantic doors – the height of three-story buildings – began to close on each other.

'If they're closing the hangars, you'll fly,' said Peter. He took us back to the Press Room for our final briefing.

'Nothing special about the Concorde,' he told us, 'except it's the best in the world. It's designed to be flown by idiots. After all, when we get world markets we'll be selling to all and sundry, and we won't be choosing the pilots. It's got four Rolls-Royce/SNECMA Olympus 593 turbojet engines mounted in paired nacelles under the wing. It's flown Mach 2 on two engines – no noticeable difference, very docile.' 'Will it fly on *one* engine?' I asked. 'Yes – presumably.'

We sat round waiting and twitching. There were still only eight of us. Where were all the others? 'You eight are the lot.' Only eight, rattling about in that great thing? 'We shall be carrying twelve tons of special electronic testing equipment. There'll just be room to pack you lot in the stern.'

We were due to take off at 11.00. There was half-an-hour's delay. Then they drove us out to the field. As I stepped down from the bus the wind ripped a 'Scandinavian Shipping Line' label off my briefcase and sent it spinning across the runway.

The Concorde was standing ready for us, its giant beak pecking earthwards, the blue maintenance-trucks beginning reverently to withdraw. Along the 200-foot fuselage was written: 'British Aircraft Corporation – Aerospatiale France'. The twin begetters, the double agents, the freak alliance that put the 'e' in 'Concorde'.

Our world, the airfield, one might say the whole of Fairford, was now dominated by the fact of this plane. I noticed that scarcely anyone in sight could take their eyes off it for a moment. Intention, power, a leap in the dimensions of gadgetry, inexorable possibility for good or ill, millions in expended treasure, and the labours of 80,000 people – all these lay sealed in the skin of this fine-spun tube, were expressed in the unearthly throb of its waiting forces.

The gangway seemed high as a fireman's ladder. I was glided towards it and climbed it without thinking. I looked back once and saw in the faces of the ground crew that they considered me inexplicably overprivileged.

From the outside, the Concorde is familiar for its dramatic clarity of line; inside, it's like a whiz-kid's attic – 'Careful how you go, don't trip on the wires, mind the switches, don't touch the explosives.'

In the rear, there were eight quite ordinary little passenger-seats, and an ordinary luggage rack, on which I bumped my head. We were settled down, strapped in, and shown where our oxygen was (if required). Then we were each given a pair of earphones. Through these we could listen in to captain and crew – though it was explained, gently, that we couldn't talk back.

So I began to eavesdrop on a mysterious litany of voices going through the long routine check before take-off. Scots' accents, Yorkshire, broad Gloucestershire, Bristolian, swapped information, asked questions, gave orders. Behind all this, God knows why, I swear I could also hear bells and bagpipes. And of course that continuous power-house whine.

The voices were relaxed and easy, especially those between captain and co-pilot, who sounded reassuringly amateurish and dotty. They might have been warming up at a friendly game of tennis, with lots of 'Oops, sorry's', and 'Let's try it again'.

Of course, my memory of the Concorde's flight-deck jargon is only of what I thought I heard; there were times when it could have been that of Indian canooists on the Upper Amazon.

Things were now hotting up anyway. Engines checked, one to four. Names and numbers reported in sequence. Occasionally there'd come a short blast of sound, deep-throated, tremendous, like Niagara being switched on and off.

'OK for steps, chief.'
'Right.'
'Electric truck away.'
'Thanks.'
Another short gust of thunder.
'Pressure gauge seems stuck.'
'It's possible. Yes.'
'Oh, well, Johnny – just give it a thump.'
More bells and bagpipes.
'Auto-pilot on. . . . Chocks away.'
'Right.' (Somebody whistled aimlessly.)
For a while we'd been poised trembling at the end of the

10,000-foot runway. Low clouds were sweeping over the ragged fields. Suddenly we came deafeningly alive, sprang forward as though kicked, gathered speed, hurled past the main buildings. I saw through my window a blurr of white figures watching, raindrops washing horizontally across the glass. I was committed now into the white palms of a power far stronger than I'd ever known.

'No transit, skipper. Bucket's in locked position.'

'Try it once more. . . . Oh, never mind, forget it.'

We tilted, rose. The wet fields leant violently backwards. In five seconds they were lost in cloud. Looking along the length of the fuselage, it seemed to sway and buckle like the vertebrae of a skeletal snake.

'No use sitting around in this stuff, Johnny. Let's get out of it quick. Hundred per cent dreadful. Reckon ceiling's 10,000. Between you and me and the Flight-Engineer. . . .' I thought it better to slip off my earphones.

In five minutes from take-off we broke the top of the cloudbank. There were still some veils of dirty stuff above. According to the map-brief we should be somewhere over Radstock, Somerset, and heading for the North Devon coast, and climbing.

They now said we could unstrap and move about if we wished. I stayed in my seat a while longer. I was in the Concorde. I felt nothing; but then I was not supposed to feel anything. I could see little; but such a plane's not for sightseeing. Presently I unbuckled and started to walk up the cabin. It was like walking up a chapel roof.

Three members of the crew, in shirt-sleeves, were sitting side by side at a bench, monitoring conditions and details of the plane's performance. Before them were computers, dials, clocks, thermometers, automatic writing needles. The more intelligible of the dials told me that we were already at 29,000 feet, and climbing at what looked like 100 feet a second; that our speed was Mach 0.94; that we were over a point of land some 150 miles from Fairford; and that we had been in the air for fifteen minutes.

'Acceleration' was to begin after we'd crossed Hartland Point, that was, in two minutes time. I stood and braced myself. We were still climbing steeply. The needle moved from 0.94 to Mach 1. I was standing facing the dials. It felt as though someone had lightly brushed against me. We had passed the speed of sound.

'Mach One-plus,' someone said. The big needle stood steady, but some of the other dials seemed suddenly to go crazy: pointers see-sawed, swung; numbers raced and clicked; indicators jerked and hiccoughed.

Nothing else appeared to happen. The crew went on with their figures. So that was that. I decided to take a look at the flight-deck. It was the closest thing I could imagine that might resemble an astronaut's command-module – instrument-packed to the point of delirium. The four crew were sitting more or less back-to-back, as though in an Irish jaunting car: pilot and co-pilot, naturally enough, up front, Flight-Engineer behind them, Navigator in a corner facing backwards. There was scarcely room in the cockpit for a visiting cat, but chairs were tilted to let me through. I spoke to the captain and his first officer (who was wearing a red-peaked cap). All was calm – we were on auto-pilot. Through the sloping windows upper-air sunlight streamed through, whitish-yellow like a narcissus.

I returned to the Navigator's corner. He was looking down into a 6-inch radar, which glowed with a sort of submarine light. The top of the screen was filled with what appeared to be a torn green leaf. 'South coast of Ireland – seventy miles off.' The Navigator indicated Cork with his pencil, then went on with his calculations. I turned unsteadily to leave him, and only then did he show the mildest alarm. 'Don't bump into any buttons,' he said.

Back at the monitoring benches I noticed we had reached 50,000 feet. That's what it said, and my ears hadn't popped. Our speed was now flickering around Mach 2. 'How fast is that?' I asked. 'Gobbledy knots,' said the crewman. 'What's that in miles?' 'Wait a sec, I'll find out.' He spoke into the intercom., then turned and scribbled in my notebook: '1,340 mph.'

We'd left the turning area off the south of Ireland and were heading down over the Bay of Biscay. Outside, the air temperature was —70 C. But the outer skin of the plane was 120 C. 'Friction,' said a pundit. 'You could fry an egg on that wing.' I'd been wondering when someone would say that.

Well over one-and-a-half times the height of Everest, and still climbing. 'Reheat's coming off at 51,600.' 'What's "reheat"?' 'Saves mucking about. We use it to get to Mach 2 quicker.'

The artificial horizon showed me we were standing on our ears, going into a starboard turn. I went back to my seat and saw the wing pointing downwards at an immense crumpled floor of cloud. A curious ghost-sun followed us, skimming across the vapour below. The windows across the cabin were filled with the opaque blue of space.

For the next half hour, at twice the speed of sound, we manoeuvred over the sea, somewhere west of the rich plains of Bordeaux, somewhere north of the rough coast of Spain. We were above a cloud-trapped world, in a thin blue air, occasionally turning and recrossing our contrails. Visibility was so clear it took in the quilted curve of the earth. I imagine there were few other civilians up there that day.

Then we were on the homeward leg, and I went for another look at the dials: 54,000 feet, steady (presumably our ceiling) and Mach 2.07 (low whistles from a fellow passenger). Oxygen, OK. No warning lights visible. About an hour in the air, and soon due to come down. We must be back off the south of Ireland. Then I noticed that we were dropping at nearly 200 feet a second – which is a deal faster than you can fall off a house. We made another steep turn and the sun changed windows. I hurried back to my seat.

Maybe I should have stayed where I was. The earphones were buzzing with problems. It seemed the weather at Fairford had closed in tight. There was talk from the captain about diverting to Manston, Kent. The question was the balance of fuel.

'I reckon I could hit Manston all right with 10,000 kilos. What else have we got? Forget about France. How's Prestwick? Gusting 40? Well, Prestwick's out, Johnny. We'll keep that for Hogmanay. How about Heathrow? Aye, there's better runways there. What's Heathrow's weather? Better ask

Gatwick.'

It was a long run back as we re-entered the cloud, and I was filled with a faint grey dread. Racing down through the storm, all bearings and dimensions lost, the Concorde now seemed ungainly, impossibly huge.

Still the flight-deck voices were chatting away in my ear. They could have been driving up the M1 on a dirty night.

'Twenty-three miles west of Radstock.'

'Ten miles.'

'Over Radstock.'

'Cut rate of descent – save juice.'

'OK, chief.'

We were now bumping a bit in the hurtling cloud. We seemed to have been flying through this stuff for ever.

'Tell you what, Johnny. We'll make one pass at two thousand. If we don't like the look of it, then we'll pull out quick.'

'Radar on. Radar on.'

'Ten miles west of airfield.'

'Two thousand. No lower, Johnny.'

Grey rain, grey cloud, nothing else in the universe. Only the huge and shining wing. We flew on for a while in silence.

'Dreadful,' murmured the captain. 'Tumpty-tum – quite dreadful. Johnny, did you switch on X?'

'Sorry, skipper – I forgot.'

Shouts of laughter, squeals. 'Better do it then, hadn't you? And remind me about the windscreen wipers. And let's bring up the Flying Manual with us next time, eh? Ha, ha! Ho, ho! Hum hum.'

More peering into the gloom. More murmurs of 'Well, well – dreadful.'

'Six miles north-west of airfield, chief.'

'*North*-west, for god's sake?' (Hysterical laughter, now.) 'All right, better put the wipers on . . . No, no! not yet! Remember last time – we switched 'em on too soon and they fell off half way along the runway.'

The countdown started. Everybody was having a ball; but I was searching the cloud for signs of good earth and Gloucestershire. We must have been at 2,000 feet, but I saw ghosts of trees and houses rush close past me as I went through false-pregnancies of landing.

'1,000 feet . . . 600 . . . Nose down . . . 500.' I had been listening, intently, and thought I'd missed something. '400 . . . 350.' I wanted to yell, 'Have you forgotten the *landing* wheels?' But there was nothing I could do about it now.

'We should see the lights. Ah, there they are.' They suddenly shone in two lines across the wet grey earth. We slid out of thick cloud at under 400 feet, turning sweetly to meet the runway. '300 . . . 200 . . . 100 . . . 50 . . . 20 . . . 5, 4, 3, 2, 1 . . .' There was a slight bump and rumble as the great aeroplane touched down, a hundred tons of it from some ten miles high. Fields and buildings rushed past us, it was Fairford all right, lines of white figures waited in the streaming rain.

An hour and three-quarters since take-off, and perhaps fifteen minutes of that confirming that our airfield was still where we left it. It had been an instrument landing, and that practically blind. Now I knew what those gadgets meant.

'Gentlemen,' someone said, as we unfastened our seat-belts. 'You have experienced a normal flight in abnormal conditions. I think you'll agree that the result of that experience is to prove that the Concorde is simply a normal aeroplane.'

My own experience, I feel, might be summed up differently. True, for the first time I had travelled faster than sound. I had even reached Mach 2.07 without pain. Moreover I had travelled more miles, in that one and three-quarter hours, than in the first ten years of my life. But emotionally, in fact, I'd been nowhere, seen nothing. We might as well have been circling above cloud over Cheltenham. There is no doubt that the Concorde is a magnificent contrivance – you can leave in daylight for New York and arrive to find it waiting for sunrise, go half round the globe and find your friends still aren't quite ready for you – and that it performs with triumphant *élan*. The device is fantastic; it could telescope the world. It could also diminish our sense of distance and wonder.

MORE ABOUT PENGUINS
AND PELICANS

Penguinews, which appears every month, contains details of all the new books issued by Penguins as they are published. From time to time it is supplemented by *Penguins in Print*, which is our complete list of almost 5,000 titles.

A specimen copy of *Penguinews* will be sent to you free on request. Please write to Dept EP, Penguin Books Ltd, Harmondsworth, Middlesex, for your copy.

In the U.S.A.: For a complete list of books available from Penguins in the United States write to Dept CS, Penguin Books, 625 Madison Avenue, New York, New York 10022.

In Canada: For a complete list of books available from Penguins in Canada write to Penguin Books Canada Ltd, 2801 John Street, Markham, Ontario.

V. S. NAIPAUL

THE OVERCROWDED BARRACOON
and other articles

'*The Overcrowded Barracoon* is an extraordinarily coherent assembly of articles ... always its quickening sense of these other cultures, other fantasies and other dilemmas is superbly communicated [with] chorographs of such subtle richness, comedy, pain and discovery that you really can look across at new territory' – Dennis Potter in *The Times*

Norman Mailer in New York, Jacques Soustelle in exile, politics and power in the Caribbean, cricket, Indian film-makers and an election in Ajmer, the post-colonial inheritance of South America, India and the West Indies ... finally, Mauritius – the overcrowded barracoon itself. Throughout a generous multiplicity of subjects, V. S. Naipaul sustains the precision, wit and intimacy that proclaim him as one of the most important journalist/novelists now writing in Britain.

'Elision and precision divide the honours between them, and the prose moves as swiftly as a cat' – Francis Hope in the *Observer*

MICHAEL HOLROYD

UNRECEIVED OPINIONS

'*Unreceived Opinions* clearly classifies Michael Holroyd as an essayist in the very best sense. His writing is, not to put too fine a point on it, impeccable' – *The Times*

'Here, thank goodness, is a bonny fighter, humorous, ironic, sensitive, loyal to words, conscious of the rightness and dignity of the author's trade, the friend of all quiet toilers in that stony field, the severe enemy of the malice, contempt, bureaucracy hedging that poor ground' – *Tribune*

'No reader could fail to put it down frequently in order to ponder or laugh' – John Stewart Collis in the *Sunday Telegraph*

A collection of brilliantly witty essays on diverse literary people – among them Virginia Woolf and Bertrand Russell – and subjects – censorship, the business of a biographer, the enjoyment of unfashionable books – in which the opinions (however comic they may seem) are 'unreceived', which is to say they are entirely the author's own.

L. P. HARTLEY

THE GO-BETWEEN

'Of all the novels L. P. Hartley has written I think *The Go-Between* is the best ... It is in what is to me the best tradition of fiction' – John Betjeman in the *Daily Telegraph*

In one of the first and finest of the post-war studies of early adolescence, an old man looks back on his boyhood and recalls a summer visit to a Norfolk country house at the beginning of the century.

Not yet equipped to understand the behaviour of adults, he is guiltily involved in a tragic drama between three grown-up people. The author forcefully conveys the intensity of an emotional experience which breeds a lasting mistrust of life.

Also published in Penguins:
THE HIRELING

LAURIE LEE

AS I WALKED OUT
ONE MIDSUMMER MORNING

It was 1934. The young man walked to London from the
security of the Cotswolds to make his fortune. He was to live
by playing the violin and by a year's labouring on a London
building site. Then, knowing one Spanish phrase, he decided
to see Spain. For a year he tramped through a country in
which the signs of impending civil war were clearly visible.

Thirty years later Laurie Lee has captured the atmosphere
of the Spain he saw with all the freshness and beauty of a
young man's vision, creating a lyrical and lucid picture of the
beautiful and violent country that was to involve him inextric-
ably.

'A marvellous book' – Kenneth Allsop, *B.B.C., The World of
Books*

'A beautiful piece of writing' – John Raymond, *Observer*

LAURIE LEE

A ROSE FOR WINTER

Andalusia is a passion. Fifteen years after his last visit, Laurie Lee returns.

He finds a country broken by the Civil War, but the totems of indestructible Spain survive: the Virgin in agony, the thrilling flamenco wail ... the pride in poverty, the gypsy intensity in grey slums, the glory in the horror of the bullfight, the exultation in death, the humour in hopelessness ... the paradoxes deep in the fiery bones of Spain.

Laurie Lee writes with a beauty to match his passion.